The Settlement Of Germantown, Pennsylvania, And The Beginning Of German Emigration To North America

Saml. W. Pennypacker

The

Settlement of Germantown

Pennsylvania

and the

Beginning of German Emigration

to

North America

BY

HON SAMUEL WHITAKER PENNYPACKER, LL.D.

PRESIDENT JUDGE OF THE PHILADELPHIA COURT OF COMMON PLEAS, NO 2, AND SENIOR VICE-PRESIDENT OF THE HISTORICAL SOCIETY OF PENNSYLVANIA

WILLIAM J CAMPBELL,
PHILADELPHIA.
1899

THREE HUNDRED COPIES PRINTED
FROM TYPE

PRESS OF
THE NEW ERA PRINTING COMPANY
LANCASTER, PA

PREFACE.

AS it seemed to be a duty which could not be avoided, I have written the following history of the settlement of one of the most interesting of the American burghs. A descendant of Hendrick Pannebecker, Abraham Op den Graeff, Paul Kuster, Cornelius Tyson, Peter Conrad, Hendrick Sellen, Hans Peter Umstat and probably of William Rittenhouse, all of them among the early residents of Germantown, for thirty years I have been gradually gathering the original materials from over the world. The task was one of great difficulty, presenting obstacles not encountered elsewhere and requiring the examination of almost inaccessible books and papers in the Dutch, German, French and Latin, as well as the English languages. An article written by me in 1880, since copied en masse as to facts, language and notes, in Cassel's History of the Mennonites, and used by other authors, has here been reconstructed. The careful and thorough investigations of the late Dr. Oswald Seidensticker, the work of Julius F. Sachse upon the German Pietists, the papers of the late Horatio Gates Jones and the article of H. P. G. Quack, of Amsterdam, upon Plockhoy's Sociale Plannen have been used freely. I am indebted likewise to Mr. Sachse for the production of the illustrations.

NOTE—Initial from Plockhoy's Kort en Klaer Ontwerp.

LIST OF ORIGINAL ILLUSTRATIONS.

THE SETTLEMENT OF GERMANTOWN, PA., AND THE BEGINNING OF GERMAN EMIGRATION TO NORTH AMERICA.

CHAPTER I.

Crefeld and the Mennonites.

Wappen von Krefeld.

THE settlement of Germantown in 1683, was the initial step in the great movement of people from the regions bordering on the historic and beautiful Rhine, extending from its source in the mountains of Switzerland to its mouth in the lowlands of Holland, which has done so much to give Pennsylvania her rapid growth as a colony, her almost unexampled prosperity, and her foremost rank in the development of the institutions of the country. The first impulse, followed by the first wave of emigration, came from Crefeld, a city of the lower Rhine within a few miles of the borders of Holland. This city has in recent years grown greatly in wealth and population, through the evolution of extensive manufactories of silk and other woven goods from the weaving industries established there centuries ago by the Mennonites.

On the 10th of March, 1682, William Penn conveyed to Jacob Telner, of Crefeld, doing business as a merchant in Amsterdam, Jan Streypers, a merchant of Kaldkirchen, a village in the vicinity, still nearer to Holland, and Dirck Sipman, of Crefeld, each five thousand acres of land to be laid out in Pennsylvania. As the deeds were executed upon that day,[1] the design must have been in contempla-

[1] Mr. Lawrence Lewis has suggested that under the system of double dating between January 1st and March 25th, which then prevailed, it is probable that the date was March 10, 1682-83 The evidence pro and con is strong and conflicting. The facts in favor of 1682-3 are mainly .

1. It is manifest from an examination of the patents that the custom was, whenever a single date, as 1682, was mentioned within those limits, the latter date, 1682-83, was meant.

2. A deed to Telner, dated June 2, 1683 (Ex Rec , 8, p 655), recites as follows " Whereas, the said William Penn by indentures of lease and release, bearing date the ninth and tenth days of the month called March for the consideration therein mentioned, etc " The presumption is that the March referred to is the one immediately preceding.

3 The lease and release to Telner March 9th and 10th, 1682, and several deeds of June, 1683, are all recited to have been in the 35th year of the reign of Charles II It is evident that March 10, 1681-82, and June, 1683, could not both have been within the same year

This would be enough to decide the matter if the facts in favor of 1681-82 were not equally conclusive They are ·

1 It is probable, *a priori*, and from the German names of the witnesses that the deeds to the Crefelders, except that to Telner, were dated and delivered by Benj Furly, Penn's agent at Rotterdam, for the sale of lands In both Holland and Germany the present system of dating had been in use for over a century.

2. A patent (Ex Rec., Vol. I., p. 462) recites as follows · " Whereas, by my indentures of lease and release dated the 9 and 10 days of March Anno 1682 and whereas by my indentures date the first day of April, and year aforesaid, I remised and released to the same Dirck Sipman the yearly rent · · ." The year aforesaid was 1682, and if the

tion and the arrangements made some time before. Telner had been in America between the years 1678 and 1681, and we may safely infer that his acquaintance with the country had much influence in bringing about the purchase.[2]

On the 11th of June, 1683, Penn conveyed to Govert Remke, Lenart Arets, and Jacob Isaacs Van Bebber, a baker, all of Crefeld, one thousand acres of land each, and they, together with Telner, Streypers, and Sipman, constituted the original Crefeld purchasers. It is evident that their purpose was colonization, and not speculation. The arrangement between Penn and Sipman provided that a certain number of families should go to Pennsylvania within a specified time, and probably the other purchasers

quit rent was released April 1, 1682, the conveyance to Sipman must have been earlier. If on the 25th of March another year, 1683, had intervened, the word "aforesaid" could not have been correctly used. This construction is strengthened by the fact that the release of quit rent to Streypers, which took place April 1, 1683, is recited in another patent (Ex. Rec., 1, p. 686) as follows: "Of which said sum or yearly rent by an indenture bearing date the first day of April for the consideration therein mentioned in the year 1683 I remised and released."

3. The lease and release to Telner on March 9 and 10, 1682, are signed by William Penn, witnessed by Herbert Springett, Thomas Coxe and Seth Craske, and purport to have been executed in England. An Op den Graeff deed in the Germantown book recites that they were executed at London. Now, in March, 1681–82, Penn was in England, but in March, 1682–83, he was in Philadelphia.

4. Pastorius says that Penn at first declined to give the Frankfort Company city lots, because they had made their purchase after he (Penn) had left England and the books had been closed, and that a special arrangement was made to satisfy them. Penn left England Sept. 1, 1682. The deeds show that the Crefelders received their city lots.

[2] Hazard's Register, Vol. VI., p. 183.

entered into similar stipulations.[3] However that may be, ere long thirteen men with their families, comprising thirty-three persons, nearly all of whom were relatives, were ready to embark to seek new homes across the ocean. They were Lenart Arets, Abraham Op den Graeff, Dirck Op den Graeff, Herman Op den Graeff, Willem Streypers, Thones Kunders, Reynier Tyson, Jan Seimens, Jan Lensen, Peter Keurlis, Johannes Bleikers, Jan Lucken, and Abraham Tunes. The three Op den Graeffs were brothers, Hermann was a son-in-law of Van Bebber, they were accompanied by their sister Margaretha and their mother, and they were cousins of Jan and Willem Streypers, who were also brothers. The wives of Thones Kunders and Lenart Arets were sisters of the Streypers, and the wife of Jan was the sister of Reynier Tyson. Peter Keurlis was also a relative, and the location of the signatures of Jan Lucken and Abraham Tunes on the certificate of the marriage of a son of Thones Kunders with a daughter of Willem Streypers in 1710 indicates that they, too, were connected with the group by family ties.[4] On the 7th of June, 1683, Jan Streypers and Jan Lensen entered into an agreement at Crefeld by the terms of which Streypers was to let Lensen have fifty acres of land at a rent of a rix dollar and half a stuyver, and to lend him fifty rix dollars for eight years at the interest of six rix dollars annually. Lensen was to transport himself and wife to Pennsylvania, to clear eight acres of Streyper's land and to work for him twelve days in each year for eight years. The agreement proceeds, "I further promise to lend him a Linnen weaving

[3] Dutch deed from Sipman to Peter Schumacher in the Germantown Book, in the Recorder's office

[4] Strieper MSS in the Historical Society. The marriage certificate belonged to Dr J H Conrad

stool with 3 combs, and he shall have said weaving stool for two years . . . and for this Jan Lensen shall teach my son Leonard in one year the art of weaving, and Leonard shall be bound to weave faithfully during said year." On the 18th of June the little colony were in Rotterdam, whither they were accompanied by Jacob Telner, Dirck Sipman, and Jan Streypers, and there many of their business arrangements were completed. Telner conveyed two thousand acres of land to the brothers Op den Graeff, and Sipman made Hermann Op den Graeff his attorney. Jan Streypers conveyed one hundred acres to his brother Willem, and to Siemens and Keurlis each two hundred acres. Bleikers and Lucken each bought two hundred acres from Benjamin Furly, agent for the purchasers at Frankfort. At this time Janes Claypoole, a Quaker merchant in London, who had previously had business relations of some kind with Telner, was about to remove with his family to Pennsylvania, intending to sail in the Concord, Wm. Jeffries, master, a vessel of five hundred tons burthen. Through him a passage from London was engaged for them in the same vessel, which was expected to leave Gravesend on the 6th of July, and the money was paid in advance.[5] It is now ascertained definitely that eleven of these thirteen emigrants were from Crefeld, and the presumption that their two companions, Jan Lucken and Abraham Tunes, came from the same city is consequently strong. This presumption is increased by the indications of relationship and the fact that the wife of Jan Seimens was Mercken Williamsen Lucken. Fortunately, however, we are not wanting in evidence of a general character. Pastorius, after having an interview with Telner at Rotterdam a few weeks earlier, accompanied by four servants,

[5] Letter book of James Claypoole in the Historical Society.

who appear to have been Jacob Schumacher, Isaac Dilbeck, George Wertmuller and Koenradt Rutters, had gone to America representing both the purchasers at Frankfort and Crefeld. In his reference to the places in which he stopped on his journey down the Rhine he nowhere mentions emigrants except at Crefeld, where he says: "I talked with Tunes Kunders and his wife, Dirck Hermann and Abraham Op den Graeff, and many others who six weeks later followed me." For some reason the emigrants were delayed between Rotterdam and London, and Claypoole was in great uneasiness for fear the vessel should be compelled to sail without them, and they should lose their passage money. He wrote several letters about them to Benjamin Furly at Rotterdam. June 19th he says: "I am glad to hear the Crevill ffriends are coming." July 3d he says: "Before I goe away wch now is like to be longer than we expected by reason of the Crevill friends not coming we are fain to loyter and keep the ship still at Blackwall upon one pretence or another;" and July 10th he says: "It troubles me much that the friends from Crevillt are not yet come."[6] As he had the names of the thirty-three persons, this contemporary evidence is very strong, and it would seem safe to conclude that all of this pioneer band, which, with Pastorius, founded Germantown, came from Crefeld. Henry Melchoir Muhlenberg says the first comers were platt-deutch from the neighborhood of Cleves.[7] Despite the forebodings of Claypoole the emigrants reached London in time for the Concord, and they set sail westward on the 24th of July. While they are for the first time experiencing the dangers and trials of a trip across the ocean, doubtless sometimes looking back with regret,

[6] Letter book of James Claypoole

[7] Hallesche Nachrichten, p 665

but oftener wistfully and wonderingly forward, let us return to inquire who these people were who were willing to abandon forever the old homes and old friends along the Rhine, and commence new lives with the wolf and the savage in the forests upon the shores of the Delaware.

The origin of the sect of Mennonites is somewhat involved in obscurity. Their opponents, following Sleidanus and other writers of the 16th century, have reproached them with being an outgrowth of the Anabaptists of Munster. On the contrary, their own historians, Mehrning, Van Braght, Maatschoen and Roosen, trace their theological and lineal descent from the Waldenses, some of whose communities are said to have existed from the earliest Christian times, and who were able to maintain themselves in obscure parts of Europe, against the power of Rome, in large numbers from the 12th century downward. The subject has of recent years received thorough and philosophical treatment at the hands of S. Blaupot Ten Cate, a Dutch historian.[8]

The theory of the Waldensian origin is based mainly on a certain similarity in creed and church observances; the fact that the Waldenses are known to have been numerous in those portions of Holland and Flanders where the Mennonites arose and throve, and to have afterward disap-

[8] Geschiedkundig Onderzoek naar den Waldenzischen oorsprong van de Nederlandsche Doopsgezinden. Amsterdam, 1844

A nearly contemporary authority, which seems to have escaped the observation of European investigators, is "De vitis, sectis, et dogmatibus omnium Haereticorum, &c., per Gabrielem Prateolum Marcossium," published at Cologne in 1583, which says, p 25 · "Est perniciosior etiam tertia quae quoniam a Catholocis legitime baptizatos rebaptizat, Anabaptistorum secta vocatur De quo genere videntur etiam fuisse fratres Vualdenses; quos et ipsos non ita pridem rebaptizasse constat, quamuis eorum nonnulli, nuper adeo, sicut ipsi in Apologia sua testantur miterare Baptismum desierint, in multis tamen eos cum Anabaptistis conuenire certum est."

peared ; the ascertained descent of some Mennonite families from Waldenses ; and a marked similarity in habits and occupations. This last fact is especially interesting in our investigation, as will be hereafter seen. The Waldenses carried the art of weaving from Flanders into Holland, and so generally followed that trade as in many localities to have gone by the name of *Tisserands*, or weavers.[9] It is not improbable that the truth lies between the two theories of friend and foe, and that the Baptist movement which swept through Germany and the Netherlands in the early part of the 16th century gathered into its embrace many of these communities of Waldenses. At the one extreme of this movement were Thomas Munzer, Bernhard Rothman, Jean Matthys and John of Leyden ; at the other were Menno Simons and Dirck Philips. Between them stood Battenberg and David Joris, of Delft. The common ground of them all, and about the only ground which they had in common, was opposition to the baptism of infants. The first party became entangled in the politics of the time, and ran into the wildest excesses. They preached to the peasantry of Europe, trodden beneath the despotic heels of Church and State, that the kingdom of Christ upon earth was at hand, that all human authority ought to be resisted and overthrown, and all property be divided. After fighting many battles and causing untold commotion, they took possession of the city of Munster, and made John of Leyden a king. The pseudo-kingdom endured for more than a year of siege and riot, and then was crushed by the power of the State, and John of Leyden was torn to pieces with red hot pincers, and his bones set aloft in an iron cage for a warning.[10]

---

[9] Ten Cate's Onderzoek, p 42

[10] Catrou's Histoire des Anabaptistes, p. 462.

MENO SIMONIS. AET
M·D·C·L

Menno Simons was born in the village of Witmarsum in Friesland, in the year 1492, and was educated for the priesthood, upon whose duties early in life he entered. The beheading of Sicke Snyder for rebaptism in the year 1531 in his near neighborhood called his attention to the subject of infant baptism, and after a careful examination of the Bible and the writings of Luther and Zwinglius, he came to the conclusion there was no foundation for the doctrine in the Scriptures. At the request of a little community near him holding like views he began to preach to them, and in 1536 formally severed his connection with the Church of Rome. Ere long he began to be recognized as the leader of the *Doopsgezinde* or *Taufgesinnte*, and gradually the sect assumed from him the name of Mennonites. His first book was a dissertation against the errors and delusions in the teachings of John of Leyden, and after a convention held at Buckhold, in Westphalia, in 1538, at which Battenberg and David Joris were present, and Menno and Dirck Philips were represented, the influence of the fanatical Anabaptists seems to have waned.[11] His entire works, published at Amsterdam in 1681, make a folio volume of 642 pages. Luther and Calvin stayed their hands at a point where power and influence would have been lost, but the Dutch reformer, Menno, far in advance of his time, taught the complete severance of Church and State, and the principles of religious liberty which have been embodied in our own federal constitution were first worked out in Holland.[12]

The Mennonites believed that no baptism was efficacious

---

[11] Nippold's Life of David Joris. Roosen's Menno Simons, p. 32.

[12] Barclay's Religious Societies of the Commonwealth, pp. 78, 676; Menno's "Exhortation to all in Authority," in his works Funk's edition, Vol I, p 75; Vol II, p 303

unless accompanied by repentance, and that the ceremony administered to infants was vain. They took not the sword and were entirely non-resistant.[13] They swore not at all.[14] They practiced the washing of the feet of the brethren,[15] and made use of the ban or the avoidance of those who were pertinaciously derelict.[16] In dress and speech they were plain and in manners simple. Their ecclesiastical enemies, even while burning them for their heresies, bore testimony to the purity of their lives, their thrift, and homely virtues.[17] They were generally husbandmen and artisans, and so many of them were weavers, that we are told by Roosen, certain woven and knit fabrics were known as Mennonite goods.[18]

The shadow of John of Leyden, however, hung over them, the name of Anabaptist clung to them, and no sect, not even the early Christians, was ever more bitterly or persistently persecuted. There were put to death for this cause at Rotterdam seven persons, Haarlem ten, the Hague thirteen, Cortrijk twenty, Brugge twenty-three, Amsterdam twenty-six, Ghent one hundred and three. and Antwerp two hundred and twenty-nine, and in the last named city there were thirty-seven in 1571 and thirty-seven in 1574, the last by fire.[19] It was usual to burn the men and drown the women. Occasionally some were buried alive, and the rack and like preliminary tortures were

---

[13] Matthew, XXVI, 52

[14] Matthew, V., 32-37.

[15] John, XIII, 4, 17; I. Timothy, V, 10.

[16] Matthew, XVIII, 17, I Corinthians, V, 9 11; Thes., III, 14

[17] Says Catrou, p 269, "On ne peut disconvenir que des sectes de la sorte n'ayent eté remplies d'assez bonnes gens et assez reglées pour les moeurs." And page 103, "Leurs invectives contre le luxe, contre l'yvrognerie, et contre incontinence avoient je ne scai quoi de pathetique"

[18] Life of Gerhard Roosen, p 9

[19] Geschiedenis der Doopsgezinden in Holland, etc, Ten Cate, p 72

OLD PRINT OF JOHN OF LEYDEN.

used to extort confessions, and get information concerning the others of the sect. Ydse Gaukes gives, in a letter written to his brother from prison, a graphic description of his own treatment. After telling that his hands were tied behind his back, he continues: "Then they drew me up about a foot from the ground and let me hang. I was in great pain, but I tried to be quiet. Nevertheless, I cried out three times, and then was silent. They said *that is only child's play*, and letting me down again they put me on a stool, but asked me no questions, and said nothing to me. They fastened an iron bar to my feet with two chains, and hung on the bar three heavy weights. When they drew me up again a Spaniard tried to hit me in the face with a chain, but he could not reach; while I was hanging I struggled hard, and got one foot through the chain, but then all the weight was on one leg. They tried to fasten it again, but I fought with all my strength. That made them all laugh, but I was in great pain." He was afterward burned to death by a slow fire at Deventer, in May, 1571.[20] Their meetings were held in secret places, often in the middle of the night, and in order to prevent possible exposure under the pressure of pain, they purposely avoided knowing the names of the brethren whom they met, and of the preachers who baptized them.[21] A reward of one hundred gold guilders was offered for Menno, malefactors were promised pardon if they should capture him,[22] Tjaert Ryndertz was put on the wheel in 1539 for having given him shelter, and a house in which his wife and children had rested, unknown to its owner, was confis-

[20] Van Braght's Blutige Schauplatz oder Martyrer Spiegel. Ephrata, 1748, Vol. II, p 632

[21] Van Braght, Vol. II, p. 468

[22] A copy of the proclamation may be seen in Ten Cate's Geschiedenis der Doopsgezinden in Friesland, etc., p 63

cated. He was, as his followers fondly thought, miraculously protected, however, died peacefully in 1559, and was buried in his own cabbage garden. The natural result of this persecution was much dispersion. The prosperous communities at Hamburg and Altona were founded by refugees, the first Mennonites in Prussia fled there from the Netherlands, and others found their way up the Rhine.[23] Crefeld is chiefly noted for its manufactories of silk, linen and other woven goods, and these manufactures were first established by persons fleeing from religious intolerance.

From the Mennonites sprang the general Baptist churches of England, the first of them having an ecclesiastical connection with the parent societies in Holland, and their organizers being Englishmen who, as has been discovered, were actual members of the Mennonite church at Amsterdam.[24] It was for the benefit of these Englishmen that the well-known Confession of Faith of Hans de Ries and Lubbert Gerritz was written,[25] and according to the late Robert Barclay, whose valuable work bears every evidence of the most thorough and careful research, it was from association with these early Baptist teachers that George Fox, the founder of the Quakers, imbibed his views. Says Barclay: " We are compelled to view him as the unconscious exponent of the doctrine, practice, and discipline of the ancient and stricter party of the Dutch

[23] Life of Gerhard Roosen, p. 5 Reiswitz und Waldzeck, p 19.

[24] Barclay's Religious Societies, pp. 72, 73, 95

[25] The preface to that Confession, Amsterdam, 1686, says "Ter cause, also daer eenige Engelsche uyt Engeland gevlucht ware, om de vryheyd der Religie alhier te genieten en alsoo sy een schriftelijcke confessie (van de voornoemde) hebben begeert, want veele van hare gheselschap inde Duytsche Tale onervaren zijnde, het selfde niet en konde versteen ende als dare konde de ghene die de Tale beyde verstonde de andere onderrechten, het welche oock niet onvruchtbaer en is ghebleven, want na overlegh der saecke zijn sy met de voernoemde Gemeente vereenight."

Contemporary portrait of Caspar Schwenckfeldt, A. D. 1556.

Mennonites."[26] To the spread of Mennonite teachings in England we therefore owe the origin of the Quakers, and the settlement of Pennsylvania. The doctrine of the inner light was by no means a new one in Holland and Germany, and the dead letter of the Scriptures is a thought common to David Joris, Casper Schwenckfeldt, and the modern Quaker. The similarity between the two sects has been manifest to all observers, and recognized by themselves. William Penn, writing to James Logan of some emigrants in 1709, says: "Herewith comes the Palatines, whom use with tenderness and love, and fix them so that they may send over an agreeable character; for they are sober people, divers Mennonists, and will neither swear nor fight. See that Guy has used them well."[27] Thomas Chalkley, writing from Holland the same year, says: "There is a great people which they call Mennonists who are very near to truth, and the fields are white unto harvest among that people spiritually speaking.[28] When Ames,[29] Caton, Stubbs, Penn, and others of the early Friends went to Holland and Germany, they were received with the utmost kindness by the Mennonites, which is in strong contrast with their treatment at the hands of the established churches.

The strongest testimony of this character, however, is given by Thomas Story, the recorder of deeds in Pennsyl-

[26] P. 77.

[27] Penn Logan Correspondence, Vol. II., p. 354.

[28] Works of Thomas Chalkley, Phila., 1749, p. 70.

[29] William Ames, an accession to Quakerism from the Baptists, was the first to go to Holland and Germany, and it was he who first made the converts in Amsterdam and Kriegsheim.

vania, who made a trip to Holland and Germany in 1715. There he preached in the Mennonite meeting houses at Hoorn, Holfert, Drachten, Goredyke, Hoerveen, Jever, Oudeboone, Grow, Leeuwarden, Dokkum and Henleven, while at Malkwara no meeting was held because "a Person of note among the Menists being departed this life," and none at Saardam because of "the chief of the Mennists being over at Amsterdam." These meetings were attended almost exclusively by Mennonites, and they entertained him at their houses. One of their preachers he described as "convinced of truth," and of another he says that after a discourse of several hours about religion they "had no difference." Jacob Nordyke, of Harlingen, a "Menist and friendly man," accompanied the party on their journey, and when the wagon broke down near Oudeboone he went ahead on foot to prepare a meeting. The climax of this staid good fellowship was capped, however, at Grow. Says Story in his journal: "Hemine Gosses, their preacher, came to us and taking me by the hand he embraced me and saluted me with several kisses, which I readily answered, for he expressed much satisfaction before the people, and received us gladly, inviting us to take a dish of tea with him. . . . He showed us his garden, and gave us his grapes of several kinds, but first of all a dram lest we should take cold after the exercise of the meeting," and "treated us as if he had been a Friend, from which he is not far, having been as tender as any at meeting."

William Sewel, the historian, was a Mennonite, and it certainly was no accident that the first two Quaker histories were written in Holland.[30] It was among the Mennonites

[30] Sewel and Gerhard Croese. In my library is the copy of Burrough's works which Penn gave to Sewel's mother, containing also the autograph of Sewel

they made their converts [31] In fact, transition between the two sects both ways was easy. Quakers became members of the Mennonite church at Crefeld [32] and at Haarlem,[33] and in the reply which Peter Henrichs and Jacob Claus, of Amsterdam, made in 1679 to a pamphlet by Heinrich Kassel, a Mennonite preacher at Kriegsheim, they quote him as saying "that the so-called Quakers, especially here in the Palatinate, have fallen off and gone out from the Mennonites."[34]

These were the people who, some as Mennonites,[35] and others, perhaps as recently converted Quakers, after being unresistingly driven up and down the Rhine for a century and a half, were ready to come to the wilds of America. Of the six original purchasers Jacob Telner and Jacob Isaacs Van Bebber are known to have been members of the Mennonite Church; Govert Remke,[36] January 14. 1686, sold his land to Dirck Sipman, and had little to do with the emigration; Sipman selected as his attorneys here at various times Hermann Op den Graeff, Hendrick Sellen, and Van Bebber, all of whom were Mennonites; and Jan Streypers was represented also by Sellen, was a cousin of the Op den Graeffs, and was the uncle of Hermannus

---

[31] Sewel, Barclay, Seidensticker

[32] Life of Gerhard Roosen, p 66

[33] Story's Journal, p.490.

[34] This valuable pamphlet is in the library of A H Cassel

[35] In this connection the statement of Hortensius in his Histoire des Anabaptistes, Paris, 1695, is interesting. He says in the preface: "Car cette sorte de gens qu'on appelle aujourd hui Mennonites ou Anabaptists en Holande et ceux qui sont connus en Angleterre sous le nom de Koakres ou Trembleurs, qui sont partagés en plus de cent sortes de Sectes. ne peuvent point conter d'autre origine que celle des Anabaptistes de Munster quoi qu'a present ils se tiennent beaucoup plus en repos, et qu'ils n'ayent aucune ambition pour le governement ou l'administration des affaires temporelles, et mesme que le port ou l' usage de toute sortes d'armes soit entierement defendu parmi eux."

[36] Johann Remke was the Mennonite preacher at Crefeld in 1752

and Arnold Kuster, two of the most active of the early Pennsylvania members of that sect. Of the emigrants Dirck, Hermann and Abraham Op den Graeff were Mennonites, and were grandsons of Hermann Op den Graeff, the delegate from Crefeld to the Council which met at Dordrecht in 1632, and adopted a Confession of Faith.[37] Many of the others, as we have seen, were connected with the Op den Graeffs by family ties. Jan Lensen was a member of the Mennonite Church here. Jan Lucken bears the same name as the engraver who illustrated the edition of Van Braght published in 1685, and others of the books of that church, and the Dutch Bible which he brought with him is a copy of the third edition of Nicolaes Biestkens, the first Bible published by the Mennonites.[38] Lenart Arets, a follower of David Joris, was beheaded at Poeldyk in 1535. The name Tunes occurs frequently on the name lists of the Mennonite preachers about the time of this emigration, and Hermann Tunes was a member of the first church in Pennsylvania.

This evidence, good as far as it goes, but not complete, is strengthened by the statements of Mennonite writers and others on both sides of the Atlantic. Roosen tells us "William Penn had in the year 1683 invited the Mennonites to settle in Pennsylvania. Soon many from the Netherlands went over and settled in and about Germantown."[39] Funk, in his account of the first church, says: "Upon an invitation from William Penn to our distressed forefathers in the faith it is said a number of them emigrated either from

[37] Scheuten genealogy in the possession of Miss Elizabeth Muller, of Crefeld I am indebted for extracts from this valuable MS, which begins with the year 1562, to Frederick Muller, the celebrated antiquary and bibliophile of Amsterdam.

[38] The Bible now belongs to Adam Lukens, of North Wales, Bucks Co., Pennsylvania

[39] P 60

Holland or the Palatinate and settled in Germantown in 1683, and there established the first church in America."[40] Rupp asserts that, "In Europe they had been sorely persecuted, and on the invitation of the liberal-minded William Penn they transported themselves and families into the province of Pennsylvania as early as 1683. Those who came that year and in 1698 settled in and about Germantown."[41] Says Haldeman "Whether the first Taufgesinneten or Mennonites came from Holland or Switzerland I have no certain information, but they came in the year 1683."[42] Richard Townsend, an eminent Quaker preacher, who came over in the Welcome, and settled a mile from Germantown, calls them a "religious good people," but he does not say they were Friends, as he probably would have done had the facts justified it.[43] Abraham, Dirck, and Hermann Op den Graeff, Lenart Arets, Abraham Tunes and Jan Lensen were linen weavers, and in 1686 Jan Streypers wrote to his brother Willem inquiring "who wove my yarns, how many ells long, and how broad the cloth made from it, and through what fineness of comb it had been through."[44]

The pioneers had a pleasant voyage, and reached Philadelphia on the 6th of October. In the language of Claypoole, "The blessing of the Lord did attend us so that we had a very comfortable passage, and had our health all the way"[45] Unto Johannes Bleikers a son Peter was born while at sea. Cold weather was approaching, and they had little time to waste in idleness or curiosity. On the 12th of the same month a warrant was issued to Pastorius for six

[40] Mennonite Family Almanac for 1875
[41] History of Berks County, p. 423.
[42] Geschichte der Gemeinde Gottes, p 55
[43] Hazard's Register, Vol VI, 198
[44] Deeds, Streper MSS
[45] Claypoole letter-book

thousand acres "on behalf of the German and Dutch purchasers", on the 24th Thomas Fairman measured off fourteen divisions of land, and the next day meeting together in the cave of Pastorius they drew lots for the choice of location. Under warrant five thousand three hundred and fifty acres were laid out May 2, 1684, "having been allotted and shared out by the said Daniel Pastorius, as trustee for them, and by their own consent to the German and Dutch purchasers after named, as their respective several and distinct dividends, whose names and quantities of the said land they and the said Daniel Pastorius did desire might be herein inserted and set down, viz.: The first purchasers of Frankfort, Germany, Jacobus Van de Walle 535, Johan Jacob Schutz 428, Johan Wilhelm Uberfeld 107, Daniel Behagel 356⅔, George Strauss 178⅓, Jan Laurens 535, Abraham Hasevoet 535, in all 2675 acres of land. The first purchasers of Crefeld, in Germany, Jacob Telner 989, Jan Streypers 275, Dirck Sipman 588, Govert Remke 161, Lenert Arets 501, Jacob Isaacs 161, in all 2675 acres." In addition two hundred acres were laid out for Pastorius in his own right, and one hundred and fifty acres to Jurian Hartsfelder, a stray Dutchman or German, who had been a deputy sheriff under Andross in 1676, and who now cast his lot in with the settlers at Germantown.[46]

Immediately after the division in the cave of Pastorius they began to dig the cellars, and build the huts in which, not without much hardship, they spent the following winter. Thus commenced the settlement of Germantown. Pastorius tells us that some people making a pun upon the name called it *Armentown*, because of their lack of supplies, and adds, "it could not be described, nor would it be believed by coming generations in what want and need,

[46] Exemplification Record, Vol. I, p. 51. It is also said that Heinrich Frey was here before the landing of Penn.

and with what Christian contentment and persistent industry this Germantown-ship started."[47] Willem Streypers wrote over to his brother Jan on the 20th of 2d mo. 1684, that he was already on Jan's lot to clear and sow it and make a dwelling, but that there was nothing in hand, and he must have a year's provision, to which in due time Jan replied by sending a "Box with 3 combs, and 3 ——, and 5 shirts and a small parcel with iron ware for a weaving stool," and telling him "to let Jan Lensen weave a piece of cloth to sell, and apply it to your use." In better spirits Willem wrote Oct. 22d, 1684: "I have been busy and made a brave dwelling house, and under it a cellar fit to live in, and have so much grain, such as Indian Corn and Buckwheat that this winter I shall be better off than I was last year."[48]

[47] Seidensticker's Pastorius in the Deutsche Pioneer, Vol. II., p. 176.
[48] Streper MSS.

Arms of the Netherlands.

CHAPTER II.

THE FRANKFORT LAND COMPANY.

Die Stadt Frankfurt.

THERE was another force at work in Germany and Holland which had a conspicuous and important, though not a primary, influence upon the settlement of Germantown. In 1670 the celebrated Philip Jacob Spener, founder of the Pietists, established in the city of Frankfort a *Collegia Pietatis*, the object of which was to awaken a deeper and more heartfelt interest in religion by means of meetings of laymen for purposes of prayer and instruction. Among those who were brought within the sphere of this influence were Jacob Van de Wall, a merchant of Frankfort, to whom Neander dedicated his book of hymns; Dr. Johann Jacob Schutz, a great friend of Neander and a jurist, who was born in 1640 and died in 1690, and who wrote the beautiful hymn "Sei Lob und Ehr dem höchsten Gut": Johann William Ueberfeld, whom the church historian, Gotfried Arnold, designates as "brother Ueberfeld"; Daniel Behagel, merchant in Frankfort; Casper Merian, George Strauss, Abraham Hasevoet and Jan

Laurens, an intimate friend of Telner, who appears to have lived at Rotterdam.[49] In November, 1682, these eight

men, all of them of influence and distinction, had discussed at their meetings in Frankfort the subject of the purchase of a tract of land in Pennsylvania and had concluded

to make the venture. The motive which determined this action is no doubt expressed by Pastorius when he

[49] Max Goebel's Geschichte des Christlichen Lebens, Coblentz, 1852, Vol. II., p. 324–326.

Fr. Johanna Eleonora Petersen,
gebohrne von und zu Merlau
Hrn Dr. J. W. Petersen Eheliebste

says: "After I had sufficiently seen the European provinces and countries and the threatening movements of war and had taken to heart the dire changes and disturbances of the fatherland, I was impelled, through a special guidance from the Almighty, to go to Pennsylvania with the living hope that my own good, and that of my neighbor and the furthering of the honor of God, which is the chief point, would be advanced, since in Europe worldiness and sin increase from day to day and the just punishment of God cannot be much longer delayed."

Pastorius, who had been appointed their agent, bought for them when in London, between the 8th of May and the 6th of June, 1683, fifteen thousand acres of land which later was increased to twenty-five thousand acres. Before November 12, 1686, Merian, Strauss, Hasevoet and Laurens had withdrawn and their interests had become vested in Pastorius, the celebrated Johanna Eleanora Von Merlau, Dr. Gerhard Von Mastricht, Dr. Thomas Von Wylich, Johannes Le Brun, Balthasar Jawert and Dr. Johannes Kemler.

Johanna Eleanora Von Merlau was born at Frankfort in 1644, of a noble and distinguished family. She was inclined to religious thought and mysticism and early in life began to have dreams and see visions. When she was four years of age her parents, in order to escape the wars and rumors of war, had temporarily gone to Philipseck near Hettersheim. One day when her mother had been left with the three children, an older sister aged seven, Eleanora and an infant, suddenly the servants came with the cry that a troop of horse were upon them. The mother with the babe in her arms and the tots by her side, walked to Frankfort with the shouts of the soldiers and the shots of firearms resounding about her. When she reached a place of safety she fell upon her knees and gave thanks to God, whereupon the sister of seven years exclaimed: "What is the use of praying now, they cannot get at us any more."

When Eleanora was ten years old she asked permission to go to church to see her sister instructed in the mysteries of the Lord's Supper, and after she had seen it the devil put it into the head of some wicked person to accuse her of having said that if she could get hold of the cup she would drink the whole of it, as though she were fond of

wine. In her twelfth year she was taken to court to the Countess von Salms-Redelheim and in her fifteenth year to the wife of the Hertzog von Hollenstein, Countess of Hesse, who upon her first marriage became a princess. In her eighteenth year, in 1662, she saw in a dream in great golden figures upon the heavens "1685," which forecasted the disturbances and persecutions in France and also the secret of the Millennium which in that year was disclosed to her. She was married by Dr. Spener, September 17, 1680, at Frankfort, in the presence of her father, the Princess of Philipseck and thirty other persons, to one beneath her in rank, Dr. Johann Wilhelm Petersen, professor at Rostock, preacher at the church of St. Egidius in Hanover,

D. Joh. Wilhelm Petersen

J. N. J.

Hertzens-Gespräch
Mit
GOTT/
In
Zwey Theile
abgefasset/
und
Zu Aufmunterung anderer from-
men Gott-liebenden Seelen ans
Tage-Licht gestellet
von
Johanna Eleonora
Petersen/
gebohrnen von und zu Merlau.
Mit einer
Vorrede
Hn. Christian Kortholtens/
der H. Schrifft Doctoris, und bey der Kielischen Uni-
versität Prof. Prim.
Anietzo zum andernmahl gedruckt und mit
vielen schönen Kupffern gezieret.

Franckfurth und Leipzig/
Bey Johann Heinichen/. 1694.

Anleitung
zu gründlicher Verständniß
der
Heiligen
Offenbahrung
Jesu Christi
welche Er seinem Knecht und Apostel
Johanni
durch seinen Engel gesandt und gedeutet hat / sofern Sie
in ihrem eigentlichsten letzten prophetischen Sinn und Zweck
betrachtet wird/
und in ihrer völligen Erfüllung
in den allerletzten Zeiten/ denen wir nahe kommen sind/ grössten
Theils noch bevorstehet/
Nach Ordnung
einer dazu gehörigen
TABELLE,
Darinnen die heilige Offenbahrung
in der Harmonie der Dinge und Zeiten
kürtzlich entworffen ist/
Mit einer zur Vorbereitung dienlichen
Vor=Rede
und
Dreyfachem Anhange/
in wohlmeynender Liebe
nach dem Maaß der Gnade
mitgetheilet und herausgegeben
von
Johanna Eleonora Petersen/
gebohrnen von und zu Merlau.

Franckfurt und Leipzig: zu finden bey Johann Daniel Müllern, 1696.

bishop's superintendent at Lubeck, chief preacher and superintendent at Luneberg, and the author of one hundred and sixty books and pamphlets. Together they were among the founders of the Philadelphia Society at Berle-

burg, where later was published the "Geistliche Fama," containing so much information concerning early Pennsylvania. Their lives, with portraits, a book now so rare that Max Goebel, the learned author of the exhaustive history of the religious life along the Rhine, was never able to see a copy, appeared in 1717.[50] She was the author among other works of "Herzens-Gespräch mitt Gott," 12mo, 1694, and "Anleitung zu gründlicher Verstandniss der Heiligen Offenbahrung Jesu Christi," folio, 1696.

Dr. Thomas von Wylich was Secretary or Recorder of the city of Wesel and we are told that after forty years his good name there was still like a "plenteous balsam in fragrance."[51] Johannes Le Brun was a business man in Frankfort, one of those to whom Neander dedicated his hymn book, and Johannes Kemler was rector at Oldenslo

---

50 The foregoing incidents of her life are taken from my copy of this autobiography.

51 Goebel, Vol. II., p. 326.

and at Lubeck. Daniel Behagel, grandson of Jacob Behagel, was born at Hanau, November 18, 1625, and married at Muhlheim, May 20, 1654, Magdalena van Mastricht. Together with his brother-in-law, Jacob van de Wall, he in 1661 established the manufacture of faience at Frankfort.[52] Of the eleven persons interested five lived in Frankfort, two in Wesel, two in Lubeck and one in Duisburg. It was originally their intention to come to Pennsylvania, but, much to the regret of Pastorius, who complained loudly of their change of plan, this purpose was abandoned and the company formed later became only a seller of lands to the settlers whom other influences brought here, and a commercial undertaking. The twenty-five thousand acres of land bought by him constituted the most extensive single sale made by Penn in the settlement of his province.

On the 2d of April, 1685, Van de Wall, Petersen and his wife, Behagel, Schutz and Merian gave the following power of attorney to Pastorius:

"At all times and in all things the Lord be praised:

"When as Francis Daniel Pastorius, U. J. Licent'us, a German of Winsheim in Franckenland, did signify his Inclination to travel towards Pennsylvania, viz., that Province in America which heretofore was called New Neth-

[52] Notes of Henry S. Dotterer.

erland, Jacob van de Wallen of Francfort, Merchant, for himself and as attorney of John Wilhelm Petersen, of Lubeck, and of his wife Johanna Eleanora van Merlau, as also Johann Jacob Schutz of Francfort, U. J. Licent'us, and Daniel Behagel and Caspar Merian of Francfort,

Merchants, have trusted and Comited unto him the care & Administration of all their Estate, lands and Rights which they lawfully obtained there of William Penn, Govern'r in that part So that the said Pastorius, in the Name of the Constituents, shall receive and Conserve in the best form of Law the things themselves, the Possession thereof and other rights: Order the tillage of the ground and what belongs to husbandry there according to his best diligence, hire Labourers, grant part of the land to others, take the yearly Revenues or Rents; and shall and may do all what the Owners may do in administration, nevertheless all sorts of alienation and mortgaging excepted.

"To this end a certain sum of money has been delivered to his trusty hands: Of all which he shall and will yearly give an account to the Constituents or their Heirs; but the Constituents will not be obliged to any man by all his doings and Contracts: What will be reasonable shall be assigned unto him out of the expected Incomes or Rents in Pennsylvania.

"This being thus done hath been subscribed by the Parties own hands, Confirmed by Publick authority and Committed to divine blessing in Francfort on Mayn, a free city of the German Empire, in the year of Christ, according to vulgar account, 1683, the 2d day of the 2d month commonly called April.

"Jacobus Van de Walle,
For myself, and as attorney for John Wm.
Petersen and his wife Eleonora van Merlau.
"Daniel Behagel.
"John Jacob Schutz.
"Casper Merian.
"Francis Daniel Pastorius."

Another power of attorney was given to Pastorius dated May 5th, 1683, which though not extant was probably of the same purport, executed by Strauss, Hasevoet and Laurens, then interested in the purchase. On the 11th of July, 1683, Johan Wilhelm Ueberfeld sold his one thousand acres to Pastorius. The latter, who the same year came to Germantown, wrote on the 14th day of November, 1685, to Van de Wall, Schutz, Behagel and Petersen "that in case they would not free me of my promise in their Letter of Attorney, viz., to be accountable to the Constituents and their Heirs I was not at all able or willing so to do, but must lay down mine administration; for as much as they in like manner promised me to follow me to this Province the next ensuing year after my departure out of Germany, the which was not performed by them; Wherefore I expect an answer from all whether they would release unto me the sd mine obligation or not.[53]

[53] Pastorius MSS

To this request Schutz, with the approval of Petersen and wife, Van de Wall and Behagel, wrote June 30, 1686:

"Dear Brother: We thank God for thy joyful Recovery and Preservation of all the rest, Putting in so much no distrust at all in thy Fidelity and Diligence that we, especially I for mine own person, do approve thine accounts unseen: Nevertheless in case it is not against thee, only for a nearer advice sake to send such accounts over: at least to make no ill Precedent to any future successor whom perhaps we dare not fully trust without all care: It will be very pleasing to, and not against us, to approve them in optima forma."

An agreement forming what became known as the Frankfort Land Company and fixing the terms upon which its business should be conducted was executed November 12, 1686. Two printed copies of this agreement with the autographs, seals and coats-of-arms of each of the signers still exist and they are both in Philadelphia. That which was among the papers of William Penn now belongs to me and the other was recently purchased by the Historical Society of Pennsylvania, for two hundred dollars. At this time the owners were:

	Acres.
Jacob Van de Wallen	2500
Caspar Merian, now Jacob Van de Wallen	833⅓
Daniel Behagel	1666⅔
Johan Jacob Schutz	4000
Johan Wilhelm Uberfeld, now Francis Daniel Pastorius	1000
Jacob Van de Wallen	1666⅔
George Strauss, now Johanna Eleonora von Merlau, wife of Johan Wm Peterson.	1666⅔
Daniel Behagel	1666⅔
D. Gerhard von Mastricht.	1666⅔
D Thomas von Wylich	1666½
Johannes Le Brun.	1666⅔
Balthasar Jawert	3333⅓
Johannes Kemler	1666⅔

The agreement provided:

"The above said lands, wherever they are or hereafter shall be Assign'd Jointly and asunder, as also the Lots in the City, which over and above the aforementioned belong unto us, to wit, four or six places in the City of Philadelphia, for to build new houses upon, and a matter of 300 Acres in the Cities Liberty Situate before and about Philadelphia; And the land, which of late hath been bought upon the Skulkill for a Brick-kiln, together with all and every Edifices and other Improvements, which now are and hereafter in any place and quarter of all Pensilvania,

and also Victuals, Commodities, Cattle, household stuff and which we have sent thither, or bought or otherwise acquired there; and the present and future Real Rights and Privileges shall now and hereafter be and remain Comon in Equal Right according to Every One's above specified Share which he hath in the said Company.

"2. All and every Expenses for the Cultivating, Improvement and Buildings; Item for transporting of Servants, Tenants and other persons, as also Commodities, Victuals, tools, &c., and there in the sd Province for Tradesmen & labourers, &c., and universally all Charges of what Name soever, which hitherto have been spent in America and Europe, or hereafter at the next mentioned manner may be spent, shall be at Comon Costs after the rate of Every Ones Share.

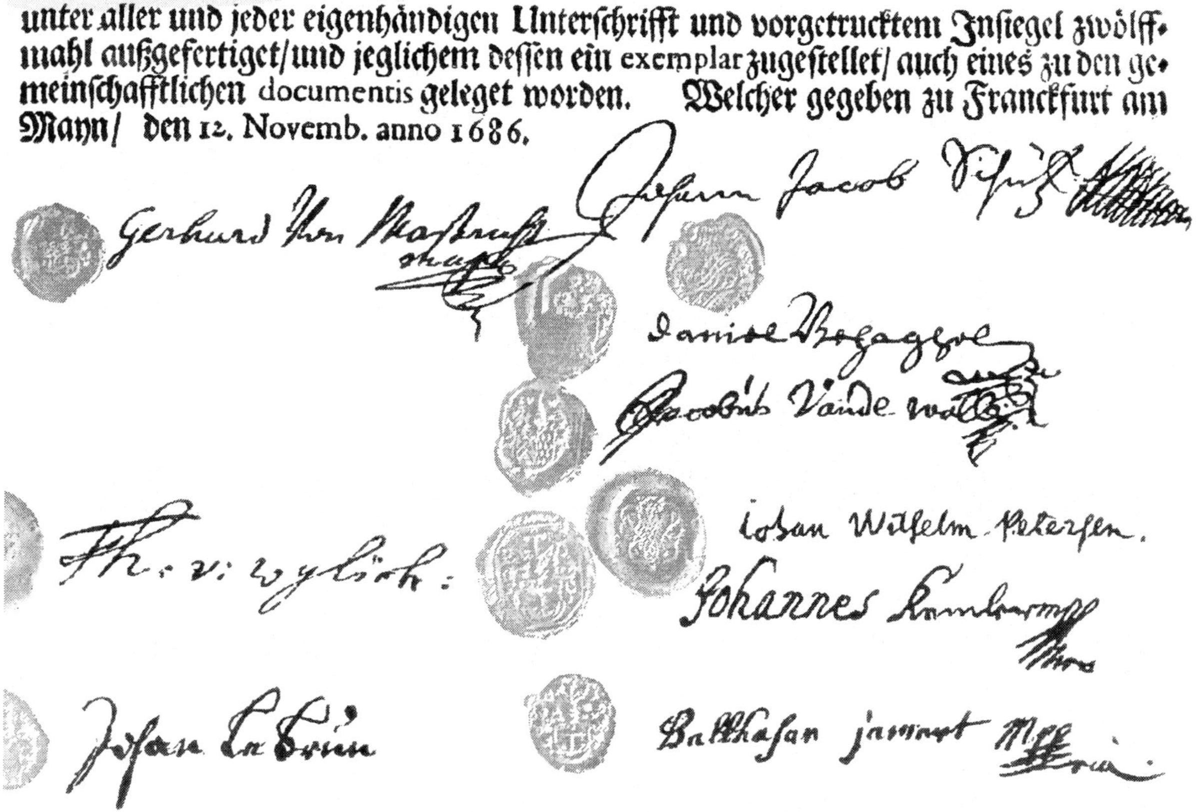
unter aller und jeder eigenhändigen Unterschrifft und vorgetrucktem Insiegel zwölff-mahl außgefertiget/und jeglichem dessen ein exemplar zugestellet/ auch eines zu den gemeinschafftlichen documentis geleget worden. Welcher gegeben zu Franckfurt am Mayn/ den 12. Novemb. anno 1686.

Gerhard von Mastricht

Johann Jacob Schütz

Daniel Behagel

Jacobus Van de walle

Th. v. Wylich

Johan Wilhelm Petersen.

Johannes Kemler

Johan Le Brün

Balthasar Jawert

AGREEMENT OF THE FRANKFORT LAND COMPANY.

"3. Per Contra all Profits, Revenues and whatsoever there is got, built, planted, tilled and brought forth, either in products of the Ground, Slaves, Cattle, manufactures &c., nothing at all Excepted, shall be Comon among all the Partners pro rata of the number of Acres.

"4. Concerning the Affairs of this Company, the five head-stems, every 5000 to be accounted for a head-stem, or as hereafter it may be otherwise Agreed upon, shall Consult among themselves, and by the Plurality of Votes (each thousand Acres having ten votes), conclude with all Convenient Speed.

"5. There in the s'd Province there shall be always an Attorney for the Company, and in case of his decease, Absence & Unableness a Substitute be appointed unto him with a Salary in writing Executed by both Parties. Both these shall yearly, under both their hands and the Company's Seal, make an Orderly Inventory of all the Companies effects there, Specifying the Cultivated and uncultivated Acres, meadows, waters, woods, houses, the bounds thereof, as also the Servants, Tenants, Cattel, fruits, Victuals, Comodities, debts Active and Passive, ready money, etc., and send the same over with their Accounts of Costs & Profits, Receipt & Disbursement, Decrease and Increase in all particulars, by one and another following Vessel with a second Original, and likewise in manner aforesaid Communicate the State of things to him, unto whom at that time the Correspondency of the Company shall be Committed.

"6. Here in these parts there shall be always Ordained by the plurality of Votes in Writing two Clerks of the Company, either of the Companions or Strangers, who shall attend the Companies Accounts & Correspondency in America; Open the letters which belong to them and Communicate the Contents thereof by way of Extract, or if need be a Copy to the head-Stems, by and from whom further all and every Partners are to receive, do & perform theirs, write down with short words yet Clearly & diligently in a Diary of the Pennsylvanian affairs out of the letters coming from thence or the Occurrencies happening here; make peculiar memorandums of what is to be done & Observed; Adjust every year ultimo Decembris the Accounts, together with the Revision of Inventories, and the Annotation of Increase & Decrease by Day and Date, as far as may be had by Letters or otherwise, and being approved by the five head-Stems or their Attornies, Record them in a Book, and keep them under two Locks, in good Order according to their Table or Index, together with the Companies Documents and Original Writings, ascribing Day & Date, as also the Copies of the Letters which they send away in a Certain Place as the Company Pleaseth, and now for the present time at Francfort upon the Mayn, where this work did first begin, and whereunto as yet the greatest part doth belong, and in all without the special consent of the five head-Stems not undertake or dispatch anything of Importance. Further they shall en-

joy for all their labour some moderate Recompense from the Company; Moreover each head-Stem may for himself & the Partners thereunto belonging extract out of such letters what he pleaseth; but the Originals shall be kept in the Archives.

"7. Hereafter the Company shall sign their letters & Contracts with a peculiar Seal to be kept along with the aforesaid Original Documents; and shall send another

Seal somewhat different in Bigness & Circumscription to their factors in Pennsilvania there to make the like use thereof. Without such Seal no Letters or Contracts shall be sent in the Companies Name thither or hither, nor be esteemed firm & good.

"8. In case any of us, or our heirs, should go to Pensilvania, or send an Attorney for himself aforehand to prepare him a Settlement and would give him or take along with himself, several proper things for his use, he or they may do the same at their own Costs and Riske; Afterwards, after the rate of his share for every thousand Acres, chuse for himself Sixty in one tract of uncleared land, So as we received the same of the Governr. And therefor he shall pay yearly a Recognition as Rent to the Company for every ten Acres One English Shilling: And if this land be not enough, but too narrow for him, there shall be further allowed unto him, proportionately to his share, 60 acres as aforesaid in consideration of each thousand for the Moiety of the Price for wch the Company useth to Let at that time upon Rent unto Strangers, And in case he should still desire more land, if the Company can spare it, at the price & on such Conditions as to a Stranger. Now upon these lands which one or the other settleth for himself alone in manner aforesd, he may act at his pleasure and use & enjoy all sorts of goods immoveable & moveable which we have in Comon there before other Strangers, Nevertheless that all this be unprejudicial to the Comon best of the Company. And those Companies which dwell in Pennsilvania shall pay the usual Rent. Wages, Payment, or Value, of all what they use of the Comon things for themselves to the Companies Factors there, whereof they are at the following Reparation to receive back their share. But if the whole Company do generally find good to let go over any of their Companions for their Comon Service and at their Comon Costs, there shall in that case be made a particular Agreement. But in every Case in all parts whatsoever the Companies there & their heirs shall be Obliged no less than those in Europe to stand to this Contract and to the further orders of the most votes.

"9. If the Clerks or else one or more by the Companies approbation as aforesaid should disburse money, such debtors shall be obliged to repay the thus disbursed principal Sum at the utmost within the space of one year with

the Yearly Interest of five per Cent, and therefor their share shall hereby in the best form of Law be engaged as a Special Pledge.

"10. If any of us or Ours soon or late shall Dye without wife & heir begotten in matrimony of his body, not having expressly & particularly declared by Testament, or other credible Disposition in Writing, or by word of mouth, what he would have done with his share of these Comon goods after his decease, his share shall accrue and be herewith assignd to the whole Company proportionably to each respective share, and shall not be otherwise accounted than as if he had reserved to himself only the use of such goods for the term of his life, and presently in the beginning Incorporated the true Property to the Company. And all deceases of the Companions, and who are their heirs in this work, shall by the Clerks then being in credible form under the attestation of all the nearest relations of the Deceased, or of other credible persons be advised with all speed, Or until the Certainty thereof the Name of the Deceased be continued in Accounts & Books, And his Contingent wc'h falls to him be kept in the Companies Case along with the Original Documents.

"11. It's not lawful for any that is a Partner in this Company to alien his land or right thereof, all or in part, to any without the Company, unless he have the Companies Consent, or at least made the first Offer to the same; But if one or other of us, our Wives, Children or whoever shall be hereafter a Partner of the Company, should be willing soon or late to alienate his Share or Portion, and none of the Company to Acquire or buy the Same, then and not otherwise the Seller shall have liberty to sell it to any other; yet with this Proviso, that always the Company, or if they will not have it, any of the Company, within three months after the Alienation is made known, shall have liberty to take to themselves that what is sold, paying down the consideration money, and for their profit to deduct or give less than such new Purchaser bought the part alien'd for Ten per Cent. of the Consideration Money, the Price whereof both Seller & Buyer shall be obliged to declare upon their Conscience.

"12. In Case, which we do not expect, be it soon or late, there should happen any misunderstanding or Cause of Contention between us, Our Heirs & Successors, Concerning these Goods & what thereon doth depend, the same shall be determined among the members of the Company, Or if both parties do not account them wholly Impartial by other than two honest Persons unanimously Chosen by the differing parties, And these two Chosen Persons shall have power to take unto them a third, if they think it necessary, in form & manner hereafter described, vizt. the chosen Arbitrators on an appointed day & place, in the presence of the differing parties or their Attornies, after the Invocation of Divine Assistance and ripe Consideration of the matter, shall determine the business by their award according to their best knowledge & Sentiment, in case they cannot bring the parties to a Composition; But if these three cannot agree, or find out the most votes, they shall send for advice to one or two of the head-Partners, and then Conceive and pronounce their Award; To the Contrary whereof afterwards in no manner or ways any thing shall be done, acted or admitted by Right or Force of no Judge or Man in the whole world in Europe or America; And if any should presume to oppose himself hereunto, eo ipso for by so doing, he shall forfeit his whole share and besides pay a fine of 200 rix Dollars to the publick Almonery (or to the poor) ipso facto without any exception or further declaration.

"All faithfully and without Covin. In true witness this present Contract, to which all Partners after a ripe Consideration did unanimously Consent, is twelve times under all & every ones own hand & Seal set forth, and an Exemplar thereof delivered to each, and one laid up with the Comon Documents.

"Given at Francfort upon Mayn the 12th November Anno 1686."

Pastorius, though with apparent reluctance, continued as the agent of the company to look after its interests until some time in the year 1700. On the 24th of January of that year Catharina Schutz, widow, the widow of Jacob Van de Wall, the heirs of Daniel Behagel, Johannes Kemler, Balthasar Jawert, Joh. Wilhelm Petersen, Gerhard von Mastricht, Johan Le Brun, and Maria Van de Wall, widow of Thomas Von Wylich, united in executing a power of attorney which set out that "because of the death of some heads of the sd Company & the Interruption of the French Warr, as also chiefly because of the absence of the Governor & the Indisposition of the sd our Factor, these our affairs in the sd Province are come to a stop, the more mentioned Mr. Pastorius having also desired by & in several of his Letters to be discharged" there was conferred full power and authority on "Mr. Daniel Falkner & Johannes Kelpius, as Inhabitants for the present in Pennsilvania, as also on Mr. Johannes Jawert, the son of one of our principals by name Mr. Balthasar Jawert of Lubeck, who hath resolved to transport himself thither."

Wir endts unterschriebene, in beiden Teutschland und
Holland, die wir zu 25000 Acker ungetheilten
Landts in Pensylvania laut deren darüber besagenden
documenten, mit besondern privilegien und Gerechtig-
keiten gesambter Handt gekaufft hat, und deßwegen eine
[illegible] 1686 beliebten brieffs, eine
Societät geschlossen, auch zur Cultivir- und Administrirung solchen Landts Herren Frantz Daniel Pastorium
U.J. Lum, besage deß unterm 2ten Aprill 1683 auß-
gefertigten procuratorii, bevollmächtiget haben; und
aber durch absterben einiger Häupter dieser unserer Compagnie und des grossen eingefallenen Frantzösischen Kriegs
wie nicht weniger wegen abwesenheit des Herren Gouverneurs und indisposition, unsers besagten factors
diese Sachen [illegible] sindt, so wegen
mehrerer Herr Pastorius auch bißhero in verschiedenen
brieffen erinnert hat, Ihme diese verwaltung wieder
abzunehmen; daß wir zu solchem Ende Volkommene
Macht und Special gewalt auffgetragen haben, Herren
Daniel Falckner, und Herrn Johann Kelpio, alß
nunmehrigen Einwohnern, in Pensylvania, wie auch
Herren Johann Jawert, alß [illegible] und principalen
Nahmen Herren Balthasar Jawert von Lübeck, welcher
[illegible] ist, also und dergestalt
daß diese unsere drey gevollmächtigte gesambter
Handt, oder in fall einer oder der andern tödtlichen Hin-
tritts, die oder der noch im leben übrig bleibende die
administrirung aller unserer da selbst habenden Güther
und Landereyen, wie und wo sie auch sambt und sonderl.
angewiesen seyn, oder noch anzuweisen, und zu zu-
messen sindt, auch deren über die 25 m Acker Landt uns
Competirenden Stattloße, nemblich der Drey oder Vierß
Plätze in der Statt Philadelphia und in circa 300 Acker
in der Statt gerechtigkeit und freyheit bey und umb
Philadelphia gelegen, und dessen an Scollkiel zur

Hypothecirung verhafften Landes, sambt allen und jeden
auffstehenden Gebäuden, und anderen meliorationen
eingesessen gefundenen, dorten gekaufften oder sonsten
erlangten Victualien, Kauffmans Wahren, Vieh, Hauß-
geräht, Werckzeug, dienstbotten, Tagelöhnern, und andern
Sachen, in optima forma, haben, auch dieselbe an
unserem Nahmen von obbesagtem unserem bißherigen
bevollmächtigten pastorio abforderen, fordern, pflegen und
abnehmen. Hiernechst alle solche unsere güther und
Effecten, da einige davon ohne unser wissen veraüssert
wären, zuforderst vindiciren, selbige überhaupt, oder
besonders, wie sich am besten wird thun lassen, verhandlen,
vertauschen, verkauffen, das geld dafür erheben, darüber quittiren, transfixiren, Documenten, auffertigen,
Wehrschafften leisten, und in Suma alles thun und
lassen sollen, was wir selbsten hiergegen, thun und lassen
solten, könten oder möchten, cum potestate substituendi
et substitutionem, toties quoties revocandi, cum ess-
clausulis, rati, grati, omnibusqe aliis, illius loci et fori,
necessariis et consuetis, und da mehr gewalt diese unsere
bevollmächtigte einiger weiterer Gewallt, als hierinn
enthalten, bedürfftig sein solten, denselben, wollen wir
ihnen gleichfalls hiemit vollmächtig hiermit ertheilet, auch
dasigen Edlen Herrn Gouverneurs und Obrigkeiten
gehörend ersucht haben, selbige dafür zu erkennen
und denenselbigen alle Obrigkeitliche Hülffe, da sie
solches benöhtiget sein würden, auff ihre ansuchen zu
leisten, dahingegen werden diese unsere bevollmächtigte
sambt und sonders angewiesen, an die beyde Hauptstämme
zu Francfurth am Mayn, wegen Herrn Jacob van de
Walle und Daniels behagels seel. Erben, von allen und jeden
ihren verrichtungen zeitlich part, bericht und Rechenschafft
zu geben; auch gelder oder wahren an dieselben über
Engellandt zu addressiren, mit ihnen zu Correspondiren
und von ihnen in Nahmen der gantzen Compagnie

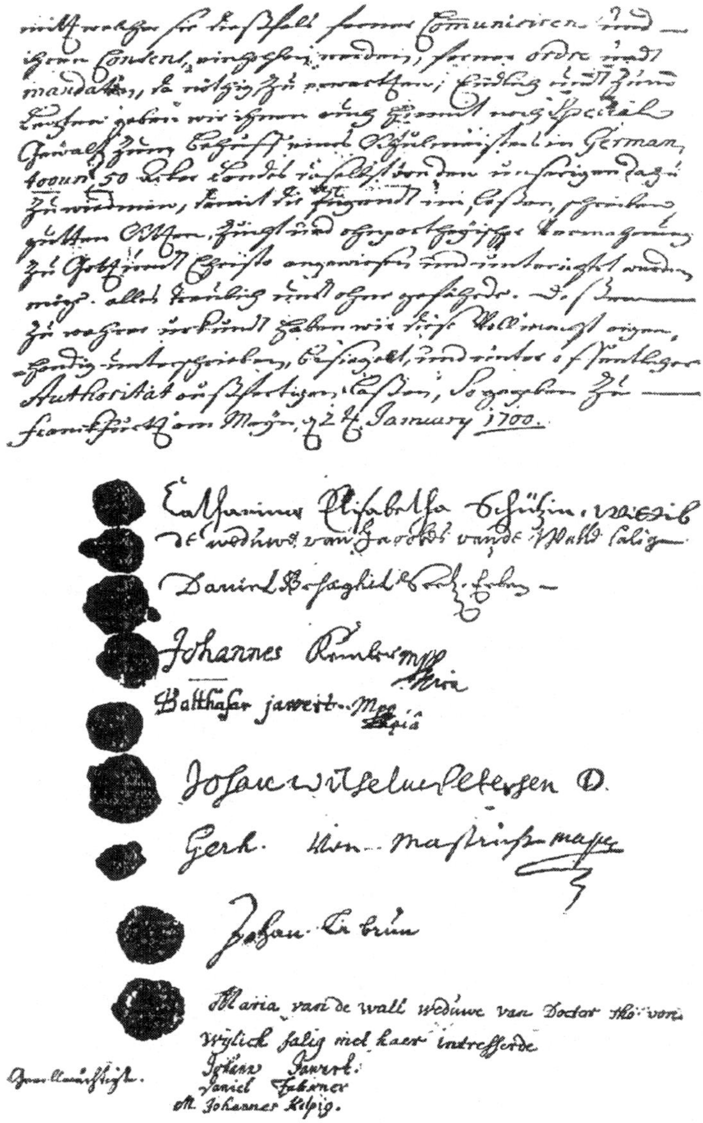

The three attorneys "Jointly or in case of the Death of one or the other they or he who remains" were to have the administration of all the goods and lands, city lots, "the land bought by the Schuylkill for a brick-kiln," to take an account from Pastorius, if any lands had been sold without their knowledge to "vindicate them" and to sell and make deeds. "Lastly we grant unto them herewith special power to appropriate fifty acres of our land in Germantown for the benefit of a schoolmaster, that the youth in reading writing & in good manners & education without partial admonishing to God and Christ may be brought up and instructed."[54]

On the first of March, 1700 (this date may be 1708), Catharine Elizabeth Schutz, widow, made a deed of gift certifying that "of a well Considered mind willingly and of my accord . . I have given as a free Gift or Present my whole Proportion or share of the 25000 acres of land purchased in Pensilvania—towit 4000 acres the wch my aforesd husband deceased hath bought of my own money,—unto some pious families and Persons who are already in Pensilvania, or Intend to go thither this year, as likewise unto such that shall follow them in time to Come, among whom Mr. Daniel Falkner, who hath settled there already, & Mr. Arnold Stork who dwells at present at Duisburg but will shortly transport himself, shall be constituted and appointed as Attornies, as well for themselves & their families to take part thereof, as also according to their good Pleasure & Conscience to Cause to participate other pious families, especially the widows among the same, viz: widow Zimmermans & other two widows with their children being of Duisburg." And she added "For as much as I also understand that George Muller of Freder-

[54] The original of this power of attorney now belongs to me

ickstadt is resolved to transport himself with his family into Pennsylvania my will is that he with his shall be one participant in this Donation."[55]

Pastorius says that in August, 1700, Daniel Falkner and Johannes Jawert having arrived they began, with Kelpius, to administer the affairs of the company, and that he delivered up to them the land, house, barn, stable, corn in and above the ground, cattle, household goods, utensils and two hundred and thirty pounds of arrears of rent, but that soon after Kelpius declined to act and Daniel Falkner "Plaid the Sot, making Bonefires of the company's flax in open street, giving a Piece of eight to one Boy to show him in his drunken Fit a house in Philada, and to another a bit to light him his Pipe, &c. In so much that his Fellow Attorney, Johannes Jawert, affixed an advertisement to the Meeting house at Germantown that nobody should pay any rent or other Debt due to the Company unto the sd Falkner. Yea, and the then Bailif and Burgesses of the Germantown corporation acquainted the sd Company of the ill Administration of this their attorney here in a letter which as they afterwards did hear miscarried."[56]

Kelpius executed the following paper witnessed by Godfried Seelig and Joh. Hendrick Sprogell:

"Whereas, upon recommendation of Mr. Daniel Falkner, the Frankfort Society hath made me ye subscribed their Plenipotentiary, together with the said Mr. Falkner & John Jawert, But my Circumstances not permitting to entangle myself in the like affairs I do Confess herewith that I do deliver all the authority, which is given unto me in the Letter of Attorney, to the said Society & him who did recommend me to the same, towit, Mr. Daniel Falk-

[55] Pastorius MSS

[56] Pastorius MSS

ner, for to act & prosecute the Case of the said Society without me with Johan Jawert upon their account according to the Letter of Attorney who attributes to one or two as much power as to three in Case of a natural or Civil Death."[57] Jawert and Falkner on March 20th, 1705, substituted and appointed George Lowther, an attorney at law in Philadelphia, the attorney in fact for the constituents. Lowther acted under the power because, on the 26th day of March, 1706, he gave notice to the tenants and other debtors to meet him on Friday, the 5th of April, at the house of Joseph Coulson in Germantown.

Meanwhile, in consequence of the notice given at the meeting house in Germantown on the 9th of November, 1705, by Jawert, no one would buy lands from Falkner, and the affairs remained in statu quo until the arrival in Pennsylvania of John Henry Sprogell, the witness to the renunciation of Kelpius. Pastorius asserts that Sprogell, "A cunning and fraudulent fellow, as appears by several letters sent from Holland after him, arrived in this Province, who one time would say that his father had some Interest in the Francfort Company, which is utterly false; and another time that he bought the Companies estate of Gerhard van Mastricht and the rest when in Germany and that the French took away his writings; which is no more true than the former. For after he was taken, he still for some weeks did lye in Holland, and so might either have had other deeds from them, or at least a letter from any of them to signify unto their attornies here that he bought the land, which he never bought one acre of, as since the said Van Mastricht did write."

[57] Ibid.

It appears that Falkner had some kind of a writing, under which he claimed the right to act alone for the company, because Pastorius says in opposition to it that it was a mere declaration signed by but two of the company and they the youngest, that it did not attempt to revoke the prior power given to the three attorneys, and that when Lowther presented it on behalf of Falkner to the court at Germantown and asked to have it recorded, the court refused upon the ground that it must be proved by two witnesses. Thereupon, Falkner, being over head and ears in debt, and having failed to sell under this authority, united with Sprogell and made a friend of David Lloyd by giving to him a thousand acres of land which belonged to Benjamin Furly, of Rotterdam.[58] Lloyd suggested an action of ejectment based upon the claim of Sprogell, and in which there could be a recovery by arrangement with Falkner acting as attorney for the company, and it is asserted by Pastorius that it was carried forward to judgment without notice to him, Jawert, or any one else interested in behalf of the company. He further complains: "And many honest men in high and low Germany, who are sincerely inclined to truth, Peace, Righteousness & Christianity, would not be occasioned to think so strange of this the Pennsylvanian Lawyers Way of Ejectment sine die; especially when they hear that one called a Quaker had a hand in it: and the sd Pastorius might at least have obtained somewhat of a salary for his Service done unto the sd Company Seventeen Years and a half, and what he disbursed of his own during that time. Now the Company being thus miserably dispossessed of their Estate, as aforementioned, the sd Pastorius one with Arnold Cassel went to David Lloyd, and Complaining of the Wrong, also de-

[58] Pastorius MSS Phœnixville now stands upon this land.

sired his Advice, presented him a small fee, which he refused to take; but told him that he the sd Pastorius & Johannes Jawert were not included in the Ejectment, which they knew already. And when the sd Pastorius further asked the sd David Lloyd what was best for him to do? David drawing his shoulders told him that his land (viz., the 1000 acres) was Involved in that of the Company, and that he must seek for it at Sprogels, which Counsel the sd Pastorius scrupled to embrace."[59]

In these proceedings and in the manner indicated a judgment in ejectment was obtained in favor of the plaintiff, execution was issued and possession given.

Sprogell immediately began to cut the timber. On the 1st of March, 1708-9 Pastorius and Jawert presented petitions to the Governor and Council Pastorius says that Sprogell "thro the contrivance or Ploting of Daniel Falkner, in ye last adjourned Court held for the County of Philada, the 15th of January, by means of Fictio juris as they term it (wherewith your petitioner is altogether unacquainted) hath gott a writt of Ejectmt, wch it doth not effect your petitioner, yet the said Sprogel would have Ejected him out of his home," and that Sprogell "gott the said Writt of Ejectmt, so as to finish this his Contrivance in the County Court, to be held third day of the next month, between wch and the former no Provincial Court doth intervene for a Writt of Error, & hath further feed or retain'd the four known lawyers of this Province, in order to deprive as well your Petitr., as likewise Johannes Jawert of all advice in law, wch sufficiently argues his cause to be none of the best."

Jawert says in his petition that Sprogell "upon his arrival from Holland first told your Petitr. that he had bought ye

[59] Pastorius MSS

said Estate of those persons residing in Germany, but afterwards denying it, again preferred to buy ye same of your Petitr., who is a partner thereof, and his joynt attorney, Danll Falkner, and when your Petitr. could not accept of his terms, he offering a very inconsiderable sum, then he promised one hundred pounds to your Petitr. gratis, or to put up for himself; but your Petitr. not willing to betray his trust, broke off: and so before he was aware & without ye least of his knowledge said Sprogel . . . ejected the said Germans out of ye said their estate . . . and besides he, ye said Sprogel & Falkner, to make this their abominable plott to bear, did fee all the known attornies, or Lawyers, of this Province, either to speak for ym, or to be silent in Court, in order to deprive your Petitr. of all advice in law, even so much as to find none to signify this, your Petitioners complaint, or to draw a Peticon to your Honour and Council in due form in our English method."[60]

The clerk of the council says that the attempt was so heinous that it was scarcely considered credible. The petitioners were called in and examined, and it then appeared that "David Lloyd was principal agent & Contriver of the whole, and it was affirmed that he had for his pay a thousand acres of Benjamin Furley's land which he the said Benjamin was so weak as to intrust to Sprogel with the disposal of." It was ordered that "notice be given by all Conveyances that may be to the Frankfort Society of Purchasers yt they forthwith send full powers to reverse ye judgment according to law."[61]

So far as we know the judgment was never reversed and Sprogell retained possession. In 1713 Jawert presented the matter to the Friends' meeting doubtless for the purpose

[60] Colonial Records, Vol. II., p 430

[61] Colonial Records, Vol II, p 432

of having some condemnation visited by them upon David Lloyd. Fortunately we have this communication which says:

"To the Monthly Meeting of those whom the world calls Quakers, at Philadelphia:

"Honorable Respected Friends: I have been informed by my Friend Pastorius that you desire to let you know the proceedings agt the Francfort Company, which Company every member of it have always bore a great respect & love to those wch the world calls Qrs for good but will take it very strange, to be used as they have been, in their Country & under their Govermt. Not that I can say or suppose that any of the real friends which fear God have had any hand in it, neither can I blame the honorable Court that was at that time, they were ignorant of the matter! But I must blame one of your friends, as he calls himself, David Lloyd, to take such dirty cause in hand for the lucre of some great reward. Respected friends, to tell you first by what power daniel Falkner did that wicked act he hath none at all, not so much as to sell one foot of the Companies land without my consent, which will appear by the letter of Attorney of which friend Pastorius has a Copie. But it seems falkner by the advice of abovsd friend D. L. produced a letter of one of the Company in Court, when they was just breaking up, which impowers him, to sell the land as he says. If this letter was a true letter it could impower him no more as if any stranger had impowered him because of the agreement between all the members of the Company to act or do nothing without the Consent & knowledge of all the members, of which I and Pastorius are 2, much lesser to sell all their land by ONE'S order. When this wicked plot was contrived by them two Children of darkness, Daniel Falkner and Sprogel, they knew well enough that they could do nothing honestly without my consent, as one of the chief owners & attourney for the said company. Now to get me in, & save the money they saw they must give the lawyers, abovesd Sprogel came to my house and offered some small sum of money for the land to wch I could not consent. So Sprogel seeing that would not do offered me hundred pounds for a bribe, of wch the rest of the company should not know, besides my share in the land. But I told him that I rather would loose all my land than betray my trust. Seeing now that their wicked design would not prevail with me they sett david to work, without doubt he was well paid for it, (for which I understand friend fuily suffers). David lloyd willing that his brethren should have a share in the buty, or else would not be seen to act alone, getts two more. Macnemary had but two periwicks, worth about ten pounds, for his fee as he told me himself. Now when it was concluded among them to fullfil their design they thought the fittest time when the Court was breaking up. According they did. But Mr. Clark being there which had had no share yet thought it very strange that such a weighty business should be called at the breaking up of the Court, asked what it was. David Lloyd finding Clark inquiring very earnestly in the matter, for fear their wicked design should be discovered, said "Thom. hold thy tongue, thou shalt have fourty shillings" And so it was done. When friend Pastorius gave me notice of this I went directly up to Philadelphia and going to the Lawyers found all their tongues bound, was therefore obliged to petition the Governor & Council to allow one Lawyer, which was Clark, who had only a promise of fourty shillings, but not received the same. But could not untie his tongue before I gave him tenn pounds ready down in silver & gold. For which ten pounds & other fast expenses I had not so much good as I had of a pott good beer & a penny roll. Friend Pastorius & Caspar Hood can tell more of it. But hope that the Lord that is the right Judge will not suffer such wickedness, but will lead the hearts of upright men to punish such wicked doings I design to be up so soon as possible & see what I can do in it with the help of God and Christian Friends. I must beg your pardon dear friends that I trouble you with such a large letter. Wish the Lord your God and my God may comfort & bless you through his son Jesus and the power of the Holy Spirit. I am respected friends your friend and servant.

"John Jawert,

"Maryland, Bohemia river, March the 25th Ano. 1713."

Some years later the survivors of the Company offered to convey such interests as they possessed to the Society in London organized for the propagation of the Gospel in foreign parts. This Society made an investigation which led to no substantial results. The efforts of the Pietists of Frankfort which began in religious enthusiasm ended in pecuniary misfortune. Wanting in that earnestness or persistency of purpose, or perhaps not driven by the same urgency of oppression, which led the purchasers at Crefeld to cross the seas, they constituted an interesting episode but not a potent factor in the early life of Germantown.

London.

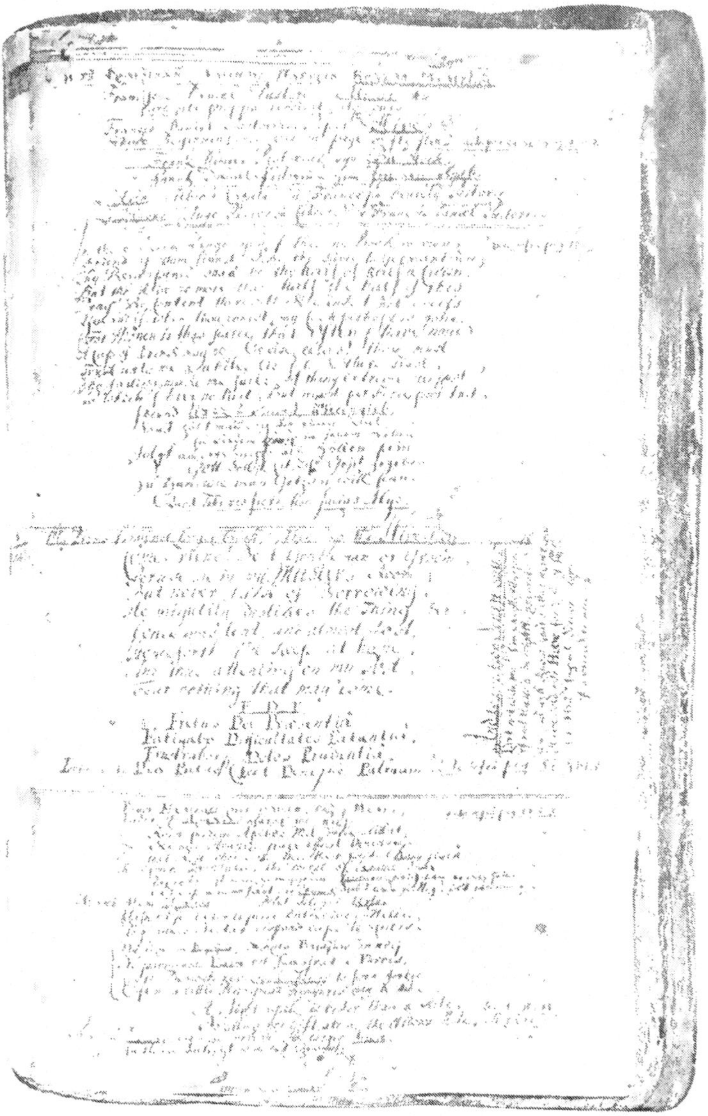

PAGE FROM THE BEE-HIVE OF PASTORIUS.
WRITTEN IN SEVEN LANGUAGES.

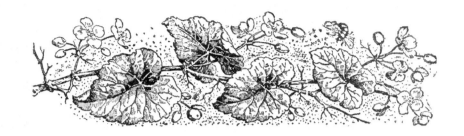

CHAPTER III.

Francis Daniel Pastorius.[62]

Pastorius.

WE now approach the career of one, who though his connection with the settlement was in a sense accidental, and though the movement which led to it cannot be ascribed to his endeavors, was nevertheless the most interesting and conspicuous figure in association with early Germantown. He well deserves an exalted place among American worthies and his life in its self abnegation, its literary productiveness and its breadth of liberality, appears the more admirable when contrasted with the narrow intelligence and restricted outlook of the leaders of the Puritan settlements

[62] The sources of this biography are Pastorius' Umständige Geographische Beschreibung Pennsylvaniae, 1700; his Thesis 1676; his MSS. in the Historical Society of Penna. and in my possession; and Dr. Seidensticker's papers in the Deutsche Pionier, Cincinnati, 1870, Vols. II. and III.

or with the tobacco-dealing and Indian robbing impulses of those who have been called Cavaliers. His grandfather, Martin Pastorius, was assessor of the Court at Erfurt. When Gustavus Adolphus captured the town the soldiers were quartered in the house, which was upon the horse-market, and plundered it, driving out the children with their drawn swords. The father rode to Mayence to make complaint, but again fell into the hands of the Swedish soldiers and was driven out naked and so badly beaten that in a few weeks afterwards he died. His wife was Brigitta, daughter of Christian Flinsberger, of Mühlhausen.

Melchior Adam, son of Martin, was born at Erfurt, then containing twenty thousand people, on the 21st of September, 1624. In his childhood he met with many misadventures. Once, when nine months old, his mother fell with him from a boat into the Rhine, and later he felt the weight of the swords of the soldiers in the army of Gustavus. He went to school at Erfurt, and studied poetry and rhetoric there, and at Wurtzburg, philosophy. He traveled to Gotha, Fulda, Frankfort, Mayence, Aschaffenburg, Wurtzburg and to Rome, where, August 26, 1644, he entered the college, and after four years was graduated Lit. Doctor. It indicates the manners of the times that once he slept in a very dark chamber of an inn, while under the bed lay the body of a dead man which emitted a dreadful odor. From Rome he went to Vienna and thence to France, and at Nancy could find no inn and walked the streets all night, hearing the dogs bark and the cocks crow. At Meaux he and his friend were arrested as spies, and when he showed his passport and letters from Cardinal Mazarine was told: "It is these books which make all the trouble and disturbance in the land." He reached Paris at a time of great tumult and unquiet, and, being compelled to keep within his room, there wrote four little books. On the 12th of June, 1649, he departed for Amiens, Lyons, Geneva and Basle, and the same year at Sommerhausen was converted to the Lutheran faith. He married Magdalena, daughter of Stephen Dietz and Margaretha Fischer, and widow of Henrich Frischman. Learned in both law and theology he settled at Windsheim, of which he wrote a history and where he held many offices, including those of burgomaster and Superior Judge.

Francis Daniel Pastorius, son of Melchior and Magdalena, was born in Sommerhausen, Sept. 26th, 1651. His sponsors in baptism were Daniel Gering, Doctor of Law at Leghitz, and Franciscus, Freyherr of Limburg, the latter of whom gave him a red scarlet coat, little sword, a hat with a feather and little white boots, "thus making a fool of me in my tender years." At eleven years of age his father took him to Windsheim and there he went to the gymnasium to school. The teacher, Tobias Schumberg, a Hungarian, knew no German, and the pupils were compelled to talk to him in Latin. On the 31st of July, 1668, he entered the school at Altdorf and from there August 11, 1670, he went to the University of Strasburg, where he began to study law and French. In July of 1672 he was at the high school at Basle, but in November returned to Windsheim. On the 13th of April, 1673, he went to Altdorf and July 2d from there to Nuremburg and Erfurt and thence to Jena, where on the 13th he renewed his study of the law and learned Italian, and in January, 1674, and again April 18, had a public discussion in that language upon some legal problem. Thereafter having visited Naumburg and Gotha he journeyed, July 31, to Regensburg in order to secure a better knowledge of jurisprudence, and on April 16, 1675, he returned from Bayreuth to Windsheim. From there, Sept. 17th, he went again to Altdorf, where finally on the 23d of November, having passed his examinations, he read his inaugural thesis and was graduated in law. His copy of this Latin thesis entitled "Disputatio inauguralis de rasura docmentorum" printed at Altdorff, and the only known copy, is now in my library. It closes with a Latin anagram upon the names of Melchior Adam Pastorius, his father, Dorothea Esther Volckmans, his stepmother, Franciscus Daniel Pastorius and Johannes Samuel Pastorius, his brother, and is explained in his own manuscript. After having taken his degree he went home to Windsheim. On the 24th of April, 1679, he made a journey to Frankfort on the Mayn and there had a private school of law for some students and practiced a little. The opportunity arose to visit Worms, Mannheim and Speyer. From December 1, 1679, to June 26, 1680, he lodged with Squire Fickard, "A merry hearted old gentleman." On the latter day he began a tour through Holland, England, France and Switzerland with Johann Bonaventura von Rodeck, "a noble young spark," whom he accompanied as tutor and to whom he had been recommended by Doctor Spener, "The brave patriarch of the Pietists," and returned to Frankfort fresh and well on the 16th of November, 1682. There he met in the house called "Saalhof" Dr. Spener, Dr. Schutz, Jacob Van de Wall and Eleanora von Merlau, and heard from his friends many reports concerning Pennsylvania. Already some God-fearing people, among whom were the Notary Christian

DISPUTATIO INAUGURALIS
De
RASURA DOCU-MENTORUM,
Qvam,
DIVINA SUFFRAGANTE GRATIA,
AUCTORITATE
MAGNIFICI
JCTORUM ORDINIS
in Incluto Noribergensium Athenæo,
pro
LICENTIA
Summos in Utroqve Jure Honores ac
Privilegia DOCTORALIA, more Majorum,
rite capessendi,
Publico Eruditorum Examini
sistit
FRANCISCUS DANIEL PASTORIUS,
Windtsheimensis.
D. 23. Novembr. A. ab incarnatione J. C.
cIↄ Iↄc LXXVI.

ALTDORFFI,
Literis HENRICI MAIERI, Univ. Typogr.

Fenda and Frau Baurin, had determined to emigrate thither and had packed their goods. A keen desire came over him to sail in their company, having seen and experienced sufficient of the frivolity of Europe to lead there a quiet and Christian life. He presented and sent his books to his brother, John Samuel, and after many letters obtained the consent of his father, together with two hundred rix dollars, and thereupon went to Kriegsheim, where he saw Peter Schumacher, Gerhard Hendricks and Arnold Kassel, and made ready for the long journey. On the 2d of April he left Frankfort and came to Cologne, where he was pleasantly received by David Van Enden, Daniel Mitz and Dotzen, the representatives there of the King of Denmark. Dotzen expressed a desire to go with him, but his wife would not consent. There she went from house to house in a carriage, but perhaps in America she would have to look after the cattle and milk the cows. On the 11th of April he went down the Rhine to Urdingen and from there on foot to Crefeld, where he spoke with Thones Kunders and his wife, and with Dirck, Hermann, and Abraham Op den Graeff and many others, who six weeks later followed him. On the 16th of April he came to Rotterdam and stopped with his friend Mariette Vettekuke, and saw there Benjamin Furly, Peter Hendricks, Jacob Telner and others. On the 4th of May he sailed from Rotterdam, and on the 8th reached London, accompanied by Tobias L. Kohlhaus. He lodged with John Hodgkins, in Lombard Street. Together with a little party of emigrants, Jacob Schumacher, George Wertmuller, Isaac Dilbeck and his wife Marieke and two boys, Abraham and Jacob, Thomas Casper, Conrad Bacher (alias Rutter) and an English maid, Frances Simpson, he on the 6th of June sailed from Gravesend, on the ship America, whose captain was Joseph Wasey, on the 7th reached Deal, on the 10th left England, and on the 16th of August arrived in the New World. Another passenger was the celebrated Thomas Lloyd, afterward Deputy Governor of Pennsylvania, with whom Pastorius established an intimate friendship. Since Lloyd did not understand German, and Pastorius was then unused to talking in English, they carried on their conversation in Latin. Upon arriving in Philadelphia he went at once to Penn, who received him with an affectionate friendship, invited him to dine, and once, after an absence of several days, came and made him promise to dine with him twice a week, and expressed much love for the Germans, which feeling he hoped would be reciprocated. Pastorius built a little house in Philadelphia, where many of the people were then living in caves, thirty feet long and fifteen wide, and made a window, for want of glass, of paper dipped in oil. Over the door he wrote: "Parva domus sed amica Bonis procul este Prophani," at which Penn, when he read it, laughed aloud. We get an idea of the condition of the new Philadelphia when we learn that Pastorius in going from the river bank to the house of the baker Cornelius Bom, a few streets off, lost his way among the bushes.

When Germantown was laid out he opened what is called the "Germantown Grund und Lager-Buch," containing the record of the conveyances of lands, and he wrote this prefatory invocation:

Salve Posteritas
Posteritas Germanopolitana
et ex argumento insequentis paginæ primitus observa
Parentes ac Majores Tuos
Alemaniam

dulce Solum quod eos genuerat, alueratque diu Voluntario exilio
deseruisse;
(oh! Patrios focos!)
ut in Silvosa hac Pennsylvania
deserta Solitudine
minus soliciti
residuum Aetatis
Germane h. e. instar fratrum transigerat
Porro etiam addiscas
Quantae molis erat
exant lato jam mari Atlantico
in Septrionali istoc Americae tractu
Germaniam condere gentem
Tuque
Series dilecta Nepotum!
ubi fuimus exemplar honesti
Nostrum imitare exemplum.
Si autem a semita tam difficili aberravimus
Quod poenitenter agnoscitur
ignosce;
Et sic te faciant aliena pericula cautem.
Vale Posteritas!
Vale Cermanitas!
Æternum Vale.

Whittier has happily rendered it in English verse as follows:

Hail to posterity!
Hail future men of Germanopolis!
Let the young generations yet to be
Look kindly upon this.
Think how your fathers left their native land,
Dear German land, O! sacred hearths and homes!
And where the wild beast roams
In patience planned

New forest homes beyond the mighty sea,
There undisturbed and free
To live as brothers of one family.
What pains and cares befell,
What trials and what fears,
Remember, and wherein we have done well
Follow our footsteps, men of coming years;
Where we have failed to do
Aright or wisely live,
Be warned by us, the better way pursue.
And knowing we were human, even as you,
Pity us and forgive.
Farewell, Posterity;
Farewell, dear Germany,
Forevermore farewell!

We gain some idea of his personal appearance from a letter of Israel Pemberton, a boy of fourteen, upon whom he had used the birch, who wrote 13th of 6 mo. 1698: "The first time I saw him I told my father that I thought he would prove an angry master. He asked me why so: I told him I thought so by his nose, for which he called me a prating boy." He describes himself as "of a melancholy choleric complexion and therefore (Juxta Culpepper p. 194) gentle, given to sobriety, Solitary, Studious, doubtful, Shamefaced, timorous, pensive, constant and true in actions, of a slow wit, with obliviousness, &c.

If any does him wrong,
He can't remember 't long."

From his father and other relations he received altogether twelve hundred and sixty-three Reichsthaler, of which he says, "Tot pereunt cum tempore Nummi."

He was thoroughly familiar with and wrote fluently in the Greek, Latin, German, French, Dutch, English, Italian and Spanish languages. Of his command of the Latin the following letter to his old teacher Tobias Schumberg gives evidence:

DE MUNDI VANITATE.

Vale mundi genebundi colorata Gloria
Tua bona, tua dona sperno transitoria
Quae externe, hodierne, splendent pulchra facie,
Cras vanescunt et liquescunt sicut Sol in glacie.
Quid sunt Reges? quorum leges terror sunt mortalibus,
Multi locis atque focis latent infernalibus.
Ubi Vani, crine cani Maximi Pontifices?
Quos honorant et adorant cardinales supplices,
Quid periti? Eruditi sunt Doctores Artium
Quid sunt Harum, vel Illarum studiosi partium?
Ubi truces Belli duces? Capita militiae?
Quos ascendit et defendit rabies saevitiae.
Tot et tanti, quanti quanti, umbra sunt et vanitas,
Omna Horum nam Decorum brevis est inanitas.
Qui vixerunt, abierunt, restant sola nomina,
Tamquam stata atque rata nostrae sortis omina.
Fuit Cato, fuit Plato, Cyrus, Croesus, Socrates,
Periander, Alexander, Xerxes et Hippocrates,
Maximinus, Constantinus, Gyges. Anaxagoras,
Epicurus, Palinurus, Daemonax, Pythagoras,
Caesar fortis, causa mortis, tot altarum partium,
Ciceronem et Nasonem nil juvabat Artium.
Sed hos cunctos jam defunctos tempore praeterito,
Non est e re, recensere. Hinc concludo merito:
Qui nunc degunt, atque regunt orbem hujus seculi,
Mox sequentur et labentur velut schema speculi.
Et dum mersi universi sunt in mortis gremium,
Vel infernum, vel aeternum sunt capturi praemium.

Hincce Dei Jesu mei invoco clementiam,
Ut is Sursum, cordis cursum ducat ad essentiam,
Trinitatis, quae beatis summam dat laetitiam.

The following letter is characteristic: "Dear Children, John, Samuel and Henry Pastorius: Though you are (*Germano sanguine nati*) of high Dutch Parents, yet remember that your father was Naturalized, and ye born in an English Colony, Consequently each of you *Anglus Natus* an Englishman by Birth. Therefore, it would be a shame for you if you should be ignorant of the English Tongue, the Tongue of your Countrymen; but that you may learn the better I have left a Book for you both, and commend the same to your reiterated perusal. If you should not get much of the Latin, nevertheless read ye the English part oftentimes OVER AND OVER AND OVER. And I assure you that *Semper aliquid haerebit.* For the Drippings of the house-eaves in time make a hole in a hard stone. Non vi sed saepe cadendo, and it is very bad Cloath that by often dipping will take no Colour.

Lectio lecta placet, decies repetita placebit
Quod Natura negat vobis Industria praestet.—F P. D."

The institution of slavery, which he saw in existence around him, called forth his earnest opposition, and at a time when in Massachusetts they were selling Indians, and white people of other creeds, to be sent to Barbados, and when even the Quakers had not yet given their testimony against the traffic in negroes, he wrote the famous protest of 1688. In German and English verse, not so well known, he said,

Allermassen ungebuhrlich
Ist der Handel dieser Zeit,

Dass ein Mensch so unnaturlich
  Andre druckt mit Dienstbarkeit.
Ich mocht einen solchen Fragen
  Ob er wohl ein Sklav mocht sein,
Ohne Zweifel wird er sagen:
  Ach, bewahr' mich Gott; nein, nein!

And also in English:

If in Christ's doctrine we abide,
Then God is surely on our side,
But if we Christ's precepts transgress,
Negroes by slavery oppress
And white ones grieve by usury,
Two evils which to Heaven cry,
We've neither God nor Christ His Son,
But straightway travel hellwards on.

He was fond of his garden and of flowers and took delight in the raising of bees, saying in his punning way that "Honey is money," and apparently found some relaxation in the pursuit of Walton. Sometimes the loneliness of the woods oppressed him, and with the disappointing sense that those who were to have been his companions had failed him, came the longing to see once more the familiar objects along the Rhine and his old home, but to a certain extent the presence of Lloyd was a recompense.

"'Twas he and William Penn that caused me to stay
In this then uncouth land and howling wilderness
Wherein I saw that I but little should possess;
And if I would return home to my father's house
Perhaps great riches and preferments would espouse."

In Germantown he looked after the affairs of the Frankfort Land Company until 1700, and not only did he never receive any compensation, but he finally, along with the rest, lost his lands. He kept the records of the Court, compiled the laws and ordinances, was bailiff of the borough when organized, a justice of the peace and County Judge, and a member of the Assembly in 1687 and 1691. As a means of gaining a livelihood he acted as a conveyancer and notary and wrote leases, mortgages, deeds, articles of agreement, wills, marriage certificates and other legal documents and sometimes letters and translations. For a lease, bond or will he charged from two to three shillings; for a deed on parchment from seven to nine shillings, and for a letter four pence. He wrote a plain flowing script and was very painstaking and careful about all of his work. Everything that he did, even the most prosy of labors, was enlivened with a certain quaint and learned humor. In opening an account with the Friends in his account book he solemnly credits them "in the first place with love." For the last twenty years of his life he also taught a school, and his Primer, of which but a single copy seems to be extant, was the first original school book printed in Pennsylvania.

In a letter still preserved acknowledging a note from Phineas Pemberton excusing the lateness of his daughters he commends "the good disposition of the two little ones" and says: "The very shadow of the rod will do more with them than the spur with others." The instruction cost from four to six pence per week. Among those who sent children to him to be taught were Lenert Arets, Benjamin Armitage, W. Baumann, Joseph Coulson, James De la Plaine, Wilhelm Dewees, Cornelius Dewees, Jan Doeden, Jan De Wilderness, Paul Engle, Jacob Gottschalk, Hans Graeff, Wilhelm Hosters, Richard Huggin, Dirck Jansen, Howell James, Conrad Jansen, Jurgen Jacobs, Tunes Kunders, Aret Klincken, Paul Kastner, Paul Kuster, Peter Keyser, Aret Kuster, Henrich Kassel, Peter Keurlis,

Anthony Klincken, Jan Lucken, Jan Lensen, Anton Loof, Matthias Milan, Benjamin Morgan, Hans Heinrich Mehls, Jan Neus, Hans Neus, Thomas Potts, Jonas Potts, Samuel Richardson, Cunrad Rutter, Claus Rittinghuysen, Hendrick Sellen, Wilhelm Strepers, Walter Simons, Peter Schumacher, George Schumacher, Isaac Schumacher, Richard Townsend, Abraham Tunes, Cornelius Tisen, Herman Tunes, Arnold Van Vossen, Isaac Van Sintern, Paul Wulff, Christian Warner and Christopher Witt.

After William Bradford, the printer, had quarreled with his Quaker friends and gone away to New York, in 1692, Pastorius thought seriously of starting a press and regretted his lack of knowledge of the art. His younger brother, Augustin Adam, had at that time in consideration the question of coming to Pennsylvania, and Pastorius wrote to him telling him before doing so to spend three months in a printing office.

When Dr. Griffith Owen died he wrote the following epitaph:

"What here of Griffith Owen lies
Is only what of all men dies.
His soul and spirit live above
With God in pure and perfect love."

On the 1st of December, 1688, he wrote to his good friend, George Leonard Modeln, Rector of the School at Windsheim, upon the subject of the education of youth, and saying that each boy, according to his capacity, in addition to his instruction in letters, should be taught light hand work, so that in case of need he could follow it in distant provinces and help himself in any part of the world without dissipating his patrimony, to the sorrow of his elders. "I myself would give one hundred rix dollars if the time I wasted upon learning the Sperling physic and metaphysics

Umständige Geogra-
phische
Beschreibung
Der zu allerletzt erfundenen
Provintz
PENSYLVA-
NIÆ,
In denen End-Gräntzen
AMERICÆ
In der West-Welt gelegen /
Durch
FRANCISCUM DANIELEM
PASTORIUM,
J.V. Lic. und Friedens-Richtern
daselbsten.
Worbey angehencket sind eini-
ge notable Begebenheiten / und
Bericht-Schreiben an dessen Herrn
Vattern
MELCHIOREM ADAMUM PASTO-
RIUM,
Und andere gute Freunde.

Franckfurt und Leipzig /
Zufinden bey Andreas Otto. 1700.

and other unnecessary sophistical *argumentationes* and *arguitiones*, I had devoted to engineer work or to book printing, which would have been useful and valuable to me and to my fellow Christians, rather than to Physics, Metaphysics and Aristotelian Elenchi and Sylochismi, by which no savage or heathen can be brought to God, much less a piece of bread can be made." This, however, was the ordinary quarrel of a man with his life and occupation. In the woods as he was, he could not desist from the writing of books. Seven of them were printed at the time.

1. His inaugural dissertation "De rasura documentorum." Altdorff, 1676.

2. Zwey Stucke aus Philadelphia, 1684.

3. A work in German dedicated to Tobias Schumberg upon four subjects of ecclesiastical history: The lives of the Saints; The Statutes of the Pontiffs; The decisions of the Councils of the Church; and the Bishops and Patriarchs of Constantinople; with the pseudo imprint Germanopolis, 1690.

4. A circumstantial geographical description of the lately founded province of Pennsylvania. Frankfort, 1700.

5. A new Primmer or Methodical Direction to attain the True Spelling, Reading and Writing of English. New York, 1698.

6. Ein Send Brieff Offenhertziger Liebsbezeugung an die sogenannte Pietisten in Hoch Teutschland. Amsterdam, 1697.

7. Henry Bernhard Koster, William Davis, Thomas Rutter and Thomas Bowyer, four Boasting Disputers of this world Rebuked and Answered according to their folly, which they themselves have manifested in a late pamphlet entitled *Advice for all* Professors and *Writers*. New York, 1697.

FRANCISCI DANIELIS PASTORII

Sommerhuſano-Franci.

Kurtze Geographiſche Beſchreibung
der letztmahls erfundenen
Americaniſchen Landſchafft

PENSYLVANIA,

Mit angehenckten einigen notablen Begebenheiten und Bericht-Schreiben an deſſen Hrn. Vattern/ Patrioten und gute Freunde.

Vorrede.

ES iſt denen Meinigen insgeſamt zur Gnüge bekandt/ auf was Weiſe ich/ von meinen Kindesbeinen an/ auf dem Wege dieſer Zeitlichkeit meinen LebensLauff gegen die frohe Ewigkeit zu/ eingerichtet und in allem meinem Thun dahin getrachtet habe/ wie ich den allein guten Willen GOttes erkennen/ ſeine hohe Allmacht fürchten/ und ſeine unergründliche Güte lieben lernen möchte. Und obwohlen ich/ nebſt andern gemeinen Wiſſenſchafften der freyen Künſte/ das Studium Juris feliciter abſolviret/ die Italiäniſch-und Franzöſiſche Sprachen ex fundamento begriffen/ auch den ſo genannten groſſen Tour durch die Landſchafften gethan/ ſo habe ich jedoch an allen Orten und Enden meinen gröſſeſten Fleiß und Bemühung an anders nichts gewendet/ als eigentlich zu erfahren/ wo

A doch

Umständige Geographische
Beschreibung
Der zu allerletzt erfundenen
Provintz
PENSYLVANIÆ,
In denen End-Gräntzen
AMERICÆ
In der West-Welt gelegen/
Durch
FRANCISCUM DANIELEM
PASTORIUM,
J. V. Lic. und Friedens-Richtern
daselbsten.
Worbey angehencket sind einige notable Begebenheiten/ und Bericht-Schreiben an dessen Herrn
Vattern
MELCHIOREM ADAMUM
PASTORIUM,
Und andere gute Freunde.

Franckfurt und Leipzig/
Zufinden bey Andreas Otto. 1704.

Vier kleine
Doch ungemeine
Und sehr nutzliche

Tractätlein

De omnium Sanctorum Vitis
I. De omnium Pontificum Statutis
II. De Conciliorum Decisionibus
V. De Episcopis & Patriarchis Constan-
tinopolitanis.
Das ist:
1. Von Aller Heiligen Lebens-Ubung
2. Von Aller Päpste Gesetz-Einführung
3. Von der Concilien Stritt-Sopirung.
4. Von denen Bischöffen und Patriarchen
zu Constantinopel.
Zum Grunde
Der künfftighin noch ferner darauf
zu bauen Vorhabender Warheit
præmittiret,
Durch
FRANCISCUM DANIELEM
PASTORIUN. J. U. L.
Aus der
In Pensylvania neulichst von mir in
Grund angelegten /. und nun mit gutem
Success aufgehenden Stadt:
G E R M A N O P O L I
Anno Christi M. DC. XC.

Kurtze

Beschreibung
Des H. R. Reichs Stadt
Windsheim/

Samt

Dero vielfältigen Unglücks-Fällen/
und wahrhafftigen Ursachen ihrer so grossen Decadenz und Erbarmungs-würdigen Zustandes/

Aus

Alten glaubwürdigen Documentis und Briefflichen Urkunden (der itzo lebenden lieben Burgerschafft/ und Dero Nachkommen/ zu guter Nachricht) also zusammen getragen/ und in den Druck gegeben

durch

Melchiorem Adamum Pastorium,
ältern Burgemeistern und Ober-Richtern in besagter Stadt.

Gedruckt zu Nürnberg
bey Christian Sigmund Froberg.
Im Jahr Christi 1692.

Ein

Send-Brieff

Offenhertziger Liebsbezeugung an die so genannte Pietisten in Hoch-Teutschland.

Zu AMSTERDAM/

Gedruckt vor Jacob Claus Buchhändler / 1697.

Henry Bernhard Koſter, William Davis, Thomas Rutter & *Thomas Boryer,*

FOUR

Boaſting Diſputers

Of this World briefly

REBUKED,

And Anſwered according to their Folly, which they themſelves have manifeſted in a late Pamphlet, entituled, *Advice for all Profeſſors and Writers.*

BY

Francis Daniel Paſtorius.

Printed and Sold by *William Bradford* at the Bible in *New-York*, 1697.

In addition to these he left forty-three works in manuscript, two of which, supposed to have been lost, are now printed in this volume. Many, no doubt, will never be recovered, but we have a catalogue of their titles.

1. Alvearium or Bee Hive, a large encyclopaedia of such matters as he thought necessary for the information of his children. 2. Academische Spar Stunden. 3. Miscellanica Theologica et Moralia. 4. Formulae Solennes, or several forms of such writings as are vulgarly in use. 5. Confusanea Geometria, oder einfaltiger Unterricht vom Landmessen. 6. A breviary of Arithmetic. 7. Lingua Anglicana or some Miscellaneous Remarks concerning the English Language. 8. Lingua Latina or Grammatical Rudiments. 9. Emblematical Recreations. 10. Semel insanivimus omnes oder Poetische Einfalle. 11. A collection of some English Manuscripts. 12. A collection of English Hymns alphabetically digested. 13. The Young Country Clerk. 14. Pennsylvanische Gesetze and Germantown Statutes. 15. Deliciae hortenses et voluptates apianae. 16. Itinerarium oder Reisebeschreibung. 17. Liber Epitaphiorum. 18. Phraseologia Teutonica. Krafft und Safft der Teutschen Helden-Sprach. 19. Miscellanea Prima oder Academischer Spar Stunden Vorlaufer. 20. Medicus Dilectus oder Artzney Buchlein. 21. Oeconomia oder Haushaltungs reguln. 22. Theologica Anglicana, in grunem Pergament eingebunden. 23. Melligo Sententia Latine. 24. Calendarium Calendariorum or a perpetual Almanack. 25. Onomastical Considerations. 26. Vademecum, or the Christian Scholars pocket book. 27. Nec tutus piscis ab Anglo; or a few observations concerning angling with several tracts on husbandry. 28. Mecum liber ibis etc or Exemplified Rules of Arithmetic and Rhythmical and Proverbial Copies. 29. The Good Order

and Discipline of the Church of Christ. 30. The Monthly Monitor, or my first born son of Husbanderia. 31. Bernh. P.-Catechism, Englished by me. 32. Aviarium oder Bienenbuchlein. 33. Wm. Penn's Fruchte der Einsamkeit von mir verteutscht. 34. English Rhymes. 35. Alvearialia. 36. Private Annotations. 37. A Fascicle of Several Manuscripts. 38. Additamenta ad Fennés Grammaticam Gallicam. 39. Additamenta ad Caffae Gram. Italicam. 40. Additamenta to the Writing Scholar's Companion. 41. Latinae primordia Linguae. 42. Law terms added to the Compleat Justice. 43. Anhang zu Tim Koll's Gartenbüchlein.

In 1713, while confined to bed with a serious illness, he wrote a lively description of his difficulties with Sprogell and Falkner over the lands of the Frankfort Land Company, which he evidently intended to print, and which first appeared, after the lapse of two hundred years, in my Pennsylvania Colonial Cases. It is here reproduced as a part of the history of Germantown and as an illustration of his style in English composition.

EXEMPLUM SINE EXEMPLO;

Or

(to borrow the Discription of one of John Wilson's Plays)

The CHEATS and the PROJECTORS.

I, Francis Daniel Pastorius, having formerly (towit these 28 years past) by Doctor Schutz & other honest men in high Germany, (Purchasers of 25000 acres of land in this Province of Pennsylvania, and known by the name of the Francfort Company) been made & Constituted their Attorney, and still being concerned as Copartner with them, to clear my Conscience (as touching the administration of their sd estate) before all People to whom the reading

SEAL OF PASTORIUS.

ENLARGED.

FROM A CONTEMPORARY DEED IN THE COLLECTION OF THE HISTORICAL SOCIETY OF PENNSYLVANIA.

hereof may come, as I always endeavoured to keep the same void of offence towards the all seeing Eyes of God, am, if it were, constrained to publish their short relation for as much as the aforesd Francfort Company is at present ejected out of their 25000 acres of land, summo jure, i, e, summa Injuria, by extreme right, extreme wrong. Now Intending Brevity, I shall let my Reader know that the sd Company being all persons of approved Integrity & learning became, at least some of them, personally acquainted with our Worthy Proprietary & Governr. William Penn, and purchased of him at a full rate the abovementioned 25000 acres, & in the very infancy of this Province disbursed large sums of money for the transporting of Servants Tenants and others; and that I, according to the best of my poor ability, (as many of the primitive Inhabitants & settlers yet surviving Swedes Dutch and English may testify) administered their affairs 17 years and a half. But conscious of my weakness, have often requested them to disburden me of this Load of theirs I took on my Shoulders by their frequent assurance to be behind my heels into this Countrey as soon as the Ice was broken. Whereupon the heirs of the sd first purchasers did appoint in my room Daniel Falkner, John Kelpius, & John Jawert, N B to act JOINTLY and not SEVERALLY. However when the sd John Kelpius had a forecast in what channel things would run he with all speed in a certain Instrument (of George Lowther's device who was the first Lawyer that unhappily got an hand into the Companies business) declared his Unwillingness to be any further concerned therein, and therefore termed Civiliter Mortuus. Then Daniel Falkner & John Jawert acted in the dual number as the sd Companies Attornies for some few years.

For the sd Jawert being married and settled in Marieland, Falkner turned into such a spendthrift and Ever-drunk-Ever-dry that he made Bonefires of the Companies flax in open street at Germantown, giving a bit of silver money to one Lad for lighting his Tobacco-pipe, and a piece of eight to another for showing him a house in Philadelphia, which in his sober fits he knew as well as his own.

Hereupon his Joint-Attorney John Jawert affixed an ADVERTISEMENT at the Meeting house of Germantown aforesd, dated the 9th of November 1705, wherein he forewarned all persons who had any Rent or other Debt to pay unto the sd Company to forbear the paying thereof &c. And all was asleep, as Dormice do in winter, till about two years agoe, one John Henry Sprogel arrived in this Province, who being HE, that by the Collusion and treachery of the sd Daniel Falkner, by the wicked assistance of the Projectors to be hereafter to be spoken of, has through I know not what Fiction of the Law Ejected the sd Company out of their real estate of 25000 acres, I think it not amiss to give some little account of him. His parents I hear are of a good report and to be pittied for such a Scandal to their Family. This Degenerate and Prodigal Child came for the first time into this Province in anno 1700, and quickly owing more than he was worth, went over to his native land in order to procure some cash of his Father whom he said to be a rich Bishop on that side. In his return he was taken by the French & carried to Dunkerk, whence he escaped with an empty Brigantine into Holland, and by the (now repented of) Recommendation of Benjamin Furly & his Bookkeeper, H. L., found so much Credit with John Van der Gaegh, Merchant at Rotterdam & others as to bee Intrusted with a deal of goods. After he departed out of harms way in that country, and could not be found when search'd for, in England, he came at last to Philada and there took his oath (as I am credibly informed) that all the said goods were his own directly or indirectly. Some of the Germantown people then visiting this their great Countryman and inquiring for letters were looked upon as Slaves, he being the only Anglified in all the Province of Pennsilvania. Howbeit none of us all (I beleeve) will ever have such a base and disloyal heart towards our Soveraign Lady the Queen of Great Britain as to get his Naturalization by the like disingenuous knack as he did, viz. :—to borrow a key & wear another man's coat as though it were his own &c.

But to return to the Francfort Companies Concern, he

the aforesd John Henry Sprogel having along with him a Letter of Attorney from the sd Benjamin Furly (afterwards though post festum revoked) sold 1000 acres of land, part of the sd Furly's purchase in this Province, unto David Lloyd at a reasonable price so as to have his Irreasonable advice in Law for the most unjust Entry upon the Companies land. For he the sd Sprogel, finding no means to satisfy his Old and Just Debts, was forced to find a new and untrodden way of Clearing his Scores, and to play the Gentleman sprung out of a Grocer's Shop. Therefore among a Swarm of tedious lies (wherewith I dare not trouble the Reader) he also spread this, that he stroke a bargain for the Companies land with Doctor Gerhard van Mastricht, one of Copartners, of whom I but newly received an extreme kind Letter to the clean Contrary thereof. Moreover the sd Sprogel to pacify the abovementioned John Jawert, who likewise had a share in the sd Company, proffered unto him 700 Pounds Pennsilvania Silver money for the land, and 100 Pounds besides as a Gratuity to himself &c. But he the sd Jawert being too honest for an Imposture and Bribe of this black stamp, Sprogel was driven to that Extremity (hap what may and let Frost & Fraud have hereafter as foul ends as they will) that he must now obtain the 25000 Acres & Arrears of Quitrents due to the Francfort Company solely & alone of Daniel Falkner, who plunged in needlessly contracted debts over head & ears, could expect no gladder tidings (as he said himself) than the same Proffer made unto him.

Here David Lloyd (whom to name again I am almost ashamed) comes in very gingerly to play his Roll FICTIONEM JURIS AD REIPSA DETRUDENDOS VEROS POSSESSORES, the which nevertheless it seems he was not bold-faced enough to do in his proper Clothes, but one Tho: Macknamara a Lawyer, if it were, started up for the purpose out of Marieland, (for a couple of Periwigs which he himself told me was all the Fee he had of this his brave Client for blushing in this Case) must be Nominally inserted in the Ejectment, lending like once the Cat her Paws to a more Crafty Creature for the drawing of the rosted Chestnuts from off the glowing coals. If any demand how this D—Ll[63] and Macknamara could possibly in so horrible a manner Circumvent the County Court, I suppose the fittest Answer I can Give to this Question is what Judge Grouden declared before our honourable Lieutenant Governor sitting in Council, viz: that at the tail of the Court Daniel Falkner and John Henry Sprogel did appear and the aforenamed d—ll and M. laid the matter before the Court, and none there to object anything &c (For this cheating trick was managed so Clandestinely that I and John Jawert were altogether ignorant thereof and when Tho: Clark the Queen's Attorney then present in Court did but rise, the others suspecting he might say somewhat in Obstruction of their hainous design, was gently pull'd down by the Sleeve and promised 40 shillings to be quiet, when he had nothing to offer) Thus they Surprised the Court and ob-et-subreptitie compassed the ejectment. Three days after the breaking up of the afresd Court I heard of this unhandsom Juggle and gave Intelligence thereof to John Jawert, who forthwith came up and putt in his Humble Bequest to our well respected Lieutenant Govrnr and his honble Council, we had the sd Tho: Clark assigned to pleade our Cause and so Jawert paid him a Fee of ten Pounds, but to this day the sd Sprogel still stirs his stumps in the Companies lands & Rents without the least controlment. Since all this there arrived divers letters from beyond the Sea, deciphering pretty fully abundance of the detestable gulleries whereby the sd Sprogel ensnared & trepan'd the Simplicity of upright & Plaindealing people in Holland, admonishing him not to persist in his Evildoings but to Confess and make reparation to the defrauded, if not fourfold as penitent Zaccheus did, yet so far as his ill gotten griff-graff gains would reach &c &c. And further there came also fresh Letters of Attorney from all the Partners of the Francfort Company, Living in Germany, Impowering some very able Men in Philada to redress their so horribly distressed Es-

[63] To ensure its not being overlooked, I call attention to this pun upon the names of David Lloyd and the Devil.

tate in this Province by one worse than the worst Land-Pirate in the world could have done, the which I hope they will undertake and heartily wish, that the Lord (who is called a Father to the Fatherless and a Judge of the Widows, whereof there are at this instant several in the abovesd Company) may prosper their just Proceedings, and all, who reverence Righteousness and Equity countenance them therein, and not be partakers of the Spoil, nor of the Curse entailed thereon with the aforesd John Henry Sprogel, for whom notwithstanding the foreign discovery of his unheard of Villanies I retain that sincere Love as to pray God Almighty to Convict & Convert him of & from his Perverseness, that he may foresake his diabolical lies, pride, bragging and boasting, and not longer continue the Vassal of Satan and heir of Hell, but become a child of Heaven and a follower of Christ, our ever-blessed Saviour, who as he is truth itself so likewise meek and lowly in heart, leading out of all cozening Practices into the way of holiness and eternal Felicity.

On the 25th of November, 1688, Pastorius married in Germantown Anna Klostermann, daughter of Dr. Hendrich Klostermann, of the Duchy of Cleves, and they had two sons, Johann Samuel, born March 30, 1690, and Heinrich, born April 1, 1692. He died February 27, 1719. There is no stone to mark his grave and no man knows where his bones lie. But Howell Powell, a Welshman, on the 21st of the 3d month, 1720, gave forth these enthusiastic verses to commemorate his merits:

What Francis Daniel Pastorius
Hath tane his flight from hence to Olympus
Lost to his Posterity, ye Germantown Specially
Loss (tho' great gains to him) it was to many,
The Hermes, Glory, Crown and Linguists gone
Who oft interpreted Teutonick Tongue,
The Scribe and Tutor, German's Polar Guide,

An Antiquarian that was far from pride
Religious, Xealous Amanuensis;
An Universal Man in Arts Sciences,
Who lov'd his Friends: the Britains; yea all Nations
Zealous for the Truth, full of Compations,
Ah! may Germanopolis be agen supplied
Of that great Loss; their Honour once, their Guide
A wise Achilles as he was be sent
Lowly, Lovely, Learn'd, Lively, Still Content,
Now free from Cares, Dire Troubles that attend
This brittle Case, the Heavenly Quire, befriend
Him still, Joyes in the Glorious Lamb, alone
Seeth the Beatifick vision
You his Family offspring take Example
By Francis, Just Sincere & Truly Humble
Tho you condole the Loss of 's Company
He got a better; be Content thereby
Tho many lost a Friend; He got; yet they
Rejoyce that he hath Nobler still for ay.
Tho dead to his Corporal Form, that Sleep, He Live
In Immortality needs no Reprieve.

Vade Diis Superis scandere Culmen Olymp
Francisce ae que vale, tu cape, carpe viam,
Opto simul quaeris vestigia recta sequi
Te pedibus verbis, te simul; esse bonos.

And a greater than Howell, William Penn, wrote in 1698–99 this merited encomium: "Irenarcha, hoc anno est aut nuperrime fuit, alias vir sobrius probus prudens et pius spectatae inter omnes inculpataeque famae."

CHAPTER IV.

Letters Home.

Letter from Francis Daniel Pastorius, March 7, 1684.[64]

Arms of William Penn.

IN order to fulfil my due obligations, as well as my promise, on setting out, I shall state somewhat circumstantially, how and what I have found and observed in this land, and, while not ignorant that through varying reports of these much is brought to light, I state at the beginning that with impartial pen, and without purpose to deceive, I will faithfully relate the discomforts of the journey and the poverty of this province, as well as the riches of the same, which have been almost too

[64] I am indebted for the above letter to the Rev. Wm. J. Hinke, who quite recently discovered it in one of the Continental libraries. Extracts from it appear in the Geographische Beschreibung and are elsewhere used in this volume, but it is so filled with hitherto unknown and graphic details that it is here translated in its entirety.

highly praised by others. Then I ask nothing more in my little corner of the earth than to walk in the footsteps of Him who is the Way, and to follow His wholesome teaching, because He is the Truth, in order that I may forever be joined to Him in life eternal.

(I) I will therefore begin with the sea voyage which is dangerous indeed on account of possible shipwreck to be feared, as well as unpleasant on account of the coarse and hard ship fare, so that from my own personal experience I can much better understand what David says in the 107th Psalm that on ship board one can search out and learn of not only the wonderful works of the Lord but also the spirit of storm. Concerning my journey hither, on the tenth of June, I sailed from Deal, with four men servants, two maids, two children and one young lad.[65] We had on the whole way mostly unfavorable wind, not twelve consecutive hours of favorable wind, much storm, and tempest. Also the foremast broke into two pieces, so that we reached here in not less than ten weeks; but *sat cito, si sat bene.*—considering that it seldom happens that any arrive much more promptly. The people from Crefeld, who reached here October 6th, were just ten weeks on the sea, and the ship that started from Deal with ours, was fourteen days longer on the way and some of the people died. Certain people from Crefeld also between Rotterdam and England lost a grown daughter, whose loss however was replaced by the birth of two children. Upon our ship no one died and no one was born. Almost all of the passen-

---

[65] It will be observed that by omitting the English maid who had left him and adding the others on this list to the thirty-three persons from Crefeld, we get the forty-two residents of Germantown mentioned later in this letter. Dilbeck was a member of the German Reformed church and a weaver. His wife was Mary Blomerse. See the valuable papers of Henry S. Dotterer in his Historical Notes Upon the Reformed Church.

gers were seasick for several days, but I, when not more than four hours out was upset by other accidents, for the two carved lions over our ship's clock struck me right on the back, and on July 9th, during a storm at night, I fell so violently upon the left side that for some days I was obliged to keep my bed. These two accidents especially recall to me the first fall, which was passed down to all posterity, by our early progenitors in Paradise; also many of those which I have experienced in this sad valley of my exile per varios casus, etc., but praised be the fatherly hand of divine mercy which so often upholds and restrains us, so that we do not quite fall into the abyss of evil. Gorg Wertmuller also fell heavily. Thomas Gasper was badly hurt. The English maid had the erysipelas and Isaac Dilbeck, who otherwise, according to external appearances, was the strongest, lay below longer than anyone else. I had also a little ship-hospital, as I alone of the Germans had taken my berth among the English. How a companion aboard was careless, and how our ship was made to tremble by the repeated attacks of a whale, I related in detail last time. The fare on board was very bad. We lived *medice ac modice.* Every ten persons received each week three pounds of butter; daily four cans of beer, and two cans of water; at noon every day in the week, meat, and fish three days at noon, which we had to dress with our own butter; and every day we had to keep enough from our dinner to make our supper upon. The worst of all was that our meat and fish were both so salty and so strong smelling, that we could scarcely half enjoy them. And if I had not prepared myself at the advice of good friends in England, with various kinds of refreshment, it might very likely have gone badly with me. Therefore it is well to suggest to those who wish to come here in the future that they either, when there are many of them, provide their own fare, or else make definite arrangements with the captain, in regard to both quantity and quality, how much and what kind they shall daily receive; and, in order to bind him to this the more closely, one should leave unpaid some little from the cost of his passage, also when possible should have himself bound over to such a ship which sails to this town of Philadelphia, since those who are left lying in Upland, undergo many trials.

My company on board consisted of many kinds of people. There was one D. Mediconae with his wife and eight children, a French captain, a pastry-cook,[66] an apothecary, a glassblower, mason, smith, cartwright, joiner, cooper, hatter, shoemaker, tailor, gardener, peasants, seamstresses, etc., in all about eighty people in the ship's company. These differ not only in their ages (our oldest woman was sixty years old, the youngest child only twelve weeks) and in their occupations just mentioned, but they were also of such different religions and stations that I might not unsuitably compare the ship which brought them hither, with the Ark of Noah, in which were found not more unclean beasts than clean (reasonable). In my company I have fallen in with the Romish Church, with the Lutheran, with the Calvinistic, with the Anabaptist and with the English, and only one Quaker.

On the 11th of Aug. we for the first time took a sounding and found that we were close upon the great sand bank, and accordingly, in order to sail around it, we must go back for over one hundred miles out of our course.

On the 16th of the same month (August, 1683) with much joy we came into sight of America, and on the 18th in the morning entered Delaware Bay, which is thirty

[66] Cornelius Bom (?)

English miles long and fifteen wide, while of such unequal depth that while our ship drew thirteen feet of water, we several times ran aground in the sand.

On the 20th we passed New Castle and Upland and Dimicum, and arrived in the dusk of evening, praised be God, happily in Philadelphia. There, on the following day I gave over to W. Penn the writings which I had with me, and was received by him with affectionate friendliness: of which very worthy gentleman and praiseworthy ruler, I should speak suitably.

(II) My pen (although it is from an eagle, which a so called savage recently brought into my house) is much too weak to express the lofty merits of this Christian, for such he is indeed. He invited me very often to his table, also to walk and ride in his always elevating society; and when I was last away from here for eight days, to bring victuals from New Castle, and he had not seen me for that length of time, he came himself to my little house, and requested that I should still come two or three times to his home, as his guest. He was very fond of the Germans and once said openly in my presence to his councillors and attendants: The Germans I am very fond of and wish that you should love them also; although I never at any other time heard a similar command from him; but these pleased me the more because they entirely conform to the command of God (vid I John 31. 23). I can now say no more than that Will. Penn is a man who honors God, and is by Him honored in return, who loves good, and is by all good men rightly loved, etc. I do not doubt that others will yet come here and learn by experience that my pen has not written enough in this direction.

(III) About the condition of the land I must in the future after one or more years acquaintance, state something more definite. The Swedes and Dutch who have cultivated the same for twenty-five years and more, are in this instance, as in most others, of two opinions, laudatur ab his, culpatur ab illis. It is certain that the ground soil lacks nothing in fertility, and will here, as well as in Europe, reward the labor of our hands, if we work upon and manure it, which two things it most needs. The above-mentioned old inhabitants are poor economists, have neither barns nor stalls, let their grain lie unthreshed under the open sky for several years, and let their cattle, horses, cows, swine, etc., run summer and winter through the thickets, though they derive little benefit therefrom. Surely the penance which God inflicted upon Adam that he should eat his bread in the sweat of his brow, extends also to his descendants in this land, and they who wish to spare their hands may remain where they are. Hic opus, hic labor est and there is no money without the disposition to work. (Swiss provincialism of to-day for "arbeiten" says "wercken") for it slips through the fingers, and I may say with Solomon; It has wings. During the past year very many people both from England and Ireland, as well as from Barbados and other American islands have come here, and this province did not produce sufficient means of subsistence for such an influx, wherefore all food became rather dear, and almost all the money went for the same out of the land. Nevertheless we hope in time to have a greater abundance of both, for W. Penn will coin money, and agriculture will be better established, etc. Farmers and laborers are most needed here, and I wish I had a dozen strong Tyrolese here to cut down the massive oak trees; for wherever one turns it may be said: Itur in antiquam sylvam. There is everywhere only forest, and little open space to be found, in which, as in other respects, my previously cherished hope was vain, for in truth, in these wild orchards there are no apples at all nor pears. And through this very cold winter no game is to be found. The wild grapes are quite small, and better to eat than to make wine from. The walnuts have exceedingly thick shells, and small kernels, so that they are scarcely worth the trouble of opening them; but the chestnuts and hazelnuts are somewhat better. Also the peaches, apples and pears are very good, and are not to be complained of, except that there are not as many of them as some desire, etc. On the other hand there are more rattle snakes (whose sting is deadly) in the land, than we like, etc. I must yet add this little tanquam testis oculatus, that on the 16th of October beautiful violets were found in the woods; Item. After I came to the town of Germantown on the 24th of October, and on the 25th of the same month, when I was coming back here with seven others, we came upon, on the way, a wild vine running over a tree, upon which hung about four hundred clusters of grapes, wherefore we thereupon cut down the tree, all eight of us had enough, and each one carried a hatful home. Item. When I was dining with W. Penn on the 25th of Aug., after the meal was finished, there was brought in a single root of barley, which had grown here in a garden, and had on it fifty stalks. But all grain does not bear in that proportion, it is as the proverb says: One swallow does not make a summer. However I do not doubt that in the future there will be more examples of such fertility, when we earnestly put these to the plow. I regret the vines, which I brought with me because, while we were still in Delaware Bay, they were soaked in sea water, and all but two were spoiled. The oft mentioned W. Penn has planted a vineyard of French vines, whose growth it is a pleasure to look upon, and which brought to my recollection, when I saw them, the one of Cap. Johannis.

(IV) Philadelphia daily increases in the number of its houses, and in population; now there is being built also a house of correction in order that those who do not wish to live as Philadelphians should, may be disciplined, for there are some here, to whom applied what our dear friend said in his letters, namely that we have more trouble with bad Christians here than with the Indians. Further, here and there towns are being built. Beside our own one by name Franckfurt, about half an hour from here, is beginning to be started, where also a mill and glass factory are built. Not far from there, namely, two hours from here, lies our Germantown, where already forty-two people live in twelve homes, who are for the most part linen weavers, and not much given to agriculture. These honest people spent all their means on their journey, so that where provision was not made for them by W. Penn, they were obliged to serve others. They have by repeated wanderings back and forth made quite a good road all the way to the said Germantown. And I can say no more for this than that it lies upon black rich earth, and is girt half way round with pleasant springs, as with a natural wall. The main street is sixty feet broad, and the cross street forty, and each family has an estate of three acres, etc.

(V) In regard to the inhabitants, I can do no better than divide them into the *natural* and the cultivated. For, if I called the former savages, and the latter Christians, I would be unjust to many of both races. Of the latter, I have already explained that the sailing ship was not to be compared to any thing but Noah's Ark. The Lutheran preacher who wants to show the Swedes the way to heaven like a statue of Mercury, is, in a word, a drunkard. Similarly there are false coiners, and other vicious persons here, whom however the breath of God's wrath will haply scatter like chaff, at his good time. Of pious God-fearing people there is also, no lack, and I can assert in all truth that nowhere in Europe have I seen, as in our Philadelphia, the notice: Such and such a thing has been found, the loser may apply; often also the opposite: Such and such a thing has been lost, whoever returns it shall receive a reward; etc. Concerning these first cultivated foreigners I will say no more now than that among them are found some Germans who have already been in this country twenty years and so have become, as it were, naturalized, namely people from Schleswig, Brandenburg, Holstein, Switzerland, etc, also, one from Nüremberg, Jan Jacquet by name, but will briefly give some information concerning these per errorem called savages. The first which came to my notice were the two who at Upland came up to our ship in a canoe. I presented them with a drink of brandy, which they wished to pay for with half a kopfstuck, and when I refused this money, they took my hand and said, thanks, brother. They are strong of limb, dark in body, and they dye their faces red, blue, etc in many ways. They go in summer quite naked, except for a cloth worn about the loins, and now in winter they hang duffels over themselves. They have coal black hair, but the Swedish children born here have snow white hair, etc. I was once dining with W. Penn when one of their kings was sitting with us at table, when W. Penn said to him (for he could

Arms of the Jacquet family of Nüremberg.

speak their language pretty readily) that I was a German, etc. He came on the 3rd of October, as also on the 12th of December there came another king and queen to my house. In like manner many of the common people come over to me very often to whom I almost always show my regard by a piece of bread and drink of beer, by which an affection is in turn aroused in them, and they everywhere call me German and Carissimo (that is Brother). N. B. Their speech is manly and partakes a little of the gravity of the Italian, as I had thought, etc. Concerning their nature and character, one must divide them, so to speak, into those who have for some time been in communication with the socalled Christians, and those who have just begun to creep out of their holes. Now the former are crafty and deceitful, for which they have to thank the above-mentioned mouth-Christians, semper enim aliquid haeret. Such a one recently offered me his belt as a pledge and assurance that he would bring me a turkey, but he brought me instead an eagle and tried to persuade me that it was a turkey, etc. When I assured him however that I had seen more eagles, he motioned to a Swede who was standing by, that he had done it to deceive, with the idea that we had just come to the country, and I would probably be not well acquainted with such birds. Another one tried the brandy in my flask thus: he stuck his finger in, and then stuck it into the fire, to see if there was water mixed with it, etc etc. The latter, on the other hand are of an honest nature, harm no one, and we have nothing at all to fear from them. One thing recently sank deep into my heart when I thought of the earnest warning of our Saviour that we His disciples should take no thought for the morrow, because thus the heathen do. Alas, thought I to myself, how everything is reversed! If we Christians had not provided for a month or more, how discouraged we would be! While these heathen cast their care on God with such wonderful trustfulness. Just then I was watching four of them eating together, the earth was at once their table and bench, pumpkins cooked in pure water, without butter or seasoning, their only dish, their spoons were mussel-shells, from which they supped the warm water, and their plates were oak leaves, which they did not have to wash after the meal, nor to take care of in case they needed them again. Ah, worthy friend, let us learn from these people the blessedness of fearing nothing, that they may not put us to shame one day before the judgment stool of Jesus Christ, etc etc.

Of the persons who came here with me already half a dozen have died, but I and mine have throughout the whole time been in healthy condition, with good appetites, except that Isaac Dilbeck for eight days has been somewhat poorly, and Jacob Schumacher on the 1st of October cut his foot badly with an axe and could not work for a week, etc. Of the people from Crefeld, no one has died except the aged mother of Herman op de Graef, who having had enough of these earthly vanities, soon after her arrival here went to enjoy the heavenly bliss. Abraham Tunes' (our tenant's) wife was lying very ill in my little house for more than two months, was for a long while unconscious, but improved gradually from day to day.

Now concerning the land bought: This is divided into three kinds, namely fifteen thousand acres together in one piece, along a navigable water. In the second place, three hundred acres in the City Liberties which strip of land is between the Delaware and Scollkill. Thirdly, three lots in the city to build houses upon. When, after my arrival, I went to W. Penn to make out warrants for the said three kinds, and to take them into possession, his first answer was concerning this;

1. The three lots in the town and the three hundred acres in the Liberties could not come to them because they were bought after he W. Penn had already started from England, and the books at London were closed, etc., but after I had represented to him that they were the forerunners of all Germans, and therefore to have more consideration etc, he let me measure off at the edge of the town three adjacent lots, from his younger son's portion.

etc. 12 11, 10 9 8 7 6 5 4 3 2 1

The double line represents the Delaware River, on which the town lies, the numbers, the following houses, and farm houses: 1. Schwed Schwan. 2. The Lutheran Church. 3. The Pastor's house. 4. An English man. 5. Schwed Anders. 6. Will Penns youngest son. 7. The .
8. Philip Fort. 9. The Society and their Trading house. 10. The Inn of the blue Anchor. 11. James Claypoole. 12 etc. are other houses whose naming is here unnecessary. They lie thus along the Delaware, for it is a wide street, upon which follows our first lot, one hundred feet wide and four hundred long, at the end of which comes a street, then our second lot, also of the same width and length. Further another street and then our third lot. Thus there can be built upon each one two houses in front, and two behind, directly alongside of each other, in all twelve houses upon the three lots, with their courts, properly, all of which front upon the street etc. But we must necessarily build, within two years, in order that such lots be not lost, three houses, that is one on each lot. I have already upon the first, together

with our servant put up a little house one-half under the earth and half above, which is indeed only thirty feet long, and fifteen broad, but when the people from Crefeld were lodging with me, it could accommodate twenty persons. Upon the window made of oiled paper, over the door I wrote, Parva Domus sed amica bonis procul este profani !—, which W. Penn read not long ago and was pleased with. Besides this I dug a cellar seven feet deep, twelve wide, and twenty long, on the Delaware stream, and am now busy building a stable. All three lots are cleared of the trees, which I have been cutting down nightly for some nights past, and I am going to sow them with Indian corn. N. B. It is especially difficult and costly to clear all the land, but we cannot do without it on account of the horses, cattle, and pigs which run loose. Also one cannot the first year in such a new land raise rye, only Indian (or as you call it Turkish) corn, which neither tastes as good nor satisfies.

(2) Concerning the three hundred acres in the city Liberties, I have given W. Penn much pressure and especially urged that B. Furly had promised them in sale to us, etc. But for a long while he would not agree to it because none had been set aside for city Liberties when he was in England, except to purchasers of five thousand acres among whom the Germans were not included At last only a few days ago, when I again delivered a memorial to him, he gave me the friendly answer that he from special favor, would have me receive those three hundred acres, but that he would have nothing more sold to any one, whosoever he might be, again, after the closing of the books. So I intend as soon as possible to start Indian corn here on these three hundred acres (which are not half an hour's distance from this town) in order the better to keep cows and pigs, and to raise more produce, and thus to help those who come after me.

(3) In regard to the fifteen thousand acres, two great difficulties present themselves, namely that W. Penn does not want to give them all in one tract, so that so great an extent of land will not be desert and vacant; also he does not want it along the Delaware River, where everything is already taken up by others. However, after I had many times by word of mouth as well as by writing represented that it would be very prejudicial for us and our German descendants, to be put under the English and had shown him the communications of B. Furly and his letters to W. Penn, in which he had promised other things to our nation, etc, he at last granted in a warrant that we should have our land altogether, in case we would, within a year's time, place thirty families upon the fifteen thousand acres, namely three townships, each of ten households, in which the three which are already here, are to be reckoned, (but in case there are not thirty families, he will not promise to give the land all in one tract). I for my part would well wish that we might have a separate little province, and be so much the more free from all oppression. Now if one of you might be free in himself to come here, and bring with him so many families, your own good would be incomparably advanced thereby. He, W. Penn said to me just day before yesterday, substantially that in this case, he would favor you before all English men who have already bought, but are not yet here, and would grant certain privileges to our new *Franckenland* (as he called the land assigned to us). But if it turned out to be too difficult to transport so many families in so short a time, my earnest suggestion would hold good, that the friend from ——should take from you a few thousand acres, and help hither several households from their great overflow, in order that the fifteen thousand acres should remain undi-

vided, and not occasional English neighbors come between us; at the same time he will not give it too far away from his town, namely on the Scollkill above the Falls, where he himself expects to build a house, and to set up for himself a little dominion. The land along the river is rather hilly, and not good for the cultivation of the vine, but further in it is level and fruitful. The greatest trouble is that one cannot go above the falls and rocky cliffs with any boat except after heavy rains, and then not without danger, etc. Now in the meantime I could not know what you might decide to do about it; also, about these oftmentioned fifteen thousand acres. They cost thirty-eight pound sterling, that is five shillings for every hundred acres, according to the measurement of this country, which money I had not at hand, and must wait until I had heard your instructions in order not to overstep the limits of my power of attorney. But that I might show the three families which had arrived to their six hundred acres I have taken up together with the Crefelders (who bought eighteen thousand acres and being all of them here could not get their land in one tract), six thousand acres in one township, of which they have three thousand, and we three thousand. This town I founded on the 24th of October, and called it *Germantown*. It lies only two hours from here, upon fruitful soil, and near pleasant springs, which I have already mentioned. This I had to do because W. Penn would give to no one his portion separately, but all must dwell together in townships or towns, and this not without excellent reasons, the most important of which, is that in this way the children are kept at school, and are much more conveniently trained well. Neighbors also offer each other a kind and helping hand, and with united voices, can in open assembly praise and honor and magnify God's goodness. N. B. You can therefore appropriate only one hundred acres to the families which you bring over in the future, and still have almost as much inheritance etc.

In regard to my household, I should like to arrange it in good German style in which Jacob Schumacher and the old Swiss are very serviceable, but the Hollanders, who are with me, are not of much use in it, especially the maid who will not agree to live with the English one; The latter will leave, because she cannot get along so well with her two children, or take them to another husband. I very much desire as soon as possible to bring here a German maid, whom I can trust better than I can do now, alas!

Now, if you wish that your hope should not be disappointed, send only Germans, for the Hollanders (as sad experience has taught me) are not so easily satisfied, which in this new land is a very necessary quality, etc. I have no carpenter among my servants. There must be a few sent therefore, for the building of houses, and it may be of use to you to know in making your contract with them, that the daily wages here are much lowered, and they receive no more daily, beside their board, than two Kopfstücke, although most of them do not work for that, and prefer to leave the country. N. B. There is a certain pay fixed for all tradesmen. Also the half of the merchant's goods must be gain although indeed there is probably little profit to be made by these in two or four years as the Society is sufficiently aware; for (1) every new comer brings with him so many clothes and goods that he needs nothing for several years. (2) There is here very little money while the desire for it with many is so much the greater. On the sixteenth of November there was a yearly market in our Philadelphia at which however I spent only a few pounds sterling. (3) One can find no return at all of goods from this country to England, etc. W. Penn intended very especially to establish weaving and vine culture. Send us, therefore, when you have a good opportunity some good vines of whose bearing there will be no doubt.—Item. All kinds of field and garden seeds, especially lentils and millet, etc. Also N. B. some large iron cooking pots and some double-boilers; item, one iron stove; because the winters here are mostly as cold as with you and the rough north wind much stronger. Item, some bed covers or mattresses, as I brought no more with me than just what I needed and have already taken one more servant. Finally will you also send here some pieces of Barchet and Osnaburg linen cloth. It can be sold with great advantage, etc. A tanner can begin his trade with great advantage as we can obtain enough skins in the country around us, exchanging one dressed for two undressed and also keep the best for a pair of shoes etc. But a certain amount of capital must be employed for it; and then, through a little money scattered in a short time a rich harvest would be reaped. Reflect on this with due consideration. The two most necessary things are 1, to build upon the lots in this town comfortable houses, which may be leased for a good deal of money, and yearly twelve per cent. may be made, 2, to found a tile bakery for which W. Penn has promised to give us a suitable place, for as long as we bake no stone, our building is entirely of wood. Other tradesmen may still wait several years etc. etc.

To the four questions I give these brief answers; (1) W. Penn has laid a good foundation for a wise rule and published from time to time useful laws. (2) He keeps up neighborly friendship with all governors around him. He also hopes that the threatening contention with Baldimor will as soon as possible be brought to a close and removed by royal decree. (3) The said W. Penn is loved and praised by all people; even the old vicious inhabitants must recognize that they have never seen such a wise ruler. Oh, what strong and impressive sighs this dear man sent up on the first day of this again recurring New Year on high and to the throne of our Emmanuel, because the true Philadelphia and brother love is not to be met with as freely in this our Philadelphia, as he on his part desires, and for the furthering of which he is industriously working like a true father of his country. (4) The Indians (of whose nature some little is stated in the foregoing) decrease in numbers here daily and withdraw several hundred miles farther into the country etc.

Now perhaps you might ask whether I with a clear, unbiased conscience would advise one and another of you to travel hither. I answer with careful reflection that I would very gladly from my heart have the advantage of your dear presence: nevertheless if (1) you do not find in yourselves the freedom of conscience and (2) you cannot resign yourselves to the difficulties and dangers of the long journey and (3) to the lack of most comforts to which you have been accustomed in Germany such as stone houses, agreeable food and drink etc. for one or two years, then follow my advice and remain yet awhile where you are; but if these above-mentioned considerations do not seem too hard to you, then go, the sooner the better, out of the European Sodom and think then of Lot's wife who indeed went forward with her feet but left behind her heart and inclinations. Oh, worthy friend, I wish indeed that with this eagle's plume I could express to you the love I feel for you and indeed convince you that it is not a mere lip love but one which wishes more good to you than to myself. My heart is bound unto yours in a bond of love. Let us now grow together like trees which the right hand of God has planted by streams of water so that we bring forth not only leaves but fruit at the proper time, the fruit of repentance, the fruit of peace, the fruit of justice. For of what advantage is such a useless tree, although the Gardener spares it for some years longer, digs and works about it with all care, he at last when it shows no improvement cuts it down and casts it into the fire. Forgive me this comparison, dear friend. We find here daily such unfruitful trees and cut them down and use them for firewood. It is entirely a heartfelt warning which can do no harm. I recommend you altogether to the divine influence without which our fruitfulness is imperfect. May the Lord who has given the will give also the fulfilment! Amen.

I send enclosed a sample of the Indian coin in common use here, of which six white ones and three black ones make an English farthing; and now certain Indians will sell nothing more for silver money but will only be paid in their own coin, because they for the most part are leaving this country and want to retire several hundred miles into the woods. Then they hold certain superstitions that just as many Indians must die annually as there are Europeans who come here, etc.

Now I have to state this, according to the measure of my duty, and I take the greatest care to be truthful, of which W. Penn and other honest people as well as my own conscience, which I prize more than thousands, can give irreproachable witness. That it is pretty hard for me in this expensive country, almost without provisions to take care of so many servants and dependents, you can easily imagine; but trust in our Heavenly Father overcomes all things.

Give my hearty greeting to all my other acquaintances.

LETTER FROM JORIS WERTMULLER.[67]

March 16th, 1684.

The blessing of the Lord be all times with you, dearly beloved brother-in-law, Benedict Kunts, and your household companion and all good friends who shall inquire for me, and especially all those who are from the land of Berne. Through the Blessing of God I greet you all very heartily, giving you to know that I arrived here in good health, and God be praised!—find myself still very well, earnestly wishing that I may receive the same information concerning you.

The city of Philadelphia covers a great stretch of country, and is growing larger and larger. The houses in the country are better built than those within the city. The land is very productive, and raises all kinds of fruits. All kinds of corn are sown. From a bushel of wheat, it is said, you may get sixty or seventy, so good is the land. You can keep as many cattle as you wish, and there is provender enough for them and as many swine as you want, since there are multitudes of oak trees, which produce an abundance of acorns to make them fat, and other wild nuts. You find here householders who have a hundred cows and innumerable hogs, so that a man can have as much pork as he wants. There are all kinds of wild animals, such as deer, roes, etc; all kinds of birds, some tame and others wild, by the thousand, together with an exceptionally great quantity of fish. The land lies in a good climate and is very healthy. You seldom see mists or fogs. There are many great and small rivers that are navigable, beautiful springs, fountains, mountains and valleys. The farmers or husbandmen live better than lords. If a workman will

[67] Biography of Hendrick Pannebecker, p 27

only work four or five days in a week, he can live grandly. The farmers here pay no tithes nor contributions. Whatever they have is free for them alone. They eat the best and sell the worst. You can find as many wild vineyards as you wish, but no one troubles himself to look after their safety or take care of them. The vines bear so many bunches that from one vine many hundred bottles of wine should be made. Handicraftsmen earn here much money, together with their board and drink, which are very good. The natives or Indians are blackish like the heathen, who through Germany and Holland have disappeared. They are stronger and hardier than the Christians, and very mild. They go almost entirely naked, except that they cover their loins. They use no money, except *kraaltjes* and little shells like those one finds on the bridles of the train horses in Holland. If any one is inclined to come here, let him look for a good ship-master, since he cannot believe everything that they say. The freight from England to Pensilvania is five pound sterling, about fifty-six Holland guldens, but I should advise you rather to go with a Holland shipmaster to Manhates, formerly called New Amsterdam, and now New York, two or three days' journey from Pensilvania, and I should advise you to take with you what you need upon the ship, especially brandy, oranges, lemons, spices and sugar since the sea may be very trying. See that you are well supplied with clothes and linen, and it will be better than to have money, since what I bought in Holland for ten guldens, I here sold again for thirty guldens; but you must not buy too dear.

I have written to my brother in Amsterdam that he send me a chest full of clothes. If you or any one else from the Hague, come here and are willing to bring it along and take care of the transportation, I shall compensate you well for your trouble. So if you bring or send to me here one or two of my sons who are with my brother I shall pay all the costs. If anyone can come here in this land at his own expense, and reaches here in good health, he will be rich enough, especially if he can bring his family or some man-servants, because servants are here dear. People bind themselves for three or four years' service for a great price, and for women they give more than for men because they are scarce. A good servant can place himself with a master for a hundred guldens a year and board.

Brother-in-law B. K., if you come into these regions bring a woman with you, and if you bring two for me, Joris Wertmuller, I shall be glad, because then we shall live like lords. My brother, who lives in Amsterdam, is named Jochem Wertmuller. He lives in Ree Street in the *Three Gray Shoes.* I have many more things to write to you, but time does not permit. Meanwhile I commend you all to God the Father Almighty, through our Lord and Saviour Jesus Christ. Amen.

I, Joris Wertmuller, Switzer by birth, at present in Pensilvania.

N. B. If anyone comes in this land or wishes to write letters, let them be addressed to Cornelius Bom in Pensilvania, in the city of Philadelphia, cake baker, who used to live in Haarlem in Holland, and who came here in the same ship with me and knows where in the country I dwell.

Letter from Cornelius Bom, October 12, 1684.

Jan Laurens, well beloved friend:

I duly received yours of the 22nd of April, 1684, and have read it through with heartfelt pleasure, as an evidence of your love to me and to the Lord. Well, Jan, I have not forgotten you since I have been away from you, but you have many times been in my thoughts. I have

Miſſive van
CORNELIS BOM,
Geſchreven uit de Stadt
PHILADELPHIA.
In de Provintie van
PENNSYLVANIA,
Leggende op d'Ooſtzyde van de
Zuyd Revier van Nieuw Nederland,
Verhalende de groote Voortgank
van de ſelve Provintie.
Waer by komt
De Getuygenis van
JACOB TELNER.
van Amſterdam.

Tot Rotterdam gedrukt, by Pieter va
Wijnbrugge, in de Leeuweſtraet. 168

not written to you, but remembered you in the letter I sent to Rotterdam. My business has been urgent, and I have had little time for writing many letters. You want to know how it goes with me here, and how I like it, and whether things are prosperous with the people, and you want to learn the condition of the country. Concerning these things I should answer you briefly and truthfully as follows: the country is healthful and fruitful, and the conditions are all favorable for its becoming through the blessing of the Lord and the diligence of men a good land—better than Holland. It is not so good now but daily grows better and better. The increase here is so great that, I believe, nowhere in history can be found such an instance of growth in a new country. It is as if the doors had been opened for its progress. Many men are coming here from many parts of the world, so that it will be overflowed with the nations. Our Governor's authority is respected by all and is very mild, so that I trust the Lord will bless this land more if we continue to walk in his way. The people in general have so far been prosperous in their business, so that those who are industrious daily expect to do better and have reason to live in hope; but many have found it hard to get along, especially those who did not bring much with them and those who went into the land to clear it for themselves and did not go to work for hire by the day. Many of those who have sat down to their trades alone [68] have had it somewhat hard. Carpenters and masons have got along the best. During the first year or two men spent what they had saved, but now almost everything is improving. As for myself, I went through and endured great difficulties, unaccustomed hardships and troubles before I got as far as I am now, but now I am above many, in good shape, and do not consider that I have less of my own than when I left Hol-

[68] So that people who are far from the city can obtain necessary accommodations.

land, and am in all respects very well-to-do. I have here a shop of many kinds of goods and edibles; sometimes I ride out with merchandise and sometimes bring something back, mostly from the Indians, and deal with them in many things. I have no servants except one negro whom I bought. I have no rent or tax or excise to pay. I have a cow which gives plenty of milk, a horse to ride around, my pigs increase rapidly, so that in the summer I had seventeen when at first I had only two. I have many chickens and geese, and a garden and shall next year have an orchard if I remain well; so that my wife and I are in good spirits and are reaching a condition of ease and prosperity in which we have great hopes. But when we first came it was pretty hard in many respects. Those who come now come as in the summer in what there is to be done, since now anything can be had for money. The market is supplied with fresh mutton and beef at a reasonable price, in a way that I would have not thought could have occurred in so short a time. Sometimes there is a good supply of partridges for half a stuiver apiece, pigeons, ducks and teals, and fish in great quantities in their seasons. There are not many roads yet made in order to receive from and bring to market, but these things are now beginning to get into order. In a few years, if it continues in the same way, everything here will be more plentiful than in other lands. The commerce and trade are close at the door, to the Barbados, Bermudas and other West India Islands that will bring this country into a good condition. Time will best show this to be the case. Nevertheless I do not advise any one to come here.[69] Those who come ought to come

[69] And in this he acts wisely and with foresight, for how could any one in such a matter, especially if unrequested, give advice: for it may hap-

after Christian deliberation, with pure intentions in fear of the Lord, so that the Lord may be their support, for before a man here reaches ease he must exercise great patience, resignation and industry, the one as much as the others. Therefore, whoever comes, let him come with a constant mind, having his eyes fixed upon the commands of the God above him. This none can do except those who have the Lord with them in the matter and so are cleansed from fleshly and worldly views and they have good counsel by them in all things.

It is hard to them, if trials come, they look to the Lord and are clear in themselves, so that to them all things are for the best. For my own part I have no regrets that I came here, but all the while we have a good hope that everything was sent for my good, and being clear before the Lord that I have had no views which displeased him, and having faith in the great God over the sea and the land. He has not forgotten me, but has shown his fatherly care over me and mine. Truly he is a God over those who are upright of heart and looks upon many of their weaknesses leniently.

So, my dearly beloved friend, not knowing whether I shall see your face in the flesh again, I take my leave of you for the present in the tender love of our Father who has shown his love for us through his Son, the true light through which he daily seeks to unite us with him. O great love of our God! O let us not forget or think little of him, but daily answer him by submitting ourselves to his wishes and

pen to one well to another badly, and no one affair, land, place, state or manner of living is equally pleasant to all. It is not a vain proverb which says an affair may be equally open to all men but the outcome be very different So that he who such a journey undertakes does well to consider whether he is able to endure the possibilities of failure as well as of success.

the power of his mercy which he shows us! O let us hold him here in love, and above all remember him and cling to him! O that we might daily perceive, that our hearts more and more cling to the Lord! That we still more and more might be united with him in that his spirit might witness that we are his children, and so his heirs! Then shall we be able to say with the Apostle Paul that we know whenever this earthly house is broken, we have a building with God everlasting in Heaven. O great cause worthy of consideration above all causes!

So, true friend, I commend you to the Lord and to his word of mercy, which is mighty to build up you and me to the end. So with love, I remain your unchangeable friend,

Cornelius Bom.

In Philadelphia, the 12th of October, 1684.

Here are it is supposed, four hundred houses great and small.

Information from Jacob Telner, of Amsterdam.

Jacob writes to me that he supposes there are many who are desirous of knowing how he and his family are and how it had fared with them, and requesting me to inform such persons briefly out of his letters. He says that they have had a long and hard voyage (that is to say, to New York, hitherto New Amsterdam); that they were twelve weeks under way, others having made the trip in five, six, or seven weeks; that they had very contrary winds and calms; that they therein found and experienced remarkably the presence and protection of the Lord; that on their arrival they were received by all their acquaintances with much love and affection; that his wife has now forgotten the hardships of the sea; that he found it a very pleasant country, overflowing with everything (that is to say, in New York, where he was), where people can live much better and with less expense than in Holland; that if men are industrious in what they undertake, and live in a Christian manner, they need not work many days in the week; that he had heard a good report of Pennsylvania; and that there was a very wonderful increase in the production of everything in proportion to the time, although it was impossible in a short time to have things as abundant as in New York; that when he went to Pennsylvania he hoped to give a true report of everything there. Since then he made a journey there and has again returned to New York. He writes, December 12, 1684, that he found a beautiful land with a healthy atmosphere, excellent fountains and springs running through it, beautiful trees from which can be obtained better firewood than the turf of Holland, and that in all things it might be considered an exceptionally excellent land, and that those who belittle it are unworthy of attention; that Philadelphia grows rapidly, having already several hundred houses of stone and wood and cottages; that he, with his family, intends to move there in the spring, and further, that he is very well, and that his wife and especially his daughters are in good health and fat.[70]

Letter of Johann Samuel and Heinrich Pastorius.

On the 4th of March, 1699, Johann Samuel and Heinrich Pastorius, the one nine and the other seven years of age, wrote this letter to their grandfather in Windsheim:
"Dearly Beloved Grandfather:

To withstand thy overflowing love and inclination to us,

[70] These letters from Bom and Telner in Dutch were printed in Rotterdam in 1685. But one copy is known

our father says is as impossible as to swim against the stream which neither of us two is able to do. We give our heartfelt thanks for it, and as for the little picture you sent over to us we never saw anything like it before. There is an unknown bird in it whose tail is bigger than himself. It is like, we are told, those proud people from whose faults may God protect us. There is also a little boy in a red coat who fell from a globe of the world. Whether this was so slippery or whether the poor child did not know how to hold himself up we shall perhaps learn by experience when we have grown older. The rhymes you wrote on the back of it pleased our parents very much and they wish that we shall never forget them especially the close of the verse.

Christum Jesum recht zu lieben
Und in Guten uns zu uben.

We often wish that we were with thee or that thou lived here in our house in Germantown which has a beautiful front garden and at this time stands empty because we are in Philadelphia and must spend eight hours every day in school except the last day of the week when we can stay home in the afternoon. Since we cannot now have the hope that we will see our dear grandfather here with us we pray thee to give us some account of thy origin and our elders. So that if one of us should by God's will, go to Germany we can ask after our relations. Will thee also give our friendly greeting to our dear cousins and aunts and show them this so that they often write letters to us which after our father leaves the world will be very pleasant to us and we shall not fail through the help of other pious people to continue the correspondence.

Meanwhile we greet thee again most lovingly wishing from our hearts that you have every earthly and eternal good and remain through life under God's true protection, dear Grandfather,

Thy obedient grandchildren,
Johann Samuel and
Henricus Pastorius."

To this request for information concerning his antecedents the pleased grandfather replied, and thus happily through the inquiry of these boys was preserved much of the information we possess relating to the family.[71]

[71] Pastorius Beschreibung, p. 101.

Seal of William Penn.

CHAPTER V.

Kriegsheim.

Arms of the Palatinate.

IN addition to the emigration from Crefeld, and the association at Frankfort, there was a third impulse which was of moment in the settlement of Germantown. On the upper Rhine, two hours' journey from Worms, one of the most interesting and historic cities of Germany, the scene in our race legends of the events of the Nibelungenlied, later the home of Charlemagne, and hallowed as the place where Luther uttered the memorable words "So hilf mich Gott, hier stehe ich. Ich can nicht anders," lies the rural village of Kriegsheim. It is situated in the midst of the beautiful and fertile Palatinate and is forever identified in its traditions, religion and people, with our Pennsylvania life. When I was there, in 1890, it had a population of perhaps two or three hundred people who lived upon one street. About it were the remains of an ancient wall, and within it was an old-time hostelry, in whose stable the village gauger watched over his hogsheads of wine, the representatives of an important local industry. In this obscure and distant village of simple German peasants we trace the ancestry of many of the ladies who now dance in the assemblies of Philadelphia, and many of the men who have been her mayors and judges and filled her most important municipal stations.

Quakerism obtained a foothold upon the continent in a most remarkable manner. Some of the followers of that then aggressive sect had been banished to the Island of Barbados, and had been put upon a British vessel to be transported. England and Holland were then at war and after the vessel had sailed out to sea it was captured by a Dutch privateer, and the useless Quakers were put on shore on the coast of Holland. As we are prettily told by the chronicler, "They acquiesced in their poverty," and though they had been in no repute among their own people, either for riches or endowments, "they increased their small fortunes to a considerable bulk," and like the trees and plants "the which the more they were shaken with the winds, the deeper and faster root they take," they propagated their doctrines in Holland and Germany. [72]

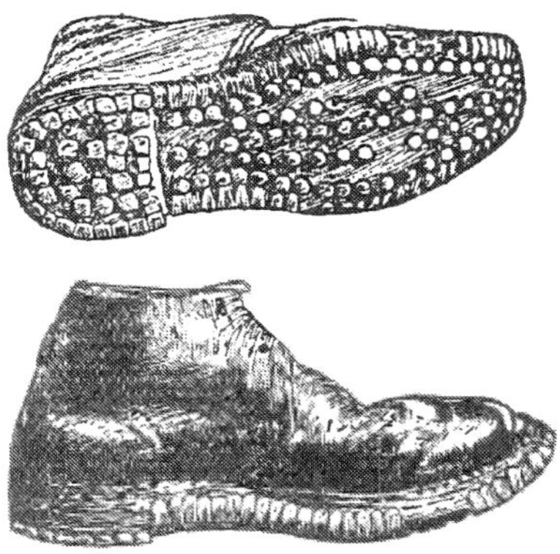

Shoes of the Early Palatines.

The meetings established were visited by preachers sent out by Fox, among others by William Ames, who spoke Dutch and German. In 1657 Ames and George Rolfe

[72] Gerhard Croese's History of the Quakers. Book 2, p. 15.

Gerhard Croesens Quaker=Historie/

Von deren Ursprung/
biß auf jüngsthin entstandene
Trennung;
Darinnen vornemlich von
den Hauptstiftern dieser Secte/
derselben Lehrsätzen/und anderen
ihres gleichen zu dieser Zeit auf=
gebrachten Lehren/ erzehlet
wird.

Berlin/
bey Johann Michael Rüdigern.
1696.

went to Kriegsheim and succeeded in making some converts among the Mennonites living there. It was the farthest outpost of Quakerism in Germany and was cherished by them with the most careful zeal. The conversion of seven or eight families was the reward of their indefatigable energy and effort. This success alarmed the clergy and incited the rabble "disposed to do evil, to abuse those persons by scoffing, cursing, reviling, throwing stones and dirt at them, and breaking their windows." The magistrates directed that any one who should entertain Ames or Rolfe should be fined forty rix dollars. In 1658, for refusing to bear arms, the goods of John Hendricks to the value of fourteen rix dollars were seized and he was put in prison. In 1660, for the same reason, his goods valued at about four and-half rix dollars were seized. In 1663 the authorities took from him two cows, and from Hendricks Gerritz two cows, from the widow of John Johnson a cow, from George Shoemaker bedding worth seven rix dollars, from Peter Shoemaker goods worth two guilders. In 1664 George Shoemaker lost pewter and brass worth three and a-half guilders, Peter Shoemaker three sheets worth three guilders, and John Hendricks three sheets worth three guilders. In 1666, John Shoemaker, Peter Shoemaker and John Hendricks each lost a cow.[73] William Caton paid a visit to them in 1661, and on the 30th of Eleventh Month wrote from there a letter to friends in London in which he says, that the Catholic, Lutheran and Calvinist clergy regarded them "as the offensivest, the irregularest, and the perturbatiousest people that are of any sect." He helped them "to gather their grapes, it being the time of vintage."

Stephen Crisp says in July, 1669: "But the Lord pre-

[73] Besse's Sufferings of the Quakers Vol. II, p 450

GERARDI CROESI

HISTORIA QUAKERIANA,

Sive

De vulgò dictis QUAKERIS,
Ab ortu illorum usque ad recèns
natum schisma,

LIBRI III.

In quibus præsertim agitur de ipsorum præcipuis antecessoribus, & dogmatis (ut & similibus placitis aliorum hoc tempore) factisque ac casibus memorabilibu.

AMSTELODAMI,
Apud HENRICUM & Viduam
THEODORI BOOM. 1695.

served me and brought me on the 14th day of that month to Griesham near Worms, where I had found divers who had received the Everlasting Truth and had stood in a testimony for God about ten years, in great sufferings and tribulations, who received me as a servant of God; and my testimony was as a seed upon the tender grass unto them. I had five good meetings among them and divers heard the truth and several were reached and convinced and Friends established in the faith." Just at this time they were in sore trouble because of the fact that the Prince of the land, or Pfaltzgraff, had imposed an unusual fine of four rix dollars upon every family for attending meetings, and upon failure to pay, goods of three times the value were taken. Crisp went to Heidelberg to see the Prince and warned him of the danger of persecution. The Prince received him graciously, discoursed with him about general topics, and promised him that the fines should be remitted, which was accomplished.[74]

On the 22d of August, 1677, William Penn left Frankfort on his way to Kriegsheim. The magistrate of the village, upon the instigation of the clergyman, attempted to prevent him from preaching, but with the friends there and a "coachful from Worms," he had a quiet and comfortable meeting. From there he walked to Mannheim, in an effort to see the Prince concerning the oppressions of the Quakers, which had been renewed. Failing to find him, he wrote to him a vigorous letter upon the subject. On the 26th Penn walked out from Worms, six English miles, and held a meeting, lasting five hours, in the course of which "The Lord's power was sweetly opened to many of the inhabitants." He describes them as "Poor hearts; a little handful surrounded with great and mighty countries

---

[74] Travels of Stephen Crisp, p 29.

THE

General History OF THE QUAKERS:

CONTAINING

The Lives, Tenents, Sufferings, Tryals, Speeches, and Letters

Of all the most

Eminent Quakers,

Both Men and Women;

From the first Rise of that SECT, down to this present Time.

Collected from Manuscripts, &c.

A Work never attempted before in English.

Being Written Originally in *Latin*
By *GERARD CROESE.*

To which is added,

A LETTER writ by *George Keith*, and sent by him to the Author of this Book: Containing a Vindication of himself, and several Remarks on this History.

LONDON, Printed for John Dunton, at the *Raven* in *Jewen-street.* 1696.

of darkness." The meeting was held in a barn. The magistrate listened from behind the door and subsequently reported that he had discovered no heresies and had heard nothing that was not good. On the 27th, after two more meetings, Penn, accompanied by several grateful attendants, returned to Worms.

The climax of the story of the Quaker meeting at Kriegsheim is given by Croese. He says that having nothing of their own to lose, and hearing of the great plenty in America, and hoping to gain a livelihood by their handiwork, they in the very year that preceded the war with the French "wherein all that fruitful and delicious country was wasted with fire and sword" forsook the cottages which could scarcely be kept standing with props and stakes, and entered into a voluntary and perpetual banishment to Pennsylvania, where they lived in the greatest freedom and with sufficient prosperity.

Jacob Schumacher, the servant who accompanied Pastorius, may have been one of the family at Kriegsheim, but up to the present time no evidence of the fact has been discovered. It is not improbable.

Oct. 12, 1685, having crossed the sea in the "Francis and Dorothy" there arrived in Germantown Peter Schumacher with his son Peter, his daughters Mary, Frances and Gertrude, and his cousin Sarah; Gerhard Hendricks with his wife Mary, his daughter Sarah and his servant Heinrich Frey, the last named from Altheim, in Alsace. Peter Schumacher, an early Quaker convert from the Mennonites is the first person definitely ascertained to have come from Kriegsheim. Fortunately we know under what auspices

he arrived. By an agreement with Dirck Sipman, of Crefeld, dated August 16th, 1685, he was to proceed with the first good wind to Pennsylvania, and there receive two hundred acres from Hermann Op den Graeff, on which he should erect a dwelling, and for which he should pay a rent of two rix dollars a year.[75] Gerhard Hendricks also had bought two hundred acres from Sipman.[76] He came from Kriegsheim, and I am inclined to think that his identity may be merged in that of Gerhard Hendricks Dewees. If so, he was associated with the Op den Graeffs and Van Bebbers, and was a grandson of Adrian Hendricks Dewees, a Hollander, who seems to have lived in Amsterdam.[77] This identification, however, needs further investigation. Dewees bought land of Sipman, which his widow, Zytien, sold in 1701. The wife of Gerhard Hendricks in the court records is called Sytje. On the tax list of 1693 there is a Gerhard Hendricks, but no Dewees, though the latter at that time was the owner of land. Hendricks after the Dutch manner called one son William Gerrits and another Lambert Gerrits, and both men, if they were two, died about the same time. Much confusion has resulted from a want of familiarity on the part of local historians with the Dutch habit of omitting the final or local appellation. Thus the Van Bebbers are frequently referred to in contemporaneous records as Jacob Isaacs, Isaac Jacobs and Matthias Jacobs, the Op den Graeffs as Dirck Isaacs, Abraham Isaacs and Herman Isaacs; and Van Burklow as Reynier Hermanns.

On the 20th of March, 1686, Johannes Kassel, a weaver, and another Quaker convert from the Mennonites, aged forty-seven years, with his children, Arnold, Peter, Eliza-

[75] See his deed in Dutch in the Germantown book.

[76] Deed book E 4, vol. 7, p 180.

[77] Raths-Buch.

beth, Mary and Sarah, came to Germantown from Kriegsheim, having purchased land from members of the Frankfort Company. In the vessel with Kassel was a widow, Sarah Shoemaker, from the Palatinate, and doubtless from Kriegsheim, with her children, George, Abraham, Barbara, Isaac,[78] Susanna, Elizabeth and Benjamin. Among the Mennonite martyrs mentioned by Van Braght there are several bearing the name of Schoenmaker, and that there was a Dutch settlement in the neighborhood of Kriegsheim is certain. At Flomborn, a few miles distant, is a spring which the people of the vicinity still call the "Hollander's Spring."

I have a Dutch medical work published in 1622, which belonged to Johannes Kassel; many Dutch books from the family are in the possession of that indefatigable antiquary, Abraham H. Cassel, and the deed of Peter Schumacher is in Dutch. The Kolbs, who came to Pennsylvania later, were grandsons of Peter Schumacher, and were all earnest Mennonites. The Kassels brought over with them many of the manuscripts of one of their family, Ylles Kassel, a Mennonite preacher at Kriegsheim, who was born before 1618, and died after 1681, and some of these papers are still preserved. The most interesting is a long poem in German rhyme, which describes vividly the condition of the country, and throws the strongest light upon the character of the people and the causes of the emigration. The writer says that it was copied off with much pain and bodily suffering November 28, 1665. It begins:

"O Lord! To Thee the thoughts of all hearts are

---

[78] He married Sarah, only daughter of Gerhard Hendricks. Their son Benjamin, and their grandson Samuel, were successively Mayors of Philadelphia, and a great-granddaughter was the wife of William Rawle. I am indebted for some of these facts to the kindness of W. Brooke Rawle, Esq.

known. Into Thy hands I commend my body and soul. When Thou lookest upon me with Thy mercy all things are well with me. Thou hast stricken me with severe illness, which is a rod for my correction. Give me patience and resignation. Forgive all my sins and wickedness. Let not Thy mercy forsake me. Lay not on me more than I can bear," and continues, "O, Lord God! Protect me in this time of war and danger, that evil men may not do with me as they wish. Take me to a place where I may be concealed from them, free from such trials and cares. My wife and children too, that they may not come to shame at their hands. Let all my dear friends find mercy from Thee." After noting a successful flight to Worms, he goes on, "O dear God and Lord! to Thee be all thanks, honor and praise for Thy mercy and pity, which Thou hast shown to me in this time. Thou hast protected me from evil men as from my heart I prayed Thee. Thou hast led me in the right way so that I came to a place where I was concealed from such sorrows and cares. Thou hast kept the way clear till I reached the city, while other people about were much robbed and plundered. I have found a place among people who show me much love and kindness. . . . Gather us into Heaven of which I am unworthy, but still I have a faith that God will not drive me into the Devil's kingdom with such a host as that which now in this land with murder and robbery destroys many people in many places, and never once thinks how it may stand before God. . . . Well it is known what misery, suffering, and danger are about in this land with robbing, plundering, murdering and burning. Many a man is brought into pain and need, and abused even unto death. Many a beautiful home is destroyed. The clothes are torn from the backs of many people. Cattle and herds are taken away. Much sorrow and complaint have been heard. The beehives are broken down, the wine spilled.'[79]

On the road leading from Worms out through Kriegsheim, but perhaps five miles further from the city, is the village of Flomborn. Thither, about twenty years before the period we are considering, a Dutch family named Pannebakker, whose arms, three tiles gules on a shield argent, were cut in glass in the church window at Gorcum in Holland, came to escape the wars still raging in the Netherlands. There March 21, 1674, was born Hendrick Pannebecker. He came as a young man to Germantown, where, in 1699, he married Eve, the daughter of Hans Peter Umstat. He was a man of education, writing a dainty script and possessing a knowledge of the Dutch, German and English languages and of mathematics. He became the owner of four thousand and twelve acres of land in the province, and as a surveyor for the Penns, he ran the lines for their manors and laid out most of the old roads in Philadelphia, now Montgomery County. He died suddenly April 4, 1754. He founded here a large and influential family, which gave to the war of the rebellion two major generals, four colonels, an adjutant general, two surgeons, a lieutenant colonel, two assistant surgeons, an adjutant, nine captains, seven lieutenants, a quartermaster, a hospital steward, five sergeants, nine corporals and one hundred privates, altogether one hundred and forty-five men, so far as known, the most extensive contribution of any single American family to that struggle.

[79] These papers belong to A. H. Cassel, his descendant.

CHAPTER VI.

The Growth of the Settlement.

Note [80].

IT was the wish of the Germans, when they made their purchase from William Penn, that their lands should all be laid out in one tract and upon a navigable stream. When they arrived here they were offered a location upon the Schuylkill, where are now Manayunk and Roxborough. They objected to the hills and asked for the ground to the eastward, where it was more level. The request was granted and on the 24th of October, 1683, Thomas Fairman measured off fourteen lots. The following day the thirteen families selected by chance the places of their new homes, and at once began to dig the cellars and erect the huts in which, with some hardship, they spent the winter. Pastorius reported that the new

[80] From Townsend Ward's Walk to Germantown, Penna. Magazine, Vol. V., upon what authority unknown.

town of Germanopolis was located upon a rich black soil, well supplied with springs, that the main street was sixty feet wide, the cross street forty feet wide, and that each family had three acres of ground. It was covered with oak, chestnut and other nut trees, and there was a good meadow for the cows. Whichever way we turn, he wrote, "Itur in antiquam Sylvam," it is all overgrown with woods, and he often wished that he had a pair of strong Tyrolers to cut down the thick oak trees. On the 20th of February, 1684, the land was again surveyed by Fairman and a thousand acres which stretched to the Schuylkill were cut off. Since the contract was that their land was to be upon a ship-bearing stream, it looks as though somebody was taking an advantage of them. A more accurate survey, December 29th, 1687, determined the quantity of land in Germantown to be five thousand seven hundred acres, and for this a patent was issued. It was divided into four villages: Germantown with two thousand seven hundred and fifty acres, Crisheim (Kriegsheim) with eight hundred and eighty-four acres, Sommerhausen with nine hundred acres, and Crefeld with one thousand one hundred and sixty-six acres, and thus were the familiar places along the Rhine commemorated in the new land.

Other emigrants ere long began to appear in the little town. Cornelius Bom, a Dutch baker, whom Claypoole mentions in association with Telner and who bears the same name as a delegate from Schiedam to the Mennonite Convention at Dordrecht arrived in Philadelphia it may be with Pastorius. David Scherkes, perhaps from Muhlheim on the Ruhr, and Walter Seimens and Isaac Jacobs Van Bebber, both from Crefeld, were in Germantown November 8th, 1684. Van Bebber was a son of Jacob Isaacs Van Bebber and was followed here a few years later, 1687, by his father, and brother Matthias. About the same time

Pastorius wrote that the floors were laid for sixty-four houses. Jacob Telner, the second of the original Crefeld purchasers to cross the Atlantic reached New York, after a tedious voyage of twelve weeks' duration, and from there he wrote, Dec. 12, 1684, to Jan Laurens, of Rotterdam. He seems to have been the central figure of the whole emigration. As a merchant in Amsterdam his business was extensive. He had transactions with the Quakers in London and friendly relations with some of the people in New York. One of the earliest to buy lands here, we find him meeting Pastorius immediately prior to the latter's departure, doubtless to give instructions, and later personally superintending the emigration of the Colonists. During his thirteen years' residence in Germantown his relations both in a business and social way with the principal men in Philadelphia were apparently close and intimate. Penn wrote to Logan in 1703, "I have been much pressed by Jacob Telner concerning Rebecca Shippen's business in the town,"[81] and both Robert Turner and Samuel Carpenter acted as his attorneys. He and his daughter Susanna were present at the marriage of Francis Rawle and Martha Turner in 1689, and witnessed their certificate The harmonious blending of the Mennonite and the Quaker is nowhere better shown than in the fact of his accompanying John Delavall on a preaching and proselyting tour to New England in 1692.[82] He was the author of a "Treatise" in quarto mentioned by Pastorius, and extracts from his letters to Laurens were printed at Rotterdam in 1685.[83] About 1692 he appears to have published a paper in the contro-

[81] Penn Logan Correspondence, Vol I, p 189

[82] Smith's History, Hazard's Register, Vol VI, p 309 Smith adopts him as a Friend, but in his own letter of 1709, written while he was living among the Quakers in England, he calls himself a Mennonite

[83] The Treatise is described by Pastorius in the enumeration of his library. MS. Hist. Society.

versy with George Keith, charging the latter with "Impious blasphemy and denying the Lord that bought him."[84]

He was one of the first burgesses of Germantown, the most extensive landholder there, and promised to give ground enough for the erection of a market house, a promise which we will presume he fulfilled. In 1698 he went to London, where he was living as a merchant as late as 1712, and from there in 1709 he wrote to Rotterdam concerning the miseries of some emigrants, six of whom were Mennonites from the Palatinate, who had gone that far on their journey and were unable to proceed. "The English Friends who are called Quakers," he says, had given material assistance.[85] Doubtless European research would throw much light on his career. He was baptized at the Mennonite Church in Amsterdam, March 29, 1665. His only child, Susanna, married Albertus Brandt, a merchant of Germantown and Philadelphia, and after the death of her first husband in 1701 she married David Williams.[86] After deducting the land laid out in Germantown, and the two thousand acres sold to the Op den Graeffs, the bulk of his five thousand acres was taken up on the Skippack, in a tract for many years known as "Telner's Township."[87]

In an original letter in my possession, written in Amsterdam 17th of 5th month, 1678, by Peter Hendricks to Roger Longworth, it is said: "And (to speake it is familiarity to thee) we have also some feare concerning Jacob Tellner; he is prettie high and it does not diminish but increase, but my heart's desire is that he may be preserved."

---

84 A true account of the Scence and advice of the People called Quakers

85 Dr Scheffer's paper in the Penna. Magazine, Vol. II, p 122

86 Exemp. Record, Vol. VII., p 208.

87 Exemp. Record, Vol VIII, p 360.

THE GREAT COMET OF 1680.

(FROM CONTEMPORARY ENGRAVING.)

It appears from Keith's *True account*, London, 1694, that Telner had printed a catechism "in which said paper he

D: F:

deare friend, my love in ye Lord Jes: Chr: is unto thee, and in ye sence of a heavenly fellowship I doe embrace thee, being of [illegible] full of the [illegible] and of these former opportunities yt we weare soe sweetly refreshed togeth[er] deare friend, I was fully resolved to Come to London this time with B.V. Tongeren, to be refreshed with and amongst friends, to which end we had sent our bagges to Rotterdam, but [illegible] things would [illegible] Convenience and soe we must be Content, BV: Tong: wife gott a very sore sickness [illegible] it is now something better, and alsoe a greate hinderance to my Jorney was ye sad disaster of Cor: Roeloffs, of which thou may be informed by deare S.C. or G.D: and indeed we weare verie glad we weare here when things fell out soe with him — we have had a godlie jealousie and Care Concerning ye man a prettie while, but oh! who should have thought of such a sad thing — but what shall we say; I have said in my heart, what should be ye reason yt ye Lord should permitte such a thing, but we must leave ye thing there, but at present it is as a Cloud upon ye truth and friends and opens ye mouths of our enemies, but I hope truth and friends will Come over it in time — how it is with him now, and friends at danzik thou may understand of deare [illegible] — and (to speake it in familiarity to thee) we have alsoe some feare Concerning Jacob Tellner, [illegible] and it doth not diminish but rather increase, but my hearts desire is yt he may be preserved — ye Rotterdamers have [illegible] ye papers, and seeke to spread ye thing among friends, speaking of it almost upon all occasions, well I hope ye Lord will [illegible] above all in this time. The letter to ye king of poland and ye Councell of danzik we understand is Come to ye kings hands with deare G: ffs: letter to him, after he was departed from danzik, and it is said he hath read it himselfe — but nothing further — [illegible] at present [illegible] in which I imbrace thee, and desire thee to remember my deare love to friends where thou art free — and ye love of many fri[ends] is to thee, and I shall long to heare from thee againe [illegible] farewell: I remaine thy friend and brother in my measure

Pieter Hendriks

Amsterd: this 17th of ye 5th month 1678 — [illegible]

positively asserteth gross Antinomian Doctrines and Principles, as that men's sins are forgiven them when Christ died on the Cross."

In 1684 also came Jan Willemse Bockenogen, a Quaker cooper from Haarlem.[88]

October 12, 1685, there arrived in the ship "Francis and Dorothy" Heinrich Buchholz and his wife Mary, and Hans Peter Umstat, from Crefeld, with his wife Barbara, his son, John, and his daughters, Anna Margaretta and Eve. Umstat was the son of Nicholas Umstat, who died at Crefeld at four o'clock on the morning of October 4, 1682. He had bought two hundred acres from Dirck Sipman, which were laid out in Germantown toward Plymouth, and there he spent the remainder of his days. Among the possessions he brought across the seas with him was a Bible, printed at Nuremberg in 1568, which had belonged to his father, Nicholas, at least since 1652, and which I inherited through his daughter Eve. In it, in addition to the family entries, are among others the following: "In the year 1658 the cold was so great that even the Rhine was frozen up. On the 31st of January so great a snow fell that it continued for four days. There was no snow so great within the memory of man," and "December 16, 1680, the Comet Star with a long tail was seen for the first time." The comet which so impressed him is the one that appeared in the time of Cæsar, and with a period of about five hundred years, is the most imposing of those known to astronomers. In 1685 came also Heivert Papen and about the same time Klas Jansen. Occasionally we catch a glimpse of the home life of the early dwellers in Germantown. Willem Streypers, in 1685, had two pairs of leather breeches, two leather doublets, handkerchiefs, stockings and a new hat.

The first man to die was Jan Seimens, whose widow was again about to marry in October, 1685.[89] Bom died before

[88] Among his descendants was Henry Armitt Brown, the orator.

[89] Pastorius' Beschreibung, Leipsic, 1700, p 23, Streyper MSS.

Apocrypha: Das sind Bücher / so der heiligen Schrifft nicht gleich gehalten / vnnd doch nützlich vnd gut zu lesen sind / Als nemlich /

I.	Judith.
II.	Sapientia.
III.	Tobias.
IIII.	Sirach.
V.	Baruch.
VI.	Maccabeorum.
VII.	Stücke in Esther.
VIII.	Stücke in Daniel.

1680

1682

Das Buch Judith.

CAP. I.

Arphaxad.

1 ARphaxad der Meder König / hatte viel Land vn Leute vnder sich bracht vnd bawete eine grosse gewaltige stadt / die nennet er Ecbatana /

Ecbatana.

2 Jre mauren machet er aus eitel werckstü

ins gantze land Gesem / bis an das gebirge
10 des Morenlands. Zu den allen sandte
Nebucad Nezar der König von Assyrien
11 botschafften. Aber sie schlugens jm alle
ab / vnd liessen die boten mit schanden wider
12 heim zihē. Da ward der König Nebucad Nezar seer zornig wider alle diese lande / vnd schwur bey seinē königstul vnd reich / das er sich an allē diesen Landē rechen wolt.

CAP. II.

1689, and his daughter Agnes married Anthony Morris, the ancestor of the distinguished family of that name.[90] In 1685 Wigard and Gerhard Levering came from Muhlheim on the Ruhr,[91] a town also far down the Rhine, near Holland, which, next to Crefeld, seems to have sent the largest number of emigrants. The following year a fire caused considerable loss, and a little church was built at Germantown. According to Seidensticker it was a Quaker meeting house, and he shows conclusively that before 1692 all of the original thirteen, except Jan Lensen, had in one way or another been associated with the Quakers. In 1687 Arent Klincken arrived from Dalem, in Holland, and Jan Streypers wrote: "I intend to come over myself," which intention he carried into effect before 1706, as at that date he signed a petition for naturalization.[92] All of

[90] Ashmead MSS

[91] Jones' Levering Family

[92] Jan Strepers and his son-in-law, H J Van Aaken, met Penn at Wesel in 1686, and brought him from that place to Crefeld. Van Aaken seems to have been a Quaker Sept 30th, 1699, on which day he wrote to Penn "I understand that Derrick Sypman uses for his Servis to you, our Magistrates at Meurs, which Magistrates offers their Service to you again. So it would be well that you Did Kyndly Desire them that they would Leave out of the High Dutch proclomation which is yearly published throughout ye County of Meurs & at ye Court House at Crevel, that ye Quakers should have no meeting upon penalty, & in Case you ffinde freedom to Desire ye sd Magistrates at Meurs that they may petition our King William (as under whose name the sd proclomation is given forth) to leave out ye word Quackers & to grant Leberty of Conscience, & if they should not obtaine ye same from the said King, that then you would be Constrained for the truth's Sake to Request our King William for the annulling of ye sd proclomation Concerning the quackers, yor answer to this p next shall greatly oblige me, Especially if you would write to me in the Dutch or German tongue, god almayghty preserve you and yor wife In soule and body I myself have some thoughts to Come to you but by heavy burden of 8 Children, &c., I can hardly move, as also that I want bodyly Capacity to Clear Lands and ffall trees, as also money to undertake something Ells." An English translation of this letter in the handwriting of Matthias Van Bebber is in my collection.

the original Crefeld purchasers, therefore, came to Pennsylvania sooner or later, except Remke and Sipman. He, however, returned to Europe, where he and Willem had an undivided inheritance at Kaldkirchen, and it was agreed between them that Jan should keep the whole of it, and Willem take the lands here. The latter were two hundred and seventy-five acres at Germantown, fifty at Chestnut Hill, two hundred and seventy-five at the Trappe, four thousand four hundred and forty-eight in Bucks County, together with fifty acres of Liberty Lands and three city lots, the measurement thus considerably overrunning his purchase.

About 1687 came Jan Duplouvys, a Dutch baker, who was married by Friends ceremony to Weyntie Van Sanen, in the presence of Telner and Bom, on the 3d of 3d month of that year. Dirck Keyser, a silk merchant doing business in Printz Gracht, opposite Rees Street, in Amsterdam, and a Mennonite, connected by family ties with the leading Mennonites of that city, arrived in Germantown by way of New York in 1688. If we can rely upon tradition, he was a descendant of that Leonard Keyser, the friend of Luther, who was burned to death at Scharding in 1527, and who, according to Ten Cate, was one of the Waldenses.[93] Long after his coming to Germantown he wore a coat made entirely of silk, which was a matter for disapproval, if not a subject for envy. His father was Dirck Gerritz Keyser, a manufacturer of morocco, and his grandfather was Dircksz Keyser. His mother was Cornelia, daughter of Tobias Govertz Van den Wyngaert, one of the most noted of the early Mennonite preachers, the learned author of a number of theological works, of whom there is a fine portrait by the famous Dutch engraver A. Blootelingh. Here seems to be an appropriate place to

[93] See Pennypacker Reunion, p 13

ENGRAVED COPPERPLATE OF DIRCK KEYSER.

record a bibliographical incident of real value which deserves to be preserved. For many years the scholars of Europe, interested in the period of the Reformation, had disputed over the dates of the birth and death of Menno Simons, one coterie contending for 1492–1559 and their opponents for 1496–1561. One of the principal authorities was Gerhard Roosen, a preacher of Hamburg, who lived to a great age and died in the beginning of the 18th century, and whose testimony was regarded as of importance because his grandmother had personally known Menno. But the whole subject was left in vague uncertainty. In 1881 a man in Ohio wrote to me that he had an old book, for which he wanted two dollars. It came, and behold! it turned out to be a copy of the works of Menno, printed in 1646, which had belonged to Gerhard Roosen, and in his hand, written in 1671, in his 60th year, was an account of a visit which he, with Tobias Govertz Van den Wyngaert and Peter Jans Moyer had made to the grave of Menno. It proceeded to say that he was born in 1492 and died in 1559, and was buried in his own cabbage garden. These facts were at once embodied in a paper by Dr. J. G. DeHoop Scheffer, the historian of the Reformation in Holland, which was printed in Amsterdam, and thus was the New World able to furnish information which settled an Old World historical controversy. Who wrote the letters of Junius may yet find an answer here.

The residents in 1689, not heretofore mentioned, were Paul Wolff, a weaver from Fendern in Holstein, near Hamburg; Jacob Jansen Klumpges, Cornelius Siverts, Hans Millan, Johan Silans, Dirck Van Kolk, Hermann Bom, Hendrick Sellen, Isaac Schaffer, Ennecke Klostermann, from Muhlheim, on the Ruhr; Jan Doeden and Andries Souplis. Of these Siverts was a native of Friesland,

Opera Menno Symons, Ofte Groot Sommarie/

DAT IS.

Vergaderingh/ van ſijne Boecken en Schrif-ten/t'ſamen in een verbaet, ende in Druck vernieuwt/door som-mige Beminders der Waerheydt/ ter Eeren Godts ende haeres naesten welvaert.

Item om alle Punđten en Artijkulen, mitſgaders diverſche redenen, t'ſamen-ſprekingen, bekenteniſſe, &c. In deſen Boeck begre-pen, lichtelijcken te vinden, ſo hebben wy twee Regiſters daer by gevoecht, ende elck Boeck met ſijn eygen Tijtel, Prologe ende Voor-reden, getrouwelijck in onſe Nederduytſche Spraecke geſtelt.

Pſalm 37.30.

Den Mont der gerechtigen ſpreeckt van wyſheyt, ende ſijn lippen van Oordeelen, de Wet ſijns Godts is in ſijn herte, ſijn treden en ſlipperen niet.

Gedruckt in 't Jaer ons Heeren, Anno 1646.

TOBIAS GOVERTSZ vanden WYNGAERT Bedienaer des Goddelyken woords inde Vlaemsche
Doopsgezinde gemeente tot Amsterdam Ætatis LXXX.

TOBIAS GOVERTSZ VANDEN WYNGAERT.

M A CONTEMPORARY PRINT BY A. BLOTELINGH.

the home of Menno Simons.[94] Sellen, with his brother Dirk, were Mennonites from Crefeld, and Souplis was admitted a burgher and denizen of the city of New York, with a right to trade anywhere in his Majesty's dominions. The antecedents of the others I have not been able to ascertain. Hendrick Sellen was very active in affairs at Germantown, being the attorney in fact for Jan Streypers, gave the ground for the Mennonite church there, was a trustee for the church on the Skippack, and in 1698 made a trip across the sea to Crefeld, carrying back to the old home many business communications, and, we may well suppose, many messages of friendship. August 22, 1709, he had a pint of wine and a roll with Pastorius. He was naturalized in 1709, and owned two hundred and ninety-one and a-half acres of land, on which he built an oil mill in 1714, but before April 16, 1739, he had sold it and removed to Komupoango, in Pennsylvania. An effort at naturalization in 1691 adds to our list of residents Reynier Hermanns Van Burklow, Peter Klever, Anthony Loof, Paul Kastner, Andris Kramer, Jan Williams, Herman Op de Trap, Hendrick Kasselberg, from Backersdorf, in the county of Brugge, and Klas Jansen The last two were Mennonites, Jansen being one of the earliest preachers. Op deTrap, or Trapman, as he is sometimes called, appears to have come from Muhlheim, on the Ruhr, and was drowned at Philadelphia in 1693. Gisbert Wilhelms died the year before..

John Goodson, writing to his friends John and S. Dew in London, the 24th of 6th mo., 1690, says · "And five miles off is a town of Dutch and German people that have set up the linnen manufactory which weave and make many thousand yards of pure fine linnen cloth in a year, that in a short time I doubt not but the country will live happily."[95]

---

[94] Raths Buch.

[95] Some Letters . from Pennsylvania, London, 1691

In 1692 culminated the dissensions among the Quakers caused by George Keith and the commotion extended to the community at Germantown. At a public meeting Keith called Dirck Op den Graeff an "impudent rascal"— and since the latter was a justice of the peace in the right of his position as a burgess of Germantown it was looked upon as a flagrant attack upon the majesty of the law. Among those who signed the testimony of the yearly meeting at Burlington 7th of 7th mo., 1692, against Keith, were Paul Wolff, Paul Kastner, Francis Daniel Pastorius, Andries Kramer, Dirck Op den Graeff and Arnold Kassel. The certificate from the Quarterly meeting at Philadelphia, which Samuel Jennings bore with him to London in 1693, when he went to present the matter before the Yearly Meeting there, was signed by Dirck Op den Graeff, Reynier Tyson, Peter Schumacher and Caspar Hoedt. Pastorius wrote two pamphlets in the controversy. On the other hand, Abraham Op den Graeff was one of five persons who, with Keith, issued the *Appeal*, for publishing which William Bradford, the printer, was committed, and a testimony in favor of Keith was signed by Hermann Op den Graeff, Thomas Rutter, Cornelis Siverts, David Scherkes and Jacob Isaacs Van Bebber.[96] The last named furnishes us with another instance of one known to have been a Mennonite acting with the Friends, and Sewel, the Quaker historian, says concerning Keith: "And seeing several Mennonites of the County of Meurs lived also in Penna., it was not much to be wondered that they who count it unlawful for a Christian to bear the sword of the magistracy did stick to him."

Caspar Hoedt, then a tailor in New York, married there 6th mo. 12th, 1686, Elizabeth, eldest daughter of Nico-

[96] Potts' Memorial, p. 394

Some LETTERS AND AN Abstract of Letters FROM PENNSYLVANIA,

Containing

The State and Improvement of that Province.

Published to prevent Mis-Reports.

Printed, and Sold by *Andrew Sowe*, at the *Crooked-Billot* in *Holloway-Lane*, in *Shoreditch*, 1691.

las De la Plaine and Susanna Cresson, who were French Huguenots. James De la Plaine, a relative and probably a son of Nicolaes, came to Germantown from New York prior to August 28th, 1692, on which day he was married by Friends' ceremony to Hannah Cook. Susanna, a daughter of Nicolaes, became the wife of Arnold Kassel 9th mo. 2d, 1693.[97]

On the 2d of November, 1693, Paul Wolff conveyed a half acre on the east side and another half acre on the west side of the street "for a common burying place." In 1694 it was determined that on the "13th and 14th days of the 3d and 4th months a fair or open year market shall be held, and such shall be written to the printer in New York to have it put in his almanac."[98]

A tax list made by order of the Assembly in 1693 names the following additional residents, viz: Johannes Pettinger, John Van de Woestyne and Paulus Kuster. Kuster, a Mennonite, came from Crefeld with his sons Arnold, Johannes, and Hermannus, and his wife Gertrude. She was a sister of Wilhelm Streypers. He was by trade a mason and he died in 1707.

In 1695 Isaac Ferdinand Saroschi, a Hungarian, the first of a long line of late followers, who had formerly been a preceptor in the house of Tobias Schumberg at Windsheim, came to Germantown, but after wandering around for two years causing trouble and "Hungarorum more nur eleemosinas et donativa colligiret" he returned to Europe with no very good opinion of the country.

George Gottschalck from Lindau, Bodensee, Daniel Geissler, Christian Warmer and Martin Sell were in Germantown in 1694, Levin Harberdinck in 1696, and in 1698

[97] Notes of Walter Cresson.

[98] Rath's Buch.

THE SETTLEMENT OF GERMANTOWN

Jan Linderman came from Muhlheim, on the Ruhr. During the last year the right of citizenship was conferred upon Jan Neuss, a Mennonite and silversmith,[99] Willem Hendricks, Frank Houfer, Paul Engle, whose name is on the oldest marked stone in the Mennonite graveyard on the Skippack under date of 1723, and Reynier Jansen. Though Jansen has since become a man of note, absolutely nothing seems to have been known of his antecedents, and I will, therefore, give in detail such facts as I have been able to ascertain concerning him. On the 21st of May, 1698, Cornelius Siverts, of Germantown, wishing to make some arrangements about land he had inherited in Friesland, sent a power of attorney to Reynier Jansen, lace maker at Alkmaer, in Holland. It is consequently manifest that Jansen had not then reached this country. On the 23d of April, 1700, Benjamin Furly, of Rotterdam, the agent of Penn at that city, gave a power of attorney to Daniel and Justus Falkner to act for him here. It was of no avail, however, because as appears from a confirmatory letter of July 28th, 1701, a previous power "to my loving friend Reynier Jansen," lace maker, had not been revoked, though no intimation had ever been received that use had been made of it. It seems then that between the dates of the Siverts and Furly powers Jansen had gone to America. On the 29th of November, 1698, Reynier Jansen, who afterward became the printer, bought of Thomas Tresse twenty

[99] Penn bought from him in 1704 a half-dozen silver spoons, which he presented to the children of Isaac Norris, while on a visit to the latter.—See Journal.

acres of Liberty Lands here, and on the 7th of February, 1698–99, the right of citizenship, as has been said, was conferred by the Germantown Court upon Reynier Jansen, lace maker. These events fix with some definiteness the date of his arrival. He must soon afterward have removed to Philadelphia, though retaining his associations with Germantown, because ten months later, Dec. 23d, 1699, he bought of Peter Klever seventy-five acres in the latter place by a deed in which he is described as a *merchant* of Philadelphia. This land he as a *printer* sold to Daniel Geissler Oct. 20th, 1701. Since the book called "God's protecting providence, etc.," was printed in 1699 it must have been one of the earliest productions of his press, and the probabilities are that he began to print late in that year. Its appearance indicates an untrained printer, and a meagre font of type. He was the second printer in the middle colonies, and his books are so rare that a single specimen would probably bring at auction now more than the price for which he then sold his whole edition. He left a son, Stephen, in business in Amsterdam, whom he had apportioned there, and brought with him to this country two sons, Tiberius and Joseph, who, after the Dutch manner, assumed the name Reyniers, and two daughters, Imity, who married Matthias, son of Hans Millan, of Germantown, and Alice, who married John Piggot. His career as a printer was very brief. He died about March 1st, 1706, leaving personal property valued at £226 1s, 8d., among which was included "a p'cell of books from Wm. Bradford £4 2s. 0d."[100]

We find among the residents in 1699, Evert In den Hoffen from Muhlheim on the Ruhr, with Hermann, Ger-

[100] Raths Buch Exemp Record, Vol. VI, p 235. Deed Book E 7, p. 550. Germantown Book, pp 187, 188. Will Book C, p. 22.

hard, Peter, and Anneke, who were doubtless his children, some of whom are buried in the Mennonite graveyard on the Skippack.

Four families, members of the Mennonite Church at Hamburg, Harmen Karsdorp and family, Claes Berends and family, including his father-in-law, Cornelius Claessen, Isaac Van Sintern and family, and Paul Roosen and wife, and two single persons, Heinrich Van Sintern and the widow Trientje Harmens started for Pennsylvania, March 5, 1700, and a few months later at least four of them were here.[101] Isaac Van Sintern was a great grandson of Jan de Voss, a burgomaster at Hanschooten, in Flanders, about 1550, a genealogy of whose descendants, including many American Mennonites, was prepared in Holland over a hundred years ago. In 1700 also came George Muller and Justus Falkner, a brother of Daniel, and the first Lutheran preacher in the province. Among the residents in 1700 were Isaac Karsdrop and Arnold Van Vossen, Mennonites, Richard Van der Werf, Dirck Jansen, who married Margaret Millan, and Sebastian Bartlesen, in 1701 Heinrich Lorentz and Christopher Schlegel; in 1702 Dirck Jansen, an unmarried man from Bergerland, working for Johannes Kuster, Ludwig Christian Sprogell, a bachelor from Holland, and brother of that John Henry Sprogell, who a few years later brought an ejectment against Pastorius, and feed all the lawyers of the province, Marieke Speikerman, Johannes Rebenstock, Philip Christian Zimmerman, Michael Renberg, with his sons Dirck and Wilhelm, from Muhlheim, on the Ruhr, Peter Bun, Isaac Petersen and Jacob Gerritz Holtzhooven, both from Guelderland, in Holland, Heinrich Tibben, Willem Hosters, a Mennonite weaver from Crefeld, Jacob

[101] Mennonitische Blatter, Hamburg

Classen Arents, from Amsterdam, Jan Krey, Johann Conrad Cotweis, who was an interpreter in New York in 1709, and Jacob Gaetschalck, a Mennonite preacher; and in 1703 Anthony Gerckes, Barnt Hendricks, Hans Heinrich Meels, Simon Andrews, Hermann Dors[102] and Cornelius Tyson. The last two appear to have come from Crefeld, and over Tyson, who died in 1716, Pastorius erected in Axe's graveyard at Germantown what is, so far as I know, the oldest existing tombstone to the memory of a Dutchman or German in Pennsylvania.[103]

On the 28th of June, 1701, a tax was laid for the building of a prison, erection of a market, and other objects for the public good. A weekly market was established "in the road or highway where the cross street of Germantown goes down to the Schuylkill." October 8, 1694, Jacob De la Plaine and Jacob Telner each gave a half acre for the purpose.[104] We are told that in 1701 there were in Germantown "three score families, besides several single persons."[105]

As in all communities, the prison preceded the school house, but the interval was not long. December 30th of that year "it was found good to start a school here in Germantown," and Arent Klincken, Paul Wolff and Peter Schumacher, Jr., were appointed overseers to collect subscrip-

---

[102] "One Herman Dorst near Germantown, a Batchelor past 80 years of Age, who for a long time lived in a House by himself, on the 14th Instant there dyed by himself."—American Weekly Mercury, October 18th, 1739.

[103] It bears the following inscription.

"Obijt Meiy 9, 1716
Cornelis Tiesen
Salic sin de doon
Die in den Heie sterve
Theilric is haer Kroon
Tgloriric haer erve."

[104] Collections of the Historical Society of Pa., Vol 1, p. 274

[105] Ibid, p 283, Rath's Buch.

TOMBSTONE OF CORNELIUS TYSON.

tions and arrange with a school teacher. Pastorius was the first pedagogue. As early as January 25, 1694–95, it was ordered that stocks should be put up for the punishment of evil doers. We might, perhaps, infer that they were little used from the fact that, in June, 1702, James De la Plaine was ordered to remove the old iron from the rotten stocks and take care of it, but alas! December 30, 1703, we find that "Peter Schumacher and Isaac Schumacher shall arrange with workmen that a prison house and stocks be put up as soon as possible.[106]

February 10, 1702–3, Arnold Van Vossen delivered to Jan Neuss, on behalf of the Mennonites, a deed for three square perches of land for a church, which, however, was not built until six years later.

In 1702 began the settlement on the Skippack. This first outgrowth of Germantown also had its origin at Crefeld, and the history of the Crefeld purchase would not be complete without some reference to it. As we have seen, of the one thousand acres bought by Govert Remke, one hundred and sixty-one acres were laid out at Germantown. The balance he sold in 1686 to Dirck Sipman. Of Sipman's own purchase of five thousand acres, five hundred and eighty-eight acres were laid out at Germantown, and all that remained of the six thousand acres he sold in 1698 to Matthias Van Bebber, who, getting in addition five hundred acres and four hundred and fifteen acres by purchase, had the whole tract of six thousand one hundred and sixty-six acres located by patent, February 22, 1702, on the Skippack. It was in the present Perkiomen Township, Montgomery County, and adjoined Edward Lane and William Harmer, near what is now the village of Evansburg.[107] For the next half century, at least, it was known as Beb-

[106] Rath's Buch

[107] Exemp. Record, Vol I, p 470.

ber's Township, or Bebber's Town, and the name being often met with in the Germantown records has been a source of apparently hopeless confusion to our local historians. Van Bebber immediately began to colonize it, the most of the settlers being Mennonites. Among these settlers were Hendrick Pannebecker, Johannes Kuster, Johannes Umstat, Klas Jansen and Jan Krey in 1702; John Jacobs, in 1704; John Newberry, Thomas Wiseman, Edward Beer, Gerhard and Hermann In de Hoffen, Dirck and William Renberg, in 1706; William and Cornelius Dewees, Hermannus Kuster, Christopher Zimmerman, Johannes Scholl and Daniel Desmond, in 1708; Jacob, Johannes and Martin Kolb, Mennonite weavers from Wolfsheim, in the Palatinate, and Andrew Strayer, in 1709; Solomon Dubois, from Ulster County, New York, in 1716; Paul Fried, in 1727, and in the last year the unsold balance of the tract passed into the hands of Pannebecker. Van Bebber gave one hundred acres for a Mennonite church, which was built about 1725, the trustees being Hendrick Sellen, Hermannus Kuster, Klas Jansen, Martin Kolb, Henry Kolb, Jacob Kolb and Michael Ziegler.

The Van Bebbers were undoubtedly men of standing, ability, enterprise and means. The father, Jacob Isaacs, moved into Philadelphia before 1698, being described as a merchant in High street, and died there before 1711.[108] Matthias, who is frequently mentioned by James Logan, made a trip to Holland in 1701, witnessing there Benjamin Furly's power of attorney, July 28th, and had returned to Philadelphia before April 13th, 1702. He remained in that city until 1704, when he and his elder

[108] He had three grandsons named Jacob, one of whom was doubtless the Jacob Van Bebber who became Judge of the Supreme Court of Delaware, Nov 27th, 1764

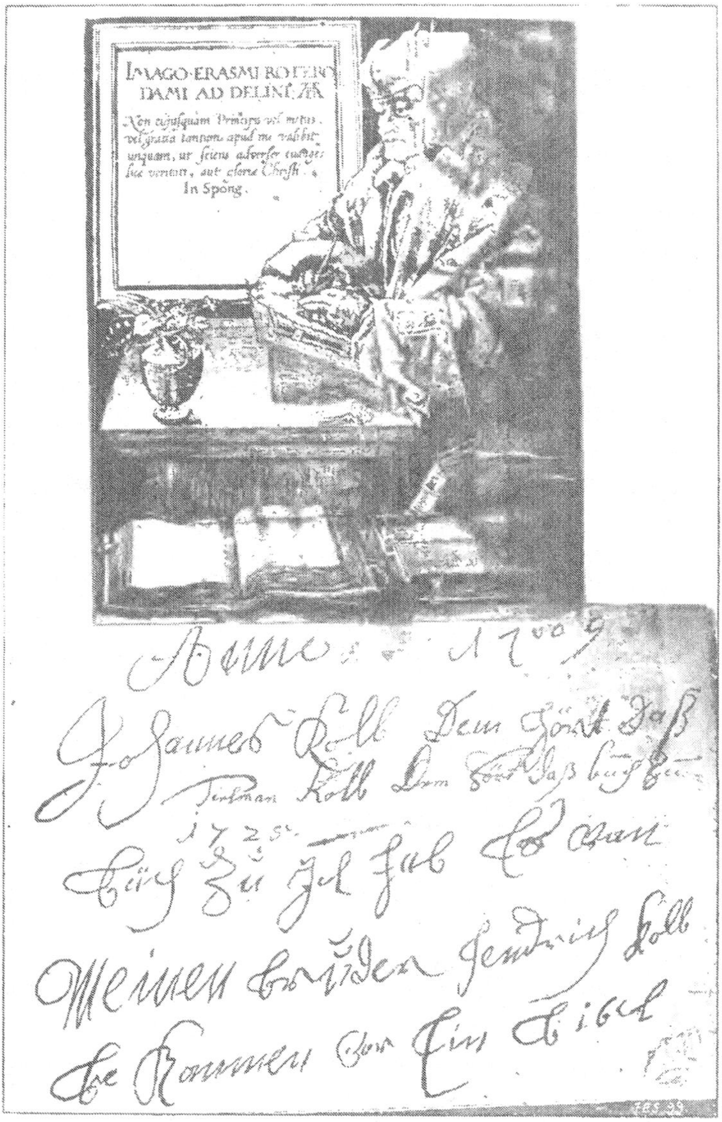

PORTRAIT OF ERASMUS BY ALBERT DURER.

FROM THE COPY OF HIS WORKS BROUGHT TO GERMANTOWN BY JOHANNES KOLB.

brother, Isaac Jacobs, accompanied by Reynier Hermanns Van Burklow, a son-in-law of Peter Schumacher, and possibly others, removed to Bohemia Manor, Cecil County, Maryland. There he was a justice of the peace, and is described in the deeds as a merchant and a gentleman. Their descendants, like many others, soon fell away from the simple habits and strict creed of their fathers; the Van Bebbers of Maryland have been distinguished in all the wars and at the bar; and at the Falls of the Kanawha, Van Bebber's rock, a crag jutting out at a great height over the river, still preserves the memory and recalls the exploits of one of the most daring Indian fighters in Western Virginia.

Arms of the Holy Roman Empire.

CHAPTER VII.

THE OP DEN GRAEFF BROTHERS AND THE PROTEST AGAINST SLAVERY.

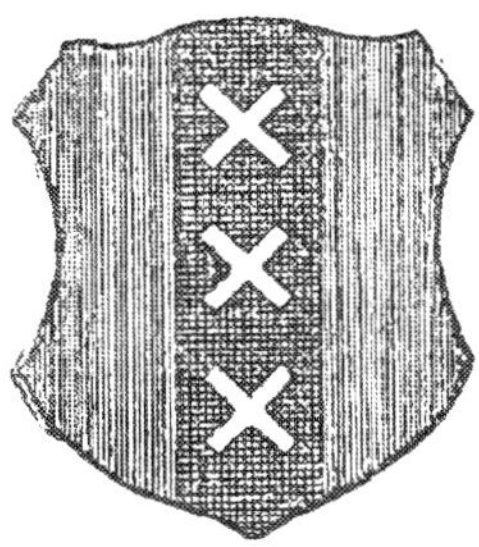

Arms of Amsterdam.

THERE was a rustic murmur in the little burgh in the year 1688 which time has shown to have been the echo of the great wave that rolls around the world. The event probably at that time produced no commotion and attracted little attention. It may well be that the consciousness of having won immortality never dawned upon any of the participants, and yet a mighty nation will ever recognize it in time to come as one of the brightest pages in the early history of Pennsylvania and the country. On the 18th day of April, 1688, Gerhard Hendricks, Dirck Op den Graeff, Francis Daniel Pastorius and Abraham Op den Graeff sent to the Friends' meeting the first public protest ever made on this continent against the holding of slaves. A little rill there started which further on became an immense torrent, and whenever hereafter men trace analytically the causes which led to Gettysburg and Appomattox they will begin with the tender consciences of the linen weavers and husbandmen of Germantown. The protest is as follows :

This is to ye Monthly Meeting held at Rigert Worrells. These are the reasons why we are against the traffick of mens-body as followeth : Is there any that would be done or handled at this manner? viz. to be sold or made a slave for all the time of his life? How fearfull & fainthearted are many on sea when they see a strange vassel being afraid it should be a Turck, and they should be tacken and sold for Slaves in Turckey. Now what is this better done as Turcks doe? yea rather is it worse for them, wch say they are Christians for we hear, that ye most part of such Negers are brought heither against their will & consent, and that many of them are stollen. Now tho' they are black, we cannot conceive there is more liberty to have them slaves, as it is to have other white ones. There is a saying, that we shall doe to all men, licke as we will be done our selves · macking no difference of what generation, descent, or Colour they are. And those who steal or robb men, and those who buy or purchase them, are they not all alicke? Here is liberty of Conscience, wch is right & reasonable, here ought to be lickewise liberty of ye body, except of evildoers, wch is an other case. But to bring men hither, or to robb and sell them against their will, we stand against. In Europe there are many oppressed for Conscience sacke ; and here there are those oppressed wch are of a black Colour. And we, who know that men must not commit adultery, some do commit adultery in others, separating wifes from their housbands, and giving them to others and some sell the children of those poor Creatures to other men. Oh, doe consider well this things, you who doe it, if you would be done at this manner? and if it is done according Christianity? you surpass Holland and Germany in this thing. This mackes an ill report in all those Countries of Europe, where they hear off, that ye Quackers doe here handel men, Licke they handel there ye Cattle; and for that reason some have no mind or inclination to come hither. And who shall maintaine this your cause or plaid for it! Truely we can not do so except you shall inform us better hereoff, viz. that christians have liberty to practise this things. Pray! What thing in the world can be done worse towarts us then if men should robb or steal us away & sell us for slaves to strange Countries, separating housband from their wife & children. Being now this is not done at that manner we will be done at, therefore we contradict & are against this traffick of men body. And we who profess that it is not lawfull to steal, must lickewise avoid to purchase such things as are stolen, but rather help to stop this robbing and stealing if possibel and such men ought to be delivred out of ye hands of ye Robbers and set free as well as in Europe. Then is Pensilvania to have a good report, in stead it hath now a bad one for this sacke in other Countries. Especially whereas ye Europeans are desirous to know in what manner ye Quackers doe rule in their Province & most of them doe loock upon us with an envious eye. But if this is done well, what shall we say, is don evil?

If once these slaves (wch they say are so wicked and stubbern men) should joint themselves, fight for their freedom and handel their masters & mastrisses, as they did handel them before; will these masters & mastrisses tacke the sword at hand & warr against these poor slaves, licke we are able to believe, some will not refuse to doe? Or have these negers not as much right to fight for their freedom, as you have to keep them slaves?

Now consider well this thing, if it is good or bad? and in case you find it to be good to handel these blacks at that manner, we desire & require you hereby lovingly that you may informe us herein, which at this time never was done, viz. that Christians have Liberty to do so, to the end we shall be satisfied in this point, & satisfie lickewise our good friends & acquaintances in our natif Country, to whose it is a terrour or fairfull thing that men should be handeld so in Pensilvania.

This was is from our meeting at Germantown hold ye 18 of the 2 month 1688 to be delivred to the monthly meeting at Richard Warrels.

gerret hendricks
derick op de graeff
Francis daniell Pastorius
Abraham op den graef.[109]

---

[109] The Friends at Germantown, through William Kite, have recently had a fac-simile copy of this protest made. Care has been taken to give it here exactly as it is in the original, as to language, orthography and punctuation. The disposition which was made of it appears from these notes from the Friends' records: "At our monthly meeting at Dublin ye 30 2 mo. 1688, we having inspected ye matter above mentioned & considered it we finde it so weighty that we think it not Expedient for us to meddle with it here, but do Rather comitt it to ye consideration of ye Quarterly meeting, ye tennor of it being nearly Related to ye truth. on behalfe of ye monthly meeting signed, pr. Jo Hart."

"This above mentioned was Read in our Quarterly meeting at Philadelphia the 4 of ye 4 mo '88, and was from thence recommended to the Yearly Meeting, and the above-said Derick and the other two mentioned therein, to present the same to ye above-said meeting, it being a thing of too great a weight for this meeting to determine.

Signed by order of ye Meeting,
Anthony Morris"

At the yearly meeting held at Burlington the 5 day of 7 mo. 1688. "A paper being here presented by some German Friends Concerning the

The men who prepared and signed this remarkable document slumbered in almost undisturbed security until the scholarly Seidensticker published his sketches, and Whittier, using the material thus collected, gave the name of Pastorius to the world in his beautiful poem. It is a little sad that Pastorius, whose life in America was spent here, and who belonged to a mental and moral type entirely our own, should become celebrated as the Pennsylvania *Pilgrim*, as though he could only obtain appreciation by the suggestion of a comparison with the men who landed at Plymouth, but no poet arose along the Schuylkill to tell the tale, and we must recognize with gratitude, if with regret, how fittingly others have commemorated the worth of one whom we had neglected.

It is the purpose of this chapter to gather into one sheaf such scattered and fragmentary facts concerning the lives of two others of those four signers as have survived the lapse of nearly two hundred years. In the Council of the Mennonite Church, which set forth the eighteen articles of their confession of faith at the city of Dordrecht, April 21, 1632, one of the two delegates from Krevelt, or Crefeld, was Hermann Op den Graeff. He was born November 26, 1585, at Aldekerk, a village of low houses, a somewhat soiled appearance, and a great church which has evidently for centuries exhausted the means of the people. It lies on the borders of Holland

Lawfulness and Unlawfulness of buying and Keeping of Negroes, It was adjudged not to be so proper for this Meeting to give a Positive Judgment in the case, It having so General a Relation to many other Parts, and, therefore, at present they forbear it "

The handwriting of the original appears to be that of Pastorius. An effort has been made to take from the Quakers the credit of this important document, but the evidence that those who sent and those who received it regarded each other as being members of the same religious society seems to me conclusive.

and later became the scene of a great battle between the French and Germans. From Aldekerk Op den Graeff removed to Crefeld, and there married a Mennonite girl, Grietjen Pletjes, daughter of Driessen Pletjes, from Kempen, the town of Thomas á Kempis He died December 27, 1642, and she died January 7, 1643. They had eighteen children, among whom was Isaac, who was born February 28, 1616, and died January 17, 1679. He had four children, Hermann, Abraham, Dirck and Margaret, all of whom emigrated to Germantown. The Dordrecht Confession of Faith appeared in the Mártyrer Spiegel of Van Braght, published at Ephrata in 1749, and has been many times reproduced in Pennsylvania. When Pastorius had concluded to cross the ocean he went to Crefeld on foot, and there talked with Thones Kunders and his wife, and with Dirck, Hermann and Abraham Op den Graeff, the three brothers. Did they have some dim and vague consciousness of the great work which they and their children, under the guidance of Providence, were to perform? Was it given to them to catch a glimpse of what that little colony, planted in an unknown land thousands of miles away, was in the course of a few generations to become, or was the hope of a religious peace alone sufficient to calm their doubts and allay their fears? Six weeks later they followed Pastorius. At Rotterdam, on the way, on the 11th of June, they bought jointly from Jacob Telner two thousand acres of land to be located in Pennsylvania. Germantown was laid out in fifty-five lots of fifty acres each, running along upon both sides of the main street, and in 1689 Dirck Op den Graeff owned the second lot on the west side going north, Hermann the third, and Abraham the fourth, with another lot further to the northward. All three were weavers of linen. Richard Frame, in a description of Pennsylvania in verse, published in 1692, refers to Germantown:

"Where lives *High German* People and *Low Dutch*
Whose Trade in weaving Linnen Cloth is much,
There grows the Flax, as also you may know
That from the same they do divide the tow;"

and Gabriel Thomas, in his account of the "Province and Country of Pennsylvania," published in 1698, says they made "very fine German Linen, such as no person of Quality need be ashamed to wear." It may be fairly claimed for Abraham op den Graeff that he was the most skilled of these artisans, doing even more than his part to have the town merit its motto of "*Vinum Linum et Textrinum*" since on the 17th of 9th month, 1686, his petition was presented to the Provincial Council, "for ye Govr's promise to him should make the first and finest pece of linnen Cloath,"[110] Upon a bond given by him to John Gibb in 1702 for £38 5s., afterward assigned to Joseph Shippen, and recorded in the Germantown book, are, among others, these items of credit: "Cloth 32 yds @ 3s, 6d," and "36-¼ Linning @ 4s," showing the prices at which these fabrics were sold.

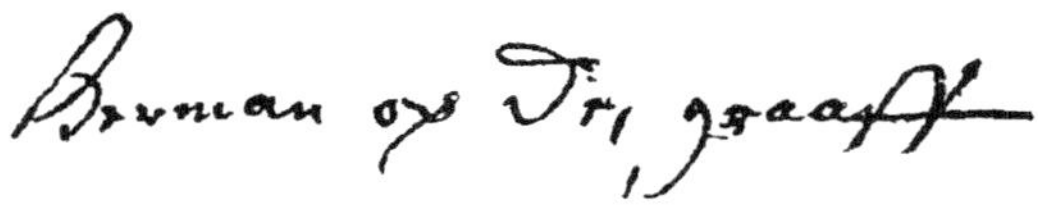

On the 12th of 6th month, 1689, Penn issued to Dirck op den Graeff, Abraham op den Graeff, Hermann op den Graeff, called "Towne President," and eight others, a charter for the incorporation of Germantown, and directed Dirck, Hermann and Thones Kunders to be the first burgesses, and Abraham, with Jacob Isaacs van Bebber,

[110] Colonial Records, Vol. I, p 193.

Johannes Kassel, Heifert Papen, Hermann Bon and Dirck Van Kolk to be the first committee-men. The bailiff and two eldest burgesses were made justices of the peace.[111] This charter, however, did not go into effect until 1691. Under it, afterward, Dirck was a bailiff in the years 1693 and 1694, and Abraham a burgess in 1692. Abraham was also elected a member of the Assembly for the years 1689, 1690 and 1692, sharing with Pastorius, who held the same position in 1687, the honor of being the only Germantown settlers who became legislators.

Their strongest claim, however, to the remembrance of future generations, is based upon the Anti-Slavery protest. It is probable, from the learning and ability of Pastorius, that he was the author of this protest, but it is reasonably certain that Dirck op den Graeff bore it to the quarterly meeting at Richard Worrall's, and his is the only name mentioned in connection with its presentation to the yearly meeting, to which it was referred as a topic of too much importance to be considered elsewhere.

A short time after this earnest expression of humanitarian sentiment had been laid away among neglected records, awaiting a more genial air and a stronger light in which to germinate, events of seemingly much more moment occurred to claim the attention of the Society of Friends. George Keith, whose memory is apostatized by them, and revered by Episcopalians, who had been one of the earliest and most effective of their preachers, began to differ with many of the leading members of the Society concerning questions of doctrine. In the nature of things, the defection of a man of such prominence was followed by that of many others. Dissension was introduced into the meetings and division and discord into families. In a

[111] Pennsylvania Archives, Vol I, p. 3

quiet and peaceable way the warfare was waged very bitterly and many harsh things were said softly. Dirck op den Graeff adhered to the cause of the Friends, but Abraham and Hermann were among the disaffected, and the three brothers seem to have been more deeply involved in the controversy than any of the other Germans. The numerous public discussions which were held only served to confirm each faction in the correctness of its own rendering of the Scriptures, the Friends who were sent to deal with George privately and to indicate to him whither he was tending made little progress, and the difficulty having become too great to be appeased, twenty-eight ministers presented a paper of condemnation against him at the monthly meeting at Frankford. Dirck op den Graeff, a magistrate in the right of his position as a burgess of Germantown, was present at the meeting and must in some way have shown an interest in the proceedings, since Keith called him publicly "an impudent Rascal." Most unfortunate words! Uttered in a moment of thoughtless wrath, and repeated in the numerous pamphlets and broadsides which the occasion called forth, they returned again and again to plague their author. Beaten out in the fervor of religious and polemic zeal, they were construed to impliedly attack the civil government in the person of one of its trusted officers. Ere long, in reply to the testimony against Keith, the celebrated William Bradford printed "An appeal from the twenty-eight Judges to the Spirit of Truth and true Judgment in all faithful Friends called *Quakers* that meet at this yearly meeting at Burlington, 7 mo., '92," signed by George Keith, George Hutcheson, Thomas Budd, John Hart, Richard Dungwoody and Abraham op den Graeff. The appeal is, in the main, an attempt to submit to the people the question which had been decided against Keith by the ministers as to whether the inner light was not alone insufficient, but it closes with the following pointed and pertinent queries:

"9. Whether the said 28 persons had not done much better to have passed Judgment against some of their Brethren at Philadelphia (some of themselves being deeply guilty) for countenancing and allowing some called *Quakers*, and owning them in so doing, to hire men to fight (and giving them a *Commission* so to do, signed by three Justices of the Peace called *Quakers*, one whereof being a Preacher among them) as accordingly they did, and recovered a Sloop, and took some Privateers by force of arms?

"10. Whether hiring men thus to fight, and also to provide the *Indians* with Powder and Lead to fight against other *Indians* is not a manifest Transgression of our principle against the use of the carnal Sword and other carnal Weapons? Whether these called Quakers in their so doing have not greatly weakened the Testimony of Friends in England, Barbadoes, &c., who have suffered much for their refusing to contribute to uphold the Militia, or any Military force? And whether is not their Practice here an evil President, if any change of government happen in this place, to bring Sufferings on faithful Friends, that for Conscience sake refuse to contribute to the Militia? And how can they justly refuse to do that under another's Government, which they have done or allowed to be done under their own? But in these and other things we stand up Witnesses against them, with all faithful Friends everywhere.

"11. Whether it be according to the Gospel that Ministers would pass sentence of Death on Malefactors, as some pretended Ministers here have done, preaching one day

Not to take an Eye for an Eye (Matt. v. 38), and another day to contradict it by taking Life?

"12. Whether there is any Example or President for it in Scripture, or in all Christendom, that Ministers should engross the worldly Government, as they do here? which hath proved of a very evil tendency."[112]

There was enough of truth in the intimations contained in these queries to make them offensive and disagreeable. According to the account of it given by Caleb Pusey, an opponent of Keith, in his "Satan's Harbinger Encountered," when Babbitt had stolen the sloop and escaped down the river, the three magistrates issued a warrant in the nature of a hue and cry, and a party of men went out in boat and captured the robbers. As they were about to depart, Samuel Carpenter, a leading and wealthy Friend, stood up on the wharf and promised them one hundred pounds in the event of success. Doubtless they used some force; but to call them militia, and the warrant a commission, was, to say the least for it, quite ingenious on the part of Keith. The Appeal had the effect of converting what had hitherto been purely a matter of Church into one of State. Bradford and John McComb were arrested and committed for printing it, but were afterwards discharged. Keith and Budd were indicted before the grand jury, tried, convicted and sentenced to pay a fine of five pounds each. These proceedings caused as much excitement as our placid forefathers were capable of feeling, and became the subject of universal comment. The justices, Arthur Cooke, Samuel Jennings, Samuel Richardson, Humphrey Murray, Anthony Morris and Robert Ewer met in private session on the 25th of 6th month, 1692, and issued the following proclamation of warning and explanation:

[112] A mutilated copy of this Appeal is in the Friends' library on Arch Street above Third

"Whereas, the government of this Province, being by the late King of England's peculiar favor, vested and since continued in Governor Penn, who thought fit to make his and our worthy friend, Thomas Lloyd, his Deputy Governor, by and under whom the Magistrates do act in the government, and whereas it hath been proved before us that George Keith, being a resident here, did, contrary to his duty, publicly revile the said Deputy Governor by calling him an impudent man, telling him he was not fit to be a Governor, and that his name would stink, with many other slighting and abusive expressions, both to him and the magistrates: (and he that useth such exorbitancy of speech towards our said Governor, may be supposed will easily dare to call the Members of Council and Magistrates impudent Rascals, as he has lately called one in open assembly, that was constituted by the Proprietary to be a Magistrate) and he also charged the Magistrates who are Magistrates here, with engrossing the magisterial power in their hands, that they might usurp authority over him: saying also, he hoped in God, he should shortly see their power taken from them: All which he acted in an indecent manner.

"And further, the said George Keith, with several of his adherents, having some few days since, with unusual insolence, by a printed sheet called an Appeal, etc., traduced and vilely misrepresented the industry, care, readiness and vigilance of some magistrates and others here, in their late proceedings against the privateers Babbitt and his crew, in order to bring them to condign punishment, whereby to discourage such assemblies for the future; and have thereby defamed and arraigned the determination of the principal judicature against murderers; and not only so, but also by wrong insinuations have laboured to possess the readers of their pamphlet that it is inconsistent for those who are Ministers of the Gospel to act as Magistrates, which, if granted, will render our said proprietary incapable of the powers given him by the King's letters patent, and so prostitute the validity of every act of government, more especially in the executive part thereof, to the courtesie and censure of all factious spirits, and malcontents under the same.

"Now forasmuch as we, as well as others, have borne and still do patiently endure the said George Keith and his adherents in their many personal reflections against us and their gross revilings of our religious Society, yet we cannot (without the violation of our trust to the King and governor, as also to the inhabitants of this government) pass by or connive at, such part of the said pamphlet and speeches, that have a tendency to sedition and disturbance of the peace, as also to the subversion of the present government, or to the aspersing magistrates thereof. Therefore for the undeceiving of all people, we have thought fit by this public writing not only to signify that our procedure against the persons now in the Sheriff's custody, as well as what we intend against others concerned (in its proper place) respects only that part of the said printed sheet which appears to have the tendency aforesaid, and not any part relating to ditterences in religion, but also these are to caution such who were well affected to the security, peace and legal administration of justice in this place that they give no countenance to any revilers and contemners of authority, magistrates or magistracy, as also to warn all other persons that they forbear the further publishing and spreading of the said pamphlets, as they will answer the contrary to their peril." [113]

---

[113] Smith's History in Hazard' Register, Vol. VI., p 281.

"What we intend against others concerned," would seem to imply that a bolt was being forged over the heads of Abraham op den Graeff and the remaining three signers of the insolent pamphlet; but it was never discharged. The yearly meeting at Burlington disowned Keith, and this action the yearly meeting at London confirmed. Dirck op den Graeff was one of those who signed the testimony against him and one of those giving a certificate to Samuel Jennings, who went to London to represent his opponents. Hermann op den Graeff, on the other hand, was among a minority of sixty-nine, who issued a paper at the yearly meeting at Burlington, favoring him. The results of this schism were extensive and grave. It placed a weapon in the hands of the enemies of Friends which they used in Europe, as well as here, without stint. Ecclesiastically it led to the foundation of the Episcopal Church in Pennsylvania. Politically it threatened to change the destinies of a Commonwealth, since it was one of the principal reasons assigned for depriving Penn of the control of his province.

The incorporation of Germantown rendered necessary the opening of a court. In its records may be traced the little bickerings and contentions which mark the darker parts of the characters of these goodly people. Its proceedings conducted with their simple and primitive ideas of judicature, written in their quaint language, are both instructive and entertaining, since they show what manner of men these were, whose worst faults appear to have consisted in the neglect of fences and the occasional use of uncomplimentary adjectives. From among them is extracted whatever, during the course of about thirteen years, relates to the Op den Graeffs.

1696. "The 3rd day of the 9th month, before the persons constituting this Court of Record, proclamation was made and the overseers of the fences did present as insufficient the fence of Hermann op den Graeff, Abraham op den Graeff, Isaac Jacobs, Johannes Pottinger, Lenert Arets and Reinert Tyson."

"The 6th day of the 9th month, after proclamation, the overseers of the fences being appointed to appear before this Court, did present as yet insufficient the fence of Hermann op den Graeff, Abraham op den Graeff, Isaac Jacobs and Johannes Pottinger."

James de la Plaine, Coroner, brought into this court the names of the jury which he summoned the 24th day of 4th month, 1701, viz: Thomas Williams, foreman; Peter Keurlis, Hermann op den Graeff, Reiner Peters, Peter Shoemaker, Reiner Tyson, Peter Brown, John Umstat, Thomas Potts, Reiner Hermans, Dirk Johnson, Hermann Tunes. Their verdict was as followeth: We, the jury, find that through carelessless the cart and the lime killed the man; the wheel wounded his back and head, and it killed him."

1700–1. "The 7th day of the 9th month, Abraham op de Graeff and Peter Keurlis were sent for to answer the complaints made against their children by Daniel Falckner and Johannes Jawert, but the said Abraham op de Graeff being not well and Peter Keurlis gone to Philadelphia, this matter was left to the next session."

20th of 11th month, 1701. "The sheriff complains against Abraham op de Graeff's son Jacob, for having taken a horse out of his custody. The said Jacob answers that he brought the horse thither again. The Court fined him half a crown, besides what his father is to pay the sheriff according to the law of this corporation."

"The sheriff, Jonas Potts, gave Abraham op de Graeff the lie for saying that the said sheriff agreed with Matthew

Peters to take for his fees 7s, 6d., which upon acknowledgement was forgiven and laid by."

December 28th, 1703. "Abraham op de Graeff did mightly abuse the Bailiff in open court, wherefore he was brought out of it to answer for the same at the Court of Record."

21st of 1st month, 1703–4. "Abraham op de Graeff being formerly committed by James de la Plaine, Bailift, for several offences mentioned in the mittimus, and the said Abraham having further, with many injurious words, abused the now Bailiff Arent Klincken in open Court of Record, held here at Germantown, the 28th day of December, 1703, was fined by this present Court the sum of two pounds and ten shillings and he to remain in the Sheriff's custody until the said fine and fees be satisfied."

13th of 4th month, 1704. "The action of Mattheus Smith against Abraham op de Graeff was called and the following persons attested as jurymen, viz: Paul Wolff, Tunes Kunders, William Strepers, Dirk Jansen, Jr., John Van de Wilderness, Dirk Jansen, Sr., Walter Simens, Henry Tubben, John Smith, Lenert Arets, Hermannus Kuster and Cornelius Dewees. The declaration of Matthew Smith being read, the answer of the defendant was that he proffered pay to the plaintiff, but that he would not accept of it, and brings for his evidences Edward Jerman and Joseph Coulson, who were both attested and said that Abraham op den Graeff came to the ordinary of Germantown, where Matthew Smith was and told to the said Smith that he should come along with him and receive his pay, and that the said Abraham had scales at home; but Smith did not go. The plaintiff asked the said German and Coulson whether they heard the defendant proffer any kind of payment: they both said no. The jury's verdict was as followeth: The jury understand that Matthew Smith refused the payment which Abraham had offered, the said Matthew is guilty; but Abraham must pay the sum which the arbitrators had agreed upon. Paul Wolff, foreman."

October 3d, 1704. "The action of Abraham op den Graeff, against David Sherkes, for slandering him, the said Abraham, that no honest man would be in his company, was called, and the bond of the said David Sherkes and Dirck Keyser, Sr., for the defendant's appearing at this Court was read; the cause pleaded, and as witnesses were attested Dirck Keyser, Sr., Dirck Keyser, Jr., Arnold Van Vosen and Hermann Dors, whereupon the jury brought in their verdict thus: We of the jury find for the defendant. The plaintiff desired an appeal, but when he was told he must pay the charges of the Court and give bond to prosecute he went away and did neither."

Dirck died about May, 1697, leaving a widow Nilcken or Nieltje, but probably no children. Hermann, about September 29, 1701, removed to Kent county, in the "Territories," now the State of Delaware, and died before May 2, 1704. In a deed made by Abraham in 1685 there is a reference to his " hausfrau Catharina," and May 16, 1704, he and his wife *Trintje* sold their brick house in Germantown. Soon afterward he removed to Perkiomen, and traces of the closing years of his life are very meagre. Of the two thousand acres purchased by the three brothers from Telner, eight hundred and twenty-eight were located in Germantown and sold, and the balance, after the deaths of Dirck and Hermann, vested in Abraham through the legal principle of survivorship. He had them laid out in the Dutch Township fronting on the Perkiomen, where he was living April 6, 1710, and where he died before March 25, 1731. On the 27th of August, 1709, he gave to his daughter Margaret and her husband Thomas Howe, a tailor of Germantown, three hundred acres of this land. In consideration of the gift Howe "doth hereby promise to maintain the within named Abraham op den Graeff if he should want livelihood at any time during his life, and to attend upon him and be dutiful to him." It is to be hoped that this covenant was more faithfully kept than sometimes happens with such promises when men in their old age drop the reins into other hands. His children beside Margaret were Isaac, Jacob, and Anne, the wife of Hermann In de Hoffen. In their youth he sent Isaac and Jacob to school to Pastorius. It is probable that after the Keith difficulty he did not renew his association with the Friends, and that his remains lie with those of the In de Hoffens (Dehaven) in the Mennonite graveyard on the Skippack near Evansburg. His name has been converted into Updegraff, Updegrave and Updegrove, but those who bear it are not numerous.

CHAPTER VIII.

WILLIAM RITTENHOUSE AND THE PAPER MILL.

Wappen von Mülheim

WILLIAM RITTENHOUSE was born in the year 1664, in the principality of Broich, near the city of Mulheim, on the Ruhr, where his brother Heinrich Nicholaus and his mother Maria Hagerhoffs were living in 1678. At this time he was a resident of Amsterdam. We are told that his ancestors had long been manufacturers of paper at Arnheim. However this may be, it is certain that this was the business to which he was trained, because when he took the oath of citizenship in Amsterdam, June 23d, 1678, he was described as a paper maker from Muhlheim. He emigrated to New York, but since there was no printer in that city, and no opportunity therefore for carrying on his business of making paper, in 1688, together with his sons Gerhard and Klaus (Nicholas) and his daughter Elizabeth, who subse-

A Short

DESCRIPTION
OF
Pennsilvania,

Or, A Relation What things are known, enjoyed, and like to be discovered in in the said Province.

…d as a Token of Good Will … of England.

By Richard Frame.

Printed and Sold by William Bradford *in* Philadelphia, 1692.

quently married Heivert Papen, he came to Germantown. There, in 1690, upon a little stream flowing into the Wissahickon, he erected the first paper mill in America, an event which must ever preserve his memory in the recollections of men. He was the founder of a family which in the person of David Rittenhouse, the astronomer, philosopher and statesman, reached the very highest intellectual rank.

In 1692 William Bradford printed a poem by Richard Frame, an early resident of Philadelphia, entitled "A Short Description of Pennsilvania or a relation of what things are known, enjoyed and like to be discovered in the said Province." In it Frame writes:

> "The German-Town of which I spoke before,
> Which is, at least in length one mile or more,
> Where lives High German People and Low Dutch,
> Whose trade in weaving linen Cloth is much,
> There grows the flax, as also you may know,
> That from the same they do divide the Tow;
> Their trade fits well within this habitation,
> We find convenience for their Occasion,
> One trade brings in imployment for another,
> So that we may suppose each trade a brother;
> From linen rags good paper doth derive,
> The first trade keeps the second trade alive;
> Without the first the second cannot be,
> Therefore since these two can so well agree,
> Convenience doth appear to place them nigh,
> One in Germantown, t'other hard by.
> A paper mill near German-Town doth stand.
> So that the flax which first springs from the land,
> First flax, then yarn, and then they must begin,
> To weave the same which they took pains to spin.
> Also when on our backs it is well worn,
> Some of the same remains ragged and Torn;
> Then of the Rags our Paper it is made;
> Which in process of time doth waste and fade:
> So what comes from the earth, appeareth plain,
> The same in Time, returneth to earth again."

While this is perhaps not very attractive as to verse, it furnishes proof of the fact that in 1692 the paper mill was in operation, and consuming to some extent the waste of linen which the weavers of Germantown were making. In 1690 Robert Turner, William Bradford, the printer in Philadelphia, Thomas Tresse and William Rittenhouse had formed a company for the purpose of erecting the mill, and Samuel Carpenter, a wealthy merchant in Philadelphia, had agreed to convey to them twenty acres of ground upon a lease for nine hundred and ninety-nine years at a rental of five shillings per annum. The mill was constructed, but no formal lease was executed.

Before February 9, 1705–6, the interests of Turner and Tresse had been purchased by Rittenhouse, who was now the sole owner, and upon that day Carpenter made a lease to him for a term of nine hundred and seventy-five years at the same rental. It was Bradford's interest in the mill which was referred to by John Holme in "A true relation to the flourishing State of Pensilvania," written in 1696, when he says:

"Here dwelt a printer and I find,
That he can both print books and bind;
He wants not paper, ink nor skill,
He's owner of a paper mill.
The paper mill is here hard by
And makes good paper frequently,
But the printer, as I do here tell,
Is gone into New York to dwell.
No doubt but he will lay up bags,
If he can get good store of rags.
Kind friends when thy old shift is rent,
Let it to the paper mill be sent."

And Gabriel Thomas in his description of Pennsylvania in 1697 says: "All sorts of very good paper are made in

Watermark used by Rittenhouse.

the German-town as also very fine German linen such as no person of quality need be ashamed to wear."

Bradford wrote to London, November 18, 1690: "Samuel Carpenter and I are building a paper mill about a mile from thy mills at Skulkill, and hope we shall have paper within less than four months."[114] But notwithstanding this modest statement, it is quite plain that Rittenhouse was the most important member of the company, upon whom the others relied for the skill both to construct the mill and to conduct the business. It was not long before Bradford had become embroiled in the schism started by Keith, had quarreled with his patrons the Quakers, who assisted him in the establishment of his press, and with Carpenter, his financial support, and had gone away to New York. In 1697 he leased his one-fourth interest for ten years to William Rittenhouse and his son Klaas upon their undertaking to furnish him "Seven ream of printing paper, Two ream of good writing paper, and two ream of blue paper" every year during the term. He was further to have the refusal of all "ye printing paper that they make and he shall take ye same at ten shillings per ream" and the refusal of "five ream of writing paper and thirty ream of brown paper yearly and every year during ye said term of ten years, ye printing paper to be at 20 s and ye brown paper at 6 s per ream." For a period of twenty years all the American paper used in Philadelphia and New York was supplied from this mill. The first watermark used was the word "Company," but this was soon superseded by the letters "W R." on one-half of the sheet, and on the other a clover leaf in a shield with a crown-like top and the word Pensilvania underneath. The clover leaf was adopted from the town seal of Germantown. The next watermark consisted of the letters "K. R.," the initials of Klaas Rittenhouse. About 1700 a sudden flood carried away the mill with a quantity of paper, material and tools, but a more substantial structure was erected to

[114] Letters from Pennsylvania, London, 1691, p 8

take its place in 1702. Bradford finally parted with his interest June 20, 1704.

Rittenhouse has still another claim to be remembered for his connection with the work of the community at Germantown. In the year 1686 a little church was built.

Although it is so described by Pastorius, there is no doubt it was a Quaker meeting house. Ere long the Mennonites began to feel that they were numerous enough to establish a distinctive organization, separate from that of the sect of the Proprietor. Rittenhouse was their first preacher. We have fortunately an account of the origin of this movement from the pen of a contemporary, Jacob Godschalks, from a city called Gog in the land of Cleeve. He says: "The beginning or the origin of the community of Jesus Christ here at Germantown, who are called Mennonites, took its rise in this way, that some friends out of Holland and other places in Germany, came here together, and although they did not all agree, since at this time the most were still Quakers, nevertheless they found it good to have exercises together, but in doing it they were to be regarded as sheep who had no shepherd, and since as yet they had no preachers, they endeavored to instruct one another. In the year 1690 more Friends from Crefeld and elsewhere came into the land, who were also of our brethren and added themselves and attended our exercises in the house of Isaac Jacobs.[115] These last mentioned friends from the first found it good, or judged it better for the building up of the community to choose by a unanimity of voters a preacher and some deacons. Thereupon was William Rittenhouse, born in Mongouerland, chosen preacher, and Jan Neues of Creveld, as deacon, and the first named entered upon the performance of

[115] Van Bebber.

his duties on the 8th of October, 1702. They undertook a second election of two preachers and Jacob Godschalks from Gog, and Hans Neues from Creveld were chosen preachers. These two last mentioned at first served the community by reading, but afterwards a difficulty arose between Hans Neues and Arnold Van Vossen, and since the first thought that he was wronged, he separated himself from the community and did not again unite with it. In the year 1707 some brethren came to us out of the Palatinate, who for a whole year kept by themselves. The 18th of February, 1708, the first chosen preacher, Willem Ruttinghausen died, to the great regret of the community. Since now Jacob Godschalks alone served the community, and the Brethren from the Palatinate had united with us, they considered it necessary to choose besides three men as deacons and overseers, which happened the 22d of March, 1708, and there were chosen Isac Van Sinteren, Hendrik Kassel and Conrad Janz. A month afterward, April 20th, there were besides two preachers chosen, to wit: Herman Casdorp and Martin Kolb. After that we remained some time living in good peace. Meanwhile some persons presented themselves in order to be taken into the community through baptism, whereupon the community, then consisting of thirty-three members, including the preachers and deacons, having consulted together, ordered that the request of these persons should be complied with, and accordingly the administration of this rite was conducted by Jacob Godschalks and water baptism performed for the first time in the land, May 9, 1708. The persons to whom baptism was administered were eleven in number, and our community increased to forty-five members. The 23d of May we celebrated the suffering and death of our Saviour by observing the Lord's Supper as instituted by the apostles. In 1709 some more Brothers and Sisters came to us throughout the Palatinate, so that on the 6th of April, 1712, our community at Germantown, and thence extending to Schippak, was so increased that we had ninety-nine members." [116]

It appears that the Mennonites wrote from Germantown to Amsterdam asking that a preacher be sent to them. The letter is lost, but it was answered by Gerhard Roosen, Pieter Van Helle, Jacob Van Kampen and Jean De Leoni in a communication addressed to Claas Berend, Paul Roosen, Heinrich van Sintern, Harmen Kasdorp and Isaac Van Sintern at Germantown, informing them that no preacher was willing to take the long and dangerous journey, advising them prayerfully to select one of their number for the performance of these duties.[117] On the 3d of September, 1708, Jacob Gaetschalk, Harman Karsdorp, Martin Kolb, Isak Van Sintern and Conrad Jansen wrote to Amsterdam "a loving and friendly request" for "some catechisms for the children and little testaments for the young." There was no bible at the meeting house, and only one copy in the whole membership. They added "that the community is still weak and it would cost much money to get them printed, while the members who come here from Germany have spent everything and must begin anew, and all work in order to pay for the conveniences of life of which they stand in need." They had asked William Bradford in New York concerning the publication of a confession of Faith, but found that it would cost so much that the purpose had to be abandoned. The letter bore fruit, because "The Christian Confession of the Faith of

[116] Life of Hendrick Pannebecker, p. 48. The original document in Dutch is in my possession.

[117] Cassel's History of the Mennonites, p. 140.

The Christian CONFESSION

Of the Faith of the harmless Christians, in the Netherlands known by the name of

MENNONISTS.

AMSTERDAM.

Printed in the Year, 1712.

The

Christian
CONFESSION

Of the Faith of the harmless *Christians*, in the *Netherlands*, known by the name of

MENNONISTS.

AMSTERDAM:
Printed, and Re-printed and Sold by *Andrew Bradford* in *Philadelphia*, in the Year, 1727.

AN

APPENDIX

TO THE

CONFESSION of FAITH

Of the Chriſtians, called,

MENNONISTS:

GIVING

A ſhort and full Account of them; becauſe of the Immagination of the Newneſs of our Religion, the Weapon and Revengeleſs Chriſtendom, and its being.

Publiſhed

Formerly in the *Low-Dutch*, and tranſlated out of the ſame into *High-Dutch*, and out of that into the *Engliſh* Language, 1725.

PHILADELPHIA:
Printed by *Andrew Bradford*, in the Year 1727.

the harmless Christians in the Netherlands known by the name of the Mennonites" was printed in Amsterdam, 1712, in English, "at the desire of some of our Fellow believers in Pensylvania" and was reprinted in Philadelphia by Andrew Bradford in 1727.[118]

Martin Kolb, one of the writers of this letter, a grandson of Peter Schumacher, was born in the village of Wolfsheim, in the Palatinate, in 1680 and came with his brothers Johannes and Jacob to Pennsylvania in the spring of 1707. He married May 19, 1709, Magdalena, daughter of Isaac Van Sintern and she may claim the distinction of having been the first genealogist in the province. Isaac Van Sintern, a great grandson of Jan de Voss, a Burgomaster at Handschooten, in Flanders, about 1550, was born September 4, 1662, and married in Amsterdam Cornelia Claassen, of Hamburg. He came with four daughters to Pennsylvania after 1687, died August 23, 1737, and was buried at Skippack. Magdalena Kolb, about 1770, when a very old woman, prepared a record of about five hundred of the descendants in Pennsylvania, which was sent to Holland and incorporated in the De Voss genealogy.

On the 10th of February, 1702–3, Arnold Van Vossen delivered to Jan Neuss on behalf of the Mennonites a deed for three square perches of land for a church. On it a log house was built, possibly at that time and certainly not later than 1708. The quantity of land was later increased, since in 1714,

Sept. 5th, Van Vossen conveyed thirty-five perches to Hendrick Sellen and Jan Neuss "for a place to erect a meeting house for the use and service of the said Men-

118 A copy of each edition is in my library

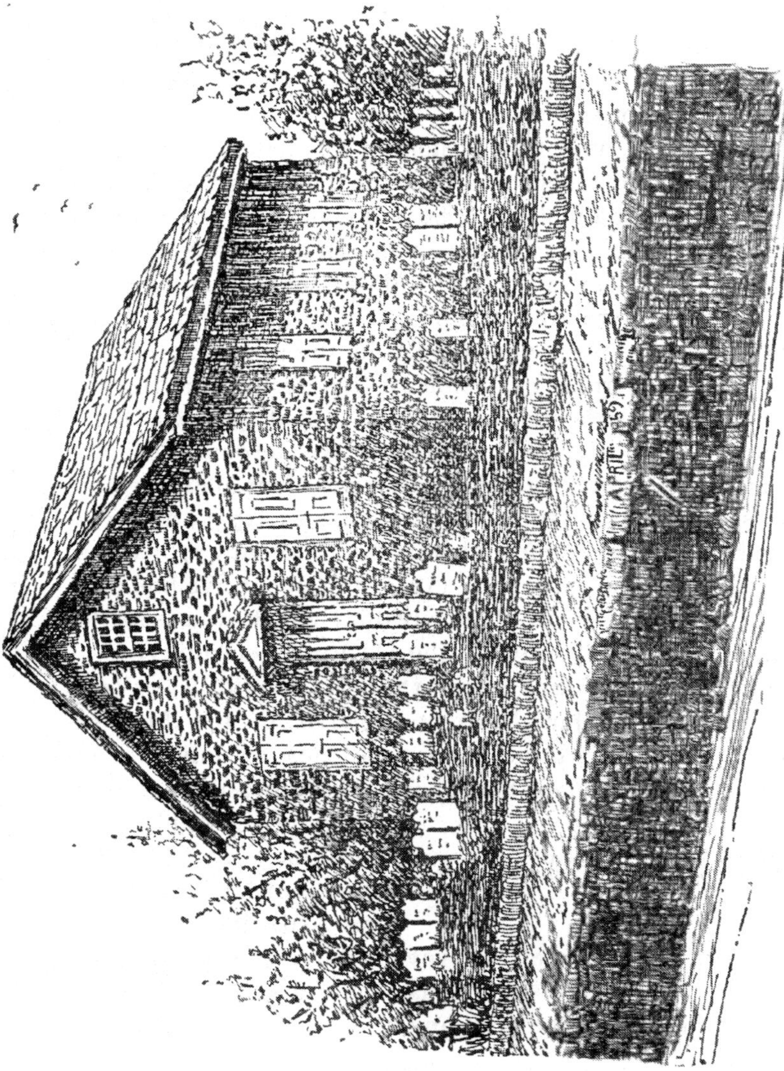

Mennonite Meeting House in Germantown. From a sketch made in 1859.

nonites (alias Menisten) and for a place to bury their dead.'

Neuss died before Dec. 8, 1724, on which day Sellen executed a declaration of trust.

The members, May 23, 1708, were Wynant Bowman, Ann Bowman, Cornelius Claassen, Peter Conrad, Gertrude Conrad, Johannes Conrad, Civilia Conrad, Jacob Godschalk and his wife, Johannes Gorgas, Margaret Huberts, Conrad Johnson and wife, Harmen Kasdorp and wife, Martin Kolb and wife, Heinrich Kassel and wife, Johannes Krey, Helena Krey, Paul Klumpges, Johannes Kolb, Jacob Kolb, Barbara Kolb, Arnold Kuster, Elizabeth Kuster, Hermannus Kuster, Peter Keyser, Catharine Kasselberg, Jan Lensen, Jan Neuss, Hans Neuss, William Rittenhouse and wife, Altien Rebenstock, Mary Sellen, Hendrick Sellen, Hermen Tuyner, (?), Mary Tuynen, Margaret Tyson, Altien Tyson, Christopher Timmerman, Civilia Van Vossen, Arnold Van Vossen, Isaac Jacobs Van Bebber, Jacob Isaacs Van Bebber, Isaac Van Sintern and wife, Sarah Van Sintern.[119]

[119] Morgan Edwards' Materials towards a History of the American Baptists. Vol. I., p. 96.

CHAPTER IX.

PETER CORNELIUS PLOCKHOY, OF ZIERIK ZEE. HIS COMMUNAL PLANS AND SETTLEMENT ON THE HOORN KILL.

Vignette from Plockhoy's Kort en klaar Ontwerp.

WE now approach the most heroic figure and the most pathetic series of incidents in connection with the early history of Germantown. It is the story of one

"Who died in the broken battle,
who lies with swordless
hand,
In the realm that the foe hath
conquered, on the edge of a
stranger land."

Robert Owen and Charles Fourier of recent years have elaborated theories of a communal life, which have attracted wide attention and discussion, and in this country led Hawthorne, Thoreau, Emerson and their companions to make the experiment at Brook Farm. This experiment, at least, had the result of leading to the production of the Blithedale Romance and other interesting literature of permanent value. The forerunner of Owen, in the suggestion of these views of life, was acknowledged by him to have been the Quaker, Robert Bellers, who in 1696 published a book in London advocating the erection of a college of labor wherein should be taught trades and housekeeping, and where the rich would get a profit, the poor a living, and the young would be properly instructed. Karl Marx praises this book as marking an epoch in the history of political economy. But as there were brave men before Agamemnon, and a book of Jasher before that of Jeremiah, so was there a precursor to Bellers, Owen and Fourier.

Peter Cornelius Plockhoy came of a Mennonite family, living at Zierik Zee, and was deeply impressed with the strong religious sentiment of the age and of the sect to which he belonged. He regarded the Christian church as a great universal union of brethren, common to all lands and to all ages, under the one head of Christ, and he says of himself that he was grieved to see the dissensions among the many sects into which this brotherhood was divided He thought over a means by which he could help to break down the walls of separation, and concluded that the man who could do the most to accomplish this object was Cromwell, the Protector of England. Thereupon he abandoned for a time his family and went to London. Cromwell, in whose character was blended the capacity for military affairs and statecraft, with strong religious impulses and tendencies, gave him a hearing and permitted him to explain his views at length. The result was that he prepared two letters to the Protector. The first of them was dated June 24, 1658. It urged upon Cromwell to see to it that he, who by his achievements had been saved from Anti-Christ, should not again fall into the hands of the little Anti-Christs. The little Anti-Christs were those sects which differ among themselves and exclude others, and the preachers of these sects. The church of Christ indicates something broad and universal. God and Christ alone are its masters. The government ought to prevent that any man should undertake to rule over another in matters of conscience. All are upon an equality in matters of religion. The government ought not to lend its authority to sects which, contrary to the Holy Scriptures, have established forms and formulas in the shape of confessions of faith, by which they bind fast the wills of mankind. No, there is one church for all. In the church differences of opinion can be permitted, but brotherhood and unity possess them all. For this common Christian church the Lord Protector ought to provide. He must cause it to be brought about that in each city, and in each county, there shall be a common Christian place of meeting, and that a great hall shall be built where the meeting shall be held, and the Holy Scriptures be read for all, and after the reading each shall have an opportunity to express briefly his opinion concerning it. The sitting places in such a hall could be arranged in the form of an amphitheatre, and with rising steps. Freedom of speech must be preserved for each. Then all sects would accustom themselves to come into one temple. Once more, there would be unity. The light would be opened in the midst of the darkness. Forbearing love would again be the custom. Freedom of conscience would be the rule.

This first letter was soon after followed by a second. The theme of a common Christian church is again set out. The result in consequence must be a separation of church and state. It is true the government must see to it that in the great hall, as they come together, everything should be done in an orderly manner, and that they who there read the Holy Scriptures should receive a certain compensation. But the Lord Protector must no more permit that preachers and leaders of the church shall be paid wages after the manner of persons employed by the state. The sects could as they chose support their own preachers. But to give tithes to the preachers must be forbidden. When this cable of hope for the preachers is cut, then is the might of the sects broken. The common church will then be able to rise up. The kingdom of Christ will then broaden out much further than England, in Holland, Denmark, Sweden and France. We shall hear no more of the mere names of men, as of Luther and Calvin Religion and statecraft will no more be mingled

Whatever may be thought of the practicability of the scheme of Plockhoy it is certain that his ideas indicate great clearness of insight and that they were far in advance of his age. It would be interesting to know how they impressed Cromwell. Fortune, however, here as elsewhere, did not favor Plockhoy. On the 3d of September, 1658, Cromwell died. This event was, no doubt, a severe blow to the hopes of the philosopher, but he did not surrender. He was ready to utilize the meeting of the Parliament which took place January 27, 1659. He had the two letters written to Cromwell put into print, and added to them a short address to the Parliament. In it he still urges the universal character of christianity. The government must support no sects. They must only take care that the truth, like the sun, has the opportunity to make itself manifest, and also in the schools and universities. A magistrate at all times must stand immovable in the midst, as a moderator between all the sects. He gave these three communications to the public in a pamphlet, a copy of which is in the university library at Ghent and whose title is "The way to the Peace and Settlement of these nations fully discovered in two letters delivered to his late Highnesse the Lord Protector, and one to the present Parliament where in the liberty of speaking (which every one desires for himself) is opposed against Anti-Christ, for the procuring of his downfall, who will not grant the same to others, and now published to awaken the publick spirit in England, and to raise up an universal magistrate in Christendome, that can suffer all sorts of people (of what religion soever they are) in any one country, as God (the great magistrate) suffers the same in all the countreys of the world." Matth. 5: 15, "Men do not light a candle and put it under a bushel, but on a candlestick, and it giveth light unto all that are in the house. By Peter Cornelius Van Zurick-Zee, a lover of truth and peace. Printed in the year 1659.' He says in it with truth that his pamphlet had little chance of success The Parliament which for the moment honored Richard Cromwell as the successor of his father, was little thinking of the separation of church and state. The army was the master of all, and the restoration was already in sight. Still Plockhoy remained in London, and cherished his dream of the brotherhood of man. He abandoned for the time the division of the kingdom of God into sects, and gave his thought to the separation of the rich and the poor. Could no way be found to fill up the gap and to better the conditions of the poor? Could no way be found for the improvement of their lives? He devoted himself to the work and the same year gave out a remarkable plan for a social union of laymen without regard to sect. A copy is in the British Museum and is entitled: "A way propounded to make the poor in these and other nations happy. By bringing together a fit, suitable and well qualified people into one hous-hold government, or little common-wealth, wherein every one may keep his Propriety, and be employed in some work or other, as he shall be fit, without being oppressed. Being the way not only to rid those and other Nations from idle, evil and disorderly persons, but also from all such that have sought and found out many inventions to live upon the labor of others. Whereunto is also annexed an invitation to this society or little Commonwealth, Psalm: Blessed is he that considereth the poor, the Lord will deliver him in time of trouble, the Lord shall preserve him and keep him alive, and he shall be blessed upon the earth. By Peter Cornelius van Zurick-zee, London, 1659. Printed for R. C. at the sign of the Black Spread Eagle at the West End of Pauls' Church Yard." [120]

The object of the plan is to increase the happiness of the poor. There must be no more oppression of others. The common life must again rest upon uprightness, upon love and upon brotherly union. No yoke shall be longer borne. There must be freedom from all idle and wrong doing persons, but above all from those who have sharpened their wits and found the means "to live from the labor of others." To accomplish this the plan provides for groups of collective house-keeping and labor combinations of working men who are willing to enter upon a common method of life. Two principles lie at the foundation. The first is the doctrine of equality. Men must abandon all ideas of greatness and desire for superior rank, and follow the example of Christ who came not to be served, but to serve, and who upon the question of his disciples, as to which

[120] I have never seen either of these pamphlets and have translated them from the Dutch of Mr H P G Quack's admirable paper on Plockhoy's Sociale plannen, Amsterdam, 1892

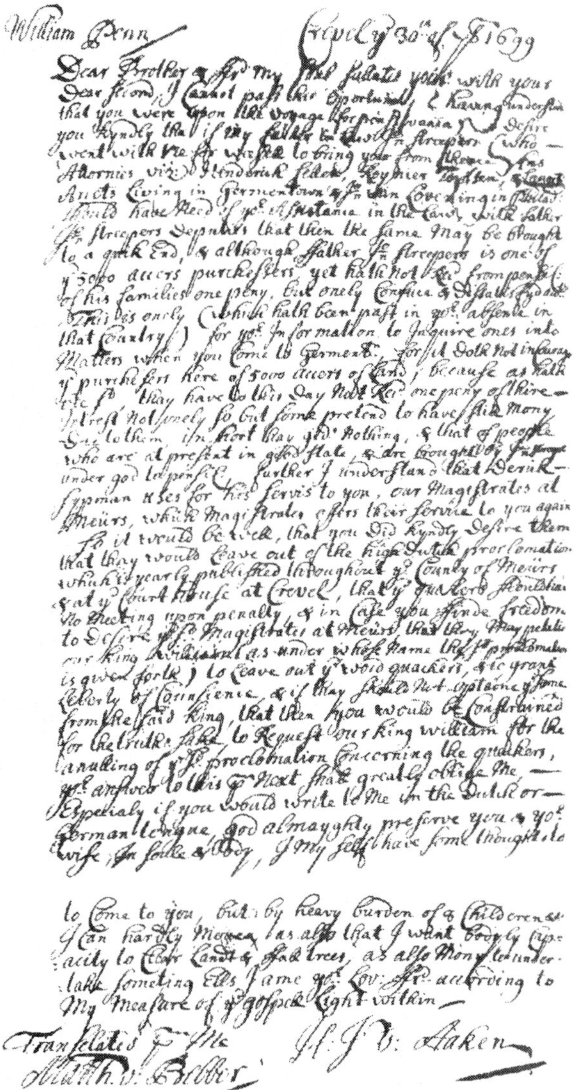

William Penn — Crevel ye 30th of 8br 1699

Dear Brother after my kind salutes your with your
Dear friend, I cannot pass this Oportunity, & having understood
that you were upon the voyage for pensilvania, I desire
you kyndly that if my father in law Jan Streepers (who
went with me for wesell to bring you from thence) his
Attornies viz: Hendrick Sellen, Reynier Tyssen, & Lenart
Arets living in Germentown & Jan van Lovening in Philad.
should have need of yor assistance in the land, with father
Jan Streepers deputies that then the same may be brought
to a quick end, & although father Jan Streepers is one of
ye 5000 acres purchessers, yet hath not rec. from pensilv.
of his families one peny, but onely Costice & desolations.
This is onely (which hath been past in yor absence in
that Country) for yor information to inquire ones into
Matters when you come to Germent. for it doth not in Luxury
ye purchesers here of 5000 acres of land; because as hath
tole so they have to this day not rec. one peny of their
intrest not onely so but some pretend to have still mony
due to them, in short they get nothing, & that of people
who are at present in good state, & are brought by such
under god to perish. further I understand that Derik
Sipman uses for his servis to you, our Magistrates at
Meurs, which Magistrates offers their service to you again
so it would be well, that you did kyndly desire them
that they would leave out of the high dutch proclamation
which is yearly published throughout ye County of Meurs
& at ye Court house at Crevel, that ye quakers should have
no meeting upon penalty, & in case you finde freedom
to desire ye sd Magistrates at Meurs, that they may petitio
our King William (as under whose name the sd proclamation
is given forth) to leave out ye word quackers, & to grant
liberty of Conscience, & if they should not optaine ye same
from the said King, that then you would be constrained
for the truths sake to request our King William for the
anulling of ye sd proclamation concerning the quakers,
yor answer to this p next shall greatly oblige me —
Especialy if you would write to me in the Dutch or —
German tongue, god almayghty preserve you & yor
wife in soule & body, I my self have some thoughts to

to come to you, but by heavy burden of 8 childeren &c
I can hardly move, as also that I want bodyly capacity to clear land & fall trees, as also mony to undertake something ells I ame yor lov. fr. according to
my measure of ye gospell light within —

Translated by me — H. J. v. Aaken
Matth. v. Bebber

LETTER OF H. J. VAN AAKEN, TRANSLATED BY MATTHIAS VAN BEBBER AND IN HIS AUTOGRAPH.

of them would be the first after his death, answered that he should be the first among them who became the servant of them all. It is therefore necessary to be careful to make the work of all equal and thus lighten the labor of the poor. Moreover, man must take heed of what the clergymen so often have in their mouths, in order to make the deaths of men so much the more serviceable to themselves. They say they care only for the soul. As though they can love the soul which they see not, and at the same time show not the least compassion for the body which they see very well. No. As well for the body of each as the soul must we be considerate, making such an order in the community that all who now scarcely have bread shall have their wants satisfied and appeased If inequality were banished, then would the mischief which arises from the difference between the rich and poor, disappear. Jealousy, superfluity, lying, and deception shall disappear from among those "who maintain equality."

The other essential idea is to bring into practice the principle of association "Neither doth anyone stand simply by himself alone." Fourier expressed the same idea in almost the identical words at the beginning of the present century. Plockhoy's view was as follows Whenever a hundred families live separately, there are necessary at least a hundred women to do the household work. Unite them and let the hundred dwell together, and then the household work can be entirely done by twenty-five women, and the other seventy-five, if they are capable, can work for the community When a hundred people live apart every day, there is a necessity for a hundred fires to prepare the mid-day meal. If they be brought together, then the great fires of four or five ovens are ample for the purpose. The objective point of the association is thus a saving. But this is only a negative gain. A positive benefit of working together is a complete development of the work or knowledge, and thus a greater result from the work. While generally in the world, he says, it is to the profit of the individual to keep his capacity and skill away from the rest, when he enters into association, he brings his knowledge and skill into the community, and devotes it to the common good. "This is the only way to find out the height, depth, length and breadth of all the affairs of the world." In order, now, to start the foundation of such a community, and Fourier says the same thing, it is necessary that some capable people should advance capital enough to buy a piece of land upon which the establishment of the community can be based. After the land has been secured, four sorts of people are necessary to unite themselves in the common household, to wit: those who understand the cultivation of the soil, merchants and tradesmen, sailors and fishermen, and finally masters in arts and trades. Tradespeople come well first, learned and scientific people last. Also, in the beginning, it is better that the majority should be unmarried. For the living and working together of all these people and for their union into one working group, he suggests certain rules. And first with respect to ownership. The time of work for all the people is fixed at ten hours a day except upon the Sabbath. They, however, who are hired servants of the community may work twelve hours upon working days while they, themselves, are members of it. Each may work in that occupation or that labor which suits him. It shall not be entirely forbidden to prepare those things which, in the view of the community, are superfluous, so long as the world remains attached to them. In all hand work the effort shall be made to secure the best masters, and they, like the others, shall work ten hours a day and lead the rest. All are bound to work. An exception can only be made in the case of those rich people who, while not belonging to the association, may desire to live there by paying for their rooms, board and clothes. Should these of their own will do any work for the community, then are they an example for all the rich "time-loosers" in this world. Those who belong to the association shall not be bound to make their goods common. There is thus not a communality of goods. Each may keep his own property. Still is it something exceptional, whenever anyone freely pours gold into the funds or capital of the community. Those who bring in lands or ground for the common work shall in the first place be secured in the holding of their title. They give up the use of it without rent and permit that the land be cultivated by the association. Unless they otherwise determine and make over the land after their death to the community, the children or relatives shall inherit it. Each receives his share in the gains of the community. In case there are no profits nothing shall be taken. So that it be well understood that those who come into the community do so not for the sake of gain. Gain is, however, more likely to be made in such an association, since the expense of living there is less than in the outside world. The living is simple and sober. Finery in dress is forbidden. The price of necessaries is less because the community buys at wholesale. Besides, the community has its own cattle, its own vegetables and fruits, catches its own fish and brews its own drink.

In order to secure the benefit of the community, and to do its work, it is necessary to have two great houses, one of them in or near the city, especially for merchants and shop-keepers, the other in the country near a river, arranged for the farmers, the seamen and sailors, the tradesmen and the learned. The house in the city shall be large enough for twenty or thirty people to live together. It shall possess stores and different compartments for merchandise, or cloth, woolen and linen goods, worsteds, clothes, shoes and all useful things. The articles produced by the work of the community can be sold at a moderate and cheap price to the public, at a less price than others, for the reason that the cost of production, as has been said, is less. The profit upon the goods shall belong to the community. The house in the city is thus mainly an office and bazaar. Business and industry are the chief features of this house. With care shall it be seen that the young people who are intended for salesmen shall attend to those things for which they are designed. In the same house dwell also the physicians, surgeons and apothecaries who must be in the city. These last can as well practice without as within the community and thus add to the profits, but they must always be ready to serve the poor without charge. Also there must be in the house in the city single persons at all times to get the clothes and other things ready daily, and to perform the daily service.

The house in the country shall be built close by a river so that there may be the opportunity to bring many goods there by water. It were best to surround the house with a ditch crossed by a drawbridge, so that it may be safer from thieves and rovers. The water of the river offers an opportunity for catching fish. Near this house a court or garden is laid out, and further away stretch fields and meadows. Here the cultivation of the land and the raising of cattle are the principal occupations, for commerce and trade have at their foundation agriculture and cattle raising.

For trade have the people of the community need of clothes, woolen and worsted goods, linen, &c. But to prepare the goods they need flax and sheep. There must be then those who understand the art, further those who can make the land fruitful, gardeners and cultivators who can make all sorts of trees, vines, roots, herbs and flowers grow. They belong in the house in the country Further must be found there masons, carpenters, smiths, and also ship-builders who can make ships and boats, to sail to Holland, Flanders, France and other lands and countries, manned with their own people from the community. If such a ship makes a bad trip, nobody blames the sailor. The families of the ship people, while the men are at sea, receive from the community all that they need. Finally in the house in the country are men skilled in all the arts and sciences, mathematics, masters in navigation, and in conclusion, teachers and their pupils.

The two houses shall be so arranged and constructed that the people there, besides their private rooms, shall find common chambers or halls. While for each man and his wife are kept a room and closet, there shall be a large hall for all those affairs which they are prepared to undertake in an orderly manner, a kitchen where all the food is made ready, a good cellar to keep provisions and drink, a hall where all eat together, a room for the children, a large room for scholars, a room for the sick, a room for the doctors and surgeons and for the preparation and preservation of drugs and medicines, a room for a library, space for maps and instruments relating to the arts and sciences, and finally a large room for the strangers, who intend some time to remain with the community and who either will do work for it or pay the expense of their maintenance. Each house shall make up its account for the half or whole year. Whatever then is found beyond what is necessary for support and furtherance shall be divided among all the men, women, youths and maidens, so that each may have enough to give to the poor, or to entertain his friends who may come to see him.

Concerning the householding arrangements and manner of living there are some directions to which attention must be given. The chief thought, however, is that in the midst of the union there is freedom. In this house, he says, each one may do his own work. The freedom within the circle of the community is recognized in all things, for example in the clothing. It is true all luxury is forbidden, but should any one desire stuff for clothing of a finer sort than that of the others, he may have it by paying so much out of his own money. No uniform, cloister like life is directed, only the recognition of community appears clearly at every point. Unity characterizes the observance of meal time The whole brotherhood and sisterhood sit down together, women and men, youths and maidens meeting each other, sitting at the dish in the order of Joseph's brethren, the women right opposite the men, the sons next to their father, the daughters next to their mother, while the young people by turns serve the table. Ceremonies and compliments are not to be taken in thought by those sitting opposite to each other, since each one is assured of the good will and friendliness of the rest.

In the matter of choosing a wife, entire freedom is permitted. The man, however, does not need to take his wife from the community. If he finds a virtuous spouse outside of this circle, he can go to live with her, or bring her into the community. In the instruction and education of the children the idea of the common life is kept steadfastly in view. All receive the same instructions, all, whether their parents be rich or poor, must learn a trade, and rather one modest trade that can keep them from want than two or three different trades. This concerns especially the children of the poor. With respect to these it is especially ordered that they be not drilled to slavish work. Also the children of the rich people who do not belong to the association, but still go to its school, shall be required to exercise themselves three hours a day at a trade, so that they, should they meet with misfortune in life, may be able to secure a livelihood. And the maidens, in addition to the care of the house-keeping and the going about with and looking after the children, shall learn some work, capable of supporting them, so that they, should they later leave the community or be married, may be in a situation to maintain themselves. The children shall not be instructed in any forms of religion prepared by men, but in the Holy Scriptures, besides in the natural sciences, arts and languages. The utmost care shall be taken that their understandings be not corrupted before they have the use of speech. They are required in spiritual matters to believe no man, since they have the spirit of God, and like the prophets and apostles work wonders. For our belief, says Plockhoy, ought not to depend upon the words of men, but upon the might of the wonderful works of God. So doing shall there no germs of sects, factions or divisions be laid in their hearts.

In this community formulas of belief shall have no control. All things wherein the kingdom of God does not exist shall, when they are not in conflict with Scripture or reason, be permitted, such as the outerly form of baptism, the Lord's Supper and such ceremonies, since there is more danger in neglecting these things than in carrying them into effect. There shall, and let this be compared with his letters to Cromwell, be built a great gathering place, a hall, in the form of an amphitheatre, with seats arranged one above the other like steps, not alone for the service of the community, but for all sensible men in common. In the hall shall the Holy Scriptures be read and thereafter shall each have the freedom to express briefly his opinion. In this manner differences of sentiment will be prevented, since there will be entire freedom of speech. The community shall strive to keep constantly in view the idea of bringing the good folks out of all sects into combination and union, so as to be together a strong guard against perversity and sin.

The direction of the association shall be in the hands of a Governor, who must be at least forty years of age He shall be chosen by the people. Next to him three men shall be named also by the people, who shall have the management and care of the money of the community. All the office holders must resign each year. Nevertheless the community shall have the power again to select them. Among these shall be chosen the overseers or directors, men and women, of the different parts or divisions of the community. The propriety of making changes by turns shall be taken into thought in such a way that a certain rank shall be given to age, and always care shall be taken that those older in service can instruct the new beginners. It is well to be understood that this association so founded is to be obedient to the government of the country where it is established. It shall pay the taxes and lovingly support the laws of the land in all things which are not contrary to the command of God.

There follow now some rules about the method of dealing with those who shall wish to leave the community. In the first place each one who shall wish to say farewell shall receive back not only what he brought with him, but his share in the gains, whatever they are, up to the time of his departure. He shall be required to make known to the community in time his intention to depart, so that the directorship can see that the sum taken by him can be provided for. A sum of twelve hundred gulden shall be set apart for this purpose. With respect to large sums, the community reserves to itself the privilege of completing the payment after the lapse of a year's time, provided a fourth part of the debt be actually paid. If a young man or a maiden leaves the community in order to get married, he or she shall receive that part of the accumulated gains made during the time of his or her life there. If no gain has been made within this time, the community will give them something. If it should unluckily turn out that the community should at some time be dissolved, then, after all the creditors have been paid, shall the land and the money which, with free will, have been given for the building up of the association, come to the poor people who have brought nothing into the community, unless there are poor relations of those who have given, out of love, capital to the association. These shall then have equal parts with the others. These are now the principal rules. In such an organization will, according to the opinion of the projector, the association present a beautiful and peaceful sight. Each of the people is received into a restful self-working community, where all is in an entire equipoise. All work for all, each finds satisfaction of his wants. Here no more shall be heard, with the eye turned upon the children who have been born, the sighing wish that he had never married, that he had never been born. There shall be no more oppression of the work people by patrons. In the outside world the contractors oppress the workmen, and these pinch, out of hard work, a small reward, while in this circle the profits of the contractors overflow and drip down to the benefit and refreshment of the work people. A feeling of calmness penetrates the union. Men shall live there without care or trouble. Losses shall be borne by all together. Safely can men advise the wanderers and ship-wrecked upon the world's sea of life to turn to the community; there can they again take heart, again raise up their heads. Honorable tradesmen and shopkeepers who are unable to support the struggle of a hard life or the wrestling with oppression may turn to this place of retreat. Brave people who, through sickness or want of work, fall into poverty can here find quiet, for here they are brought into and become parts of a vast organization. Each who works has now the assurance that he has, as the purchaser of his product, the whole association. Is the worker sick? The others work for him. He need have no anxiety for his old days, and is free from the perplexing feeling that he, after twenty or thirty years of almost intolerable work, has no prospect of any return. All extremes are absent from the association. No one is poor and no one is excessively rich. The eagerness to hunt for shadows, the uncertainty between the hope of receiving gain and the fear of making losses, are entirely absent. Moreover, is he assured that the children whom he leaves after him can here lead a quiet industrial life without care. After hazards and great risks, or substance or income, he does not reach. Still is he easy in conscience. The end finds him in peace. This equipoise of life shall also appear good to the woman who now, whether she is young and wishes to be married, or whether she is a widow and must take care of herself, depends too much upon outerly circumstances, upon the kingdom of this world, upon circumstances or fortune. First in such an association can she find security and steadfastness of life. Nevertheless, give heed to it, says Plockhoy, that this place where each, through his work, can spend a secure life, be not compared to a hospital, an old man's or woman's house where the people already aged come with their stripes, their oppositions, their deeply rooted ills, after their bodies have been lamed or stiffened from hard labor, and their spirits have been destroyed through bad habits. For the most part the people grovel away in the hard earth or sink into such a depth of ignorance that no glimmer of reason can again enlighten them.

Those who now wish to come into this association please to think, concludes our writer, that only such people shall be received who are brave, intelligent and unpartisan. All others begin to work in the association for hire and can first live in their own houses until they are prepared to come into the full union. In conclusion the writer gave the information that it was first his intention to found such an association in London, then in Bristol and afterwards in Ireland, where much land could be bought for little money, and much wood for building houses and ships and for the preparation of other essentials.

To this plan, which appeared in print in 1659, were added an invitation in English to unite with the association thus described, and a scheme "showing the excess of Christian love and the folly of those who have not considered for what end the Lord of Heaven and Earth has created them" with the quotation from Matthew, 12th Chapter, 50th verse: "For whosoever shall do the will of my Father which is in heaven, the same is my brother and sister and mother." It was a clear demonstration that such a union of men meant something since God himself joined them together. Such a society was possible in this association arranged by Peter Cornelius Plockhoy of Zierik Zee. Through such established communal life should the earthly desire for riches or idle honor be restrained. Unity of life should be considered. Real equality could be established. All the childish attention given to mere forms could be thrown aside. Such a peaceful association had been in the early times of Christianity a living truth. But the anti-Christ had known how to destroy the beautiful unity. Since had the Roman Catholic church added abuse upon abuse. Institutions such as that of the lazy monks had stolen in to produce corruption, so that the reformation had again restored the ancient truth. Now again must it be awakened in order to break the remaining strength of Satan, the enemy of mankind. We must be Christians not only in name but in fact. Therefore must men unite as true brothers and thus proceed with this scheme.

The whole was concluded with a short letter wherein the people were invited to give their money in order to raise the capital necessary to start the movement. This want was only to be the bridge, since the association, so it was expressly assured, can later stand through its own strength, according to the testimony of credible persons who gave the information that many hundred people, in Zebenbergen[121] in Hungary and in the land of the Palatinate, beginning in a small way had not only lived an agreeable life together, but had accumulated means which had enabled them to do good to others not in the association.

Such is a full summary of the social and communistic plan of Plockhoy, as it appeared in the year 1659. In it can be found all the thoughts which, written by Bellers in 1696, gave him note among economists. Presented to

[121] These people were Saxons, living in Siebenburgen (Transylvania).

Englishmen in the time of Charles II., when the pleasures and revelries of the Court gave the cue to life, and the needs of the poor had little chance of being heard, it seemed to produce no effect beyond the aspirations and philanthropic outpourings of the prospectus. It was mentioned in Sir Frederic Morton Eden's large quarto work upon "The state of the poor," published in London in 1797. It was stolen by Abraham van Akkeren, who published it under his own name and with a different title, without reference to Plockhoy, in Amsterdam in 1688. And this was apparently all. And yet in Girard College in Philadelphia to-day may be found the large hall, arranged like an amphitheatre, with rising seats where the Scriptures are read and all the formulas of sect are rigidly excluded as outlined by Plockhoy. In the large apartment houses springing up in all the modern cities may be found that economy of household labor he suggested. In his views with respect to practical Christianity, the economical utilization of labor, the separation of church and state, the education of the young, including the teaching of trades, and the practical insight which led him to permit the retention of hallowed but unessential ceremonies, he was far ahead of his age and presented much that is admirable England afforded him no opportunity and he went to Amsterdam. And, behold, the way opened up to him! The seed which would not germinate in the old and worn-out lands of Europe might produce abundant harvests when sown in the virgin soil of the new world beyond the sea. Distance and danger and difficulty did not daunt the brave spirit of Plockhoy. The Dutch were then the owners of the New Netherlands, which included the North River, now the Hudson, and the South River, now the Delaware. A site upon the Delaware became the

Kort en klaer ontwerp,
dienende tot
Een onderling Accoort,
O M
Den arbeyd / onrust en moeye-
lijckheyt/van Alderley-hand-wercx-
luyden te verlichten
D O O R
Een onderlinge Compagnie ofte
Volck-planting (onder de protectie vande H: Mo:
Heeren Staten Generael der vereenigde Neder-lan-
den; en bysonder onder het gunstig gesag van de
Achtbare Magistraten der Stad Amstelre-
dam) aen de Zuyt-revier in Nieu-ne-
der-land op te rechten; Bestaende in,

Land bouwers,
Zee-varende Persoonen,
Alderhande noodige Ambachts-luyden, en Meesters
van goede konst en en wetenschappen.

Steunende op de voor-rechten van hare Achtbaerheden (als hier na volgt) tot dien eynde verleent.

t'Samen gestelt

Door Pieter Cornelisz. Plockhoy van Zierck-zee, voor hem selven en andere Lief-hebbers van Nieu-neder-land.

t'Amsterdam gedruckt by Otto Barentsz. Smient, Anno 1662.

chosen field where his schemes for the benefit of humanity, so long thought out, were to be put in operation. The place selected was the mouth of the Hoorn Kill, where is now the town of Lewes, in the State of Delaware. The beautiful name of Swanendael, "The Valley of the Swans," has a ring of promise, could we but forget that the swan is the bird which sings once and then dies. There was another omen. In 1630 Gilles Osset had taken a little colony of thirty-three persons to the same place, all of whom had been murdered by the Indians, and their bones were scattered along the shore.

In 1662 Plockhoy published at Amsterdam a Dutch quarto volume called "Kort en Klaer Ontwerp," or, in English, "Short and clear plan, serving as a mutual contract to lighten the labor and anxiety and trouble of all kinds of handicrafts' men by the establishment of a Community or Colony on the South River in the New Netherlands, comprising agriculturists, seafaring men, all kinds of necessary tradespeople and masters of good arts and sciences, under the protection of their High Mightinesses, the Lords States-General of the United Netherlands and particularly under the favorable auspices of the Honorable Magistrates of the City of Amsterdam, depending upon the privileges of their Honors as hereinafter set forth, granted for the purpose. Brought together by Peter Cornelius Plockhoy of Zierck Zee for himself and other lovers of New Netherlands." The only copy of this book in any of the States along the Delaware is in my library. It is believed that another work "Kort Verhael van Nieu Nederlants" which appeared a few months later without a name, was written by the same author, but the evidence is not clear. The scheme which he arranged for his settlement in America was as follows:

Since men with their families living alone or scattered through the land, because they are by themselves alone and because of poverty, sickness, death, or other misfortune, are able to secure little success or advancement, have we, lovers of humanity, in order to better our own and our neighbors welfare, undertaken, under the protection of their High Mightinesses the States-General of the United Netherlands and especially under that of the Honorable Magistrates of the city of Amsterdam, to establish a mutual company or society upon the South River in New Netherlands, consisting of a peaceful united and select folk who, by aiding each other in the cultivation of the land, fisheries, trades and other useful occupations, hope to better the condition of many oppressed people who live here in great trouble. In accordance with the mutual agreement, in order that the aforesaid society may be governed in good order, we have prepared the following regulations:

First: In order that a numerous mutual company wherein each may have his goods and dwelling apart shall be under one common direction, but without being subject to the control of any individual, each shall have the freedom to use his judgment in the improvement of the established conditions by adding thereto, either by the common consent or by the votes of two-thirds of the association, thus expressly excluding such persons as wish obstinately to accomplish ends according to their own opinions.

In order to open the door for all kinds of reasonable and unpartisan men, there will be needed here first: cultivators of the soil, second, seafaring men; third, all kinds of useful tradespeople, and fourth masters of good arts and sciences, who all with a voluntary unanimity shall work for the common good and benefit like members of one family. The profits from farming, fish catching, mining or any other labor shall be divided not according to the number of families, but according to the number of individuals in such families, sick or well, who are over twenty years of age, all unmarried persons, both women and men who are not at service, receiving as much as those married; but the married who are under twenty years of age, shall begin to receive their profits from the year of their marriage. Only the men who belong to the society shall have the privilege over the women that the undivided lands shall be divided among them according to lot, when their moneys are brought to the magistrate. Those who are under twenty years of age shall like all the others, whether they can be of service or not, be supplied with necessaries out of the common goods. Those in our society who are accustomed to farming or other labor shall, when all is brought into good order, work every day except the Sabbath, six hours for the common profit, or supply others in their place. The remaining hours shall be their own for their own profit, refreshment of the body, or other useful pursuits. To which end not only married men, but also all unmarried men above twenty years of age may select out of the common grounds a piece of land for a private plantation whereon to plant or cultivate, as it may seem to them good. The seafaring persons and others whose labor cannot be accommodated to any fixed hours, in order in the overtime to secure their profit from planting or otherwise and to be on an equality with the tradesmen and farmers so far as possible, shall receive, instead of a private plantation, some other profit from the society.

So as to keep everything in good order, every year those who are thirty years old or over shall choose, by a majority of votes, the names being written on folded pieces of paper, one man for director over the whole society, who, having ruled for one year, shall give up his office and go back to the common work. But no person shall be nominated in the election who has been in the office the year before, or is not fit for the same, or not inclined to perform the duties of the office, so that no man may be selected contrary to his sense and inclination. The office, however, will not be burdensome in itself, since the rulers or directors do not have to make any rules or laws, but only to see that the regulations made or found good by the whole people are observed. So doing shall no man rule according to his own will or pleasure, except in little things for which no special order can be made. Still as he makes no more profit by ruling than the others do by working through the same time, why would he not rather work in quiet for the common profit six hours a day in accordance with our rule than to busy himself with the continually distracting cares of the many affairs of government?

Beside the director over the whole society, there shall be chosen two of the most suitable men to keep the books, one of whom shall give the order in writing, upon which the other delivers the money, wares or merchandise to the person whom the written order describes, placing the reckoning of the same in the book, in order to make good the reckoning of him who has given the order. These bookkeepers may also be used for the purpose of writing letters, journals and other matters which concern the society. No man alone, even the most important of the whole society, shall be in control of the common funds, but the three highest in the government, namely the chosen director of the whole society, and the two book-keepers aforesaid, shall at all times have the keys of the three different locks so that neither one or two in the absence of the third can open the cash. At the end of each year shall all the accounts of the society be brought into balance, and all with the knowledge of the society be well balanced, and the books with two of the keys belonging to the common cash be put in the hands of the two above-named bookkeepers and the great book with a key be given to the newly chosen director for protection.

No man shall be permitted to take away cargoes of merchandise from here or elsewhere in order to carry on a private business until he has paid the money advanced by the magistrates of the city of Amsterdam. Also shall each one be permitted to carry on business with those goods and wares which he, through his art, trade or land cultivation, has made his private property through his overtime. And in case that any person, whether a member or no member of our society, desires to pay in money, wares or merchandise in order therewith to make a profit, he shall receive a reasonable interest or the half of the profit upon his capital, wherein he is much more secure, having the common property of the society as security, than if he ventured his merchandise with a private person. In order to avoid, as much as possible, the risks of loss we shall not trust the society's money, wares or merchandise to any one to be exported or traded with in the country, unless he has capital or a wife and children, wherewith he is, as it were, anchored in the society.

The women, if their husbands die first, shall, with their children, be taken care of out of the common fund, and each person in such a family who is above twenty years of age shall, together with the mother, be paid a share of the profit which appears yearly, after the payment of the common needs. Only the profit, in order to make the common fund safe, shall be retained until the moneys needed for the Lords shall be secured. The children or persons under age shall every day work for half a day and go to school for half a day except upon the Sabbath, and, besides learning a suitable trade, shall be taught to read, write and cipher according to their age and ability, so that they may be freed from bondage and may not fall into idleness and folly.

Among all the trades and occupations the most suitable workmen shall be chosen for masters and foremen who, as well as the other people of our company, shall work six hours a day for the common good, or be busy placing in the book all that is received or paid out for the society.

The name of servant or servant-maid has no place among us, where each, head for head, watches over his share of the profits. Still if strangers, whether full grown or persons under age, not of our society, will work for another for daily hire or otherwise, and are received by one person or another or in one family or another as servant or servant maids, and work six hours a day for the community, and the overtime for their masters and mistresses privately, doing during the six hours the necessary things like others of the society, and giving the remaining work and service for the profit of their masters and mistresses, they shall receive so much money or the worth of it as is paid here or there in the country.

In matters of religion in order to arrange all well, shall each have freedom of conscience, to which and in order that no one give any offence by formulas established by men, in a common meeting house on each Sabbath day or on Sunday and holidays shall the Holy Scriptures, which all Christians recognize for truth, be read, and psalms and hymns sung. Should the number of persons so increase with lapse of time that each kind of people belonging to one sect should want its own meeting house and choose to support its own preachers, it may be done. This is a matter with which the society has nothing at all to do.[122]

The children and youths shall be taught in our common school, so that everywhere equality be regarded, no human formulas of religion, but only the Holy Scriptures, natural sciences and similar instruction enabling them to rightly use their reason and not by the inculcation of private opinions to destroy it. This must be observed that no foundation of sect or partisanship be laid in their hearts. If any one wishes to have his children taught in a private school or by a private teacher, such person may freely be guided by his own conscience, the more so that it does not in the least concern the society.

Any man who for conscientious reasons is unable to bear arms, in order to be free from service and watch, shall pay yearly a certain tax or contribution to that part of the society which protects him in case it is desired. This work, since we believe only in defensive war, is to provide officers, and maintain order when occasion demands it, and also the daily exercise of drill, the securing of ammunition, and whatever is necessary in this respect.

If any colonists, after we have worked a year or two upon the common plantation, come to us as partners and desire a part not only in the cleared land, but also in the undivided cattle and all that is common, they must enter into an agreement with the society concerning it and pay for the privilege in money or wares. If they are people who have no money or goods to pay for the privilege, but are willing to work six hours a day for the society and in this way lighten our work some hours a day, they may do so in order that, instead of showing them a favor, our own plantations and opportunities may be improved.

[122] A note of admiration cannot be withheld.

And in case any persons dwelling here in the Fatherland shall desire for themselves, their descendants or heirs to become partners in our common plantation, after we have worked upon it two, three or four years, they may make an agreement before our departure with the society, and by placing a certain sum of money or merchandise in our company obtain such a privilege and receive their part of the divided cattle and all other profits which come out of the common work in the aforesaid years.

No lordship or servile slavery shall burden our company. So shall each be held to use his diligence to work out a good example of progress. But if anyone, through unworthiness or unrighteousness, disobey the common laws and rules, and makes himself undesirable in the company, and after he has been reasoned with in a friendly way by the directors and others, he is headstrong and will not heed, he may be expelled and driven out by the votes of at least two-thirds, their opinions being written upon folded pieces of paper, but still not without giving him his part of the profit made in his time after his part of the advanced money has been paid.

The men may sell their share in the common plantation and in the undivided cattle and in everything which is coming to them from the society, or put others in their places who will bear their part of the common good. To perform the common work with the others is regarded as sufficient by the society.

If any one wishes to leave the society before the advanced moneys are paid to the magistrates, in order to return to the Fatherland, he is free at any time to do it, and to transport his family at the common expense, transferring to the society his share in the undivided land, cattle and other things coming to him. He shall only take with him his own private property, so that the remaining colonists may not be hindered from paying the money advanced by the magistrates of the city of Amsterdam.

If any one wishes to go over or to journey elsewhere at his own expense and at any time to withdraw from the society, he can do it upon first paying the moneys so far as it concerns him which he has received from the Lords by way of advancement, selling his share in the common land and everything that is in common, or if he chooses to remain a partner by putting in his place a person acceptable to the society, as has been said upon helping the others to do the common work, if it be done, he may go and dwell in any place he thinks best. The reader will be pleased to remember that we desire no wild cursers, drunkards or other such strange people in our community, but only such as we know by experience or by recommendation to be reasonable unpartisan persons. Others whom we know not may work for us as day laborers until we find out they are suitable to come into the society, which consists, as has been said, not only of farmers, seafaring persons, and masters of good arts and sciences, but also of all sorts of useful tradesmen, such as smiths, house carpenters, ship carpenters, brickmakers, masons, stonecutters, potters, tilers, dishmakers, woodsawyers, wagonmakers, chestmakers, turners, joiners, coopers, millwrights, millers, bakers, brewers, distillers, butchers, jarmakers, skindressers, leathermakers, shoemakers, glovemakers, saddlers, tailors, brushmakers, hatters, bleachers, painters, woolcombers, threadtwisters, weavers, fullers, ropemakers, sievemakers, sailmakers, netmakers, blockmakers, compassmakers, makers of sea instruments, refiners, braziers, pewterers, plumbers, tinmen, glassblowers, glassmakers, basketmakers, spectaclemakers, combmakers, soapboilers, saltboilers, glueboilers, oilmillers, needlemakers, pinmakers, cutters, sheathmakers, surgeons, druggists, etc.

All who intended to participate were to be ready to start not later than the middle of September, in 1662, and were to come to Brouwerstraet, in Amsterdam, the Boomgaert of New Netherland, between 8 and 9 o'clock in the morning, or to the Sea Dike, in the Golden Boot, in the evening between 6 and 7 o'clock, so that the number of persons could be known and provisions for a year could be secured, wares and merchandise could be brought and agreements made. The book was illustrated with a picture of a boat. It was enlivened by a ringing poem upon New Netherlands by Karel ver Loove at the beginning, and some verses at the end by Jacob Steendam, the poet of the North River, which have been somewhat roughly translated as follows:

SPURRING VERSES.[123]

You poor, who know not how your living to obtain;
You affluent, who seek in mind to be content;
Choose you New Netherland, which no one shall disdain;
Before your time and strength here fruitlessly are spent.
There have you other ends, your labor to incite;
Your work will generous soils, with usury, requite.

New Netherland's the flow'r, the noblest of all lands;
With richest blessings crowned, where milk and honey flow;
Endowed; yea, filled up full, with what may thrive and grow.
The air, the earth, the sea, each pregnant with its gift,
The needy, without trouble, from distress to lift.

The birds obscure the sky, so numerous in their flight,
The animals roam wild, and flatten down the ground.
The fish swarm in the waters, and exclude the light,

---

[123] From Henry C. Murphy's Jacob Steendam The Hague, 1861.

The oysters there, than which no better can be found,
Are piled up heap on heap, till islands they attain;
And vegetation clothes the forest, mead and plain.

You have a portion there which costs not pains or gold,
But if you labor give, then shall you also share
(With trust in Him who you from want does there uphold)
A rich reward, in time, for all your toil and care.
In cattle, grain and fruit, and every other thing;
Whereby you always have great cause His praise to sing.

What see you in your houses, towns and Fatherland?
Is God not over all? the heavens ever wide?
His blessings deck the earth—like bursting veins expand,
In floods of treasure o'er, wherever you abide;
Which neither are to monarchies nor dukedoms bound,
They are as well in one as other country found.

But there, a living view does always meet your eye
Of Eden, and of the promised land of Jacob's seed;
Who would not, then, in such a formed community,
Desire to be a freeman; and the rights decreed,
To each and every one, by Amstel's burgher Lords,
T' enjoy? And treat with honor what their rule awards?

Communities the groundwork are of every state;
They first the hamlet, village and the city make;
From whence proceeds the commonwealth; whose members great
Become, an interest in the common welfare take.
'Tis no Utopia; it rests on principles,
Which, for true liberty, prescribes you settled rules.

You will not aliens, in those far lands appear;
As formerly in Egypt, e'en was Israel,
Nor have you slavery nor tyranny to fear,
Since Joseph's eyes do see, and on the compass fall.
The civic Fathers who on th'Y, perform their labors,
Are your protectors; and your countrymen are neighbors.

New Netherland's South River—second Amazon,
For you a pleasure garden on its banks concedes.
Choose you the Swanendael, where Osset had his throne,
Or any other spot your avocation needs.
You have the choice of all; and you're left free to choose;
Keep the conditions well, and you have naught to lose.

Discard the base report, unworthy of your ear;
'Tis forged by ignorance and hate and jealous spite,
By those who are its authors, to bedim this fair
Bright morning sun before the laughing noonday light.
An accident may hinder, but not change the plan,
Whose gloss, take that away, you then may fairly scan.

'Twas but an accident, which gives them stuff to slight
That land, which, *as I know*, no proper rival has;
In order from your purpose they may you affright,
Who there desire to live, before you thither pass.
'Tis groundless, ev'ry one may easily perceive,
Who now neglects the chance, great treasures does he leave.

The plan met with the favor of the Burgomasters of Amsterdam, who entered into an agreement with Plockhoy, June 6, 1662, that he should take twenty-five persons, described as Mennonites, with him to the South River, for each of whom they were to advance one hundred guilders. The colonists were further to be free from taxes or tenths for twenty years. They were to repay the sums advanced and to make arrangements for other settlers to follow.

In due time the same year they reached the Valley of the Swans and at last the great scheme of a community founded upon the idea of the brotherhood of man, its members living together in peace and sharing equitably the results of their mutual labors, hearing the Gospel without dogma or form read in a common meeting place for all sects, was put in operation. What would have been the result had they

Burgermeeſteren ende Regeerders der Stad *A*mſtelredamme.

ALſo Wy altoos genegen blijven tot voortſettinge van deſer Stede Colonie in Nieu-Nederland; *SOO IS'T*, dat Wy met kenniſſe ende goed-vinden van de Heeren xxxvj. Raden, gereſolveert hebben tot dien eynde met Pieter Corneliſz. Plockhoy van Zierick-Zee op te rechten het na-volgende Accoort, namentlijck;

Dat hy Pieter Corneliſz. Plockhoy aen-neemt ſo dra mogelijck aen Ons voor te ſtellen vier-en-twintig Mannen, de welcke met hem makende een ſocieteyt van xxv. perſonen, haer ſullen verbinden met de eerſte gelegentheyt van Schip of Schepen te vertrecken na de voorſz deſer Stede Colonie, om haer in de ſelve metter woon neer te ſetten, en met Land-bouwerye, Viſcherye, Hand-wercken en anders te generen, 't ſelve ſo veel doenelijck beneerſtigende; niet alleen ten fijne dat ſy uyt ſodanigen arbeyt bequamelijck ſouden konnen leven, maer oock, op dat daer door voorraet voor andere aen-komende Perſonen ende Huys-geſinnen ſoude mogen toe-bereyt worden

Des ſal de voorſz ſocieteyt van xxv. Mans-perſonen (ofte van meer of minder getal, na datſe ſoude mogen komen te vermeerderen of verminderen) voor 't gemeen; mitſgaders noch daer-en-boven ider Ik van de ſelve Societeyt voor ſig ſelfs in 't particulier, van tijd tot tijd mogen uyt-kieſen, beſlaen ende aen haer nemen ſo veel Lands, niemand anders toe-komende 't ſy aen de Hoere-kil, [a] of elders, in 't Diſtrict van deſe Colonie, waer

[a] Anders genaemt Swanen-dal.

been left undisturbed, we do not know. But the times were unpropitious and the misfortunes which ever attended the steps of Plockhoy pursued him in the distant land. The hand of fate fell heavily upon him and an evil day soon came. War broke out between England and Holland, the result of which was that the Dutch surrendered the New Netherlands and retained the island of Java and other East India islands, then regarded as much the more valuable possessions. In the course of this war, when Sir Robert Carr entered the South River, on behalf of the English in 1664, he sent a boat to the Hoorn Kill and demolished the settlement and seized and carried off "what belonged to the Quaking Society of Plockhoy to a very naile." What became of the people has always been a mystery. History throws no light on the subject, and of contemporary documents there are none. In the year 1694 there came an old blind man and his wife to Germantown. His miserable condition awakened the tender sympathies of the Mennonites there. They gave him the citizenship free of charge. They set apart for him at the end street of the village by Peter Klever's corner a lot twelve rods long and one rod broad, whereon to build a little house and make a garden, which should be his as long as he and his wife should live. In front of it they planted a tree. Jan Doeden and William Rittenhouse were appointed to take up "a free will offering'" and to have the little house built. This is all we know, but it is surely a satisfaction tô see this ray of sunlight thrown upon the brow of the hapless old man as he neared his grave. After thirty years of untracked wanderings upon these wild shores, friends had come across the sea to give a home at last to one whose whole life had been devoted to the welfare of his fellows. It was Peter Cornelius Plockhoy. What recognition may be hereafter awarded to his career cannot be foretold. His efforts resulted in what the world calls failure, and for over two hundred years he has slept in the deepest obscurity, yet when we compare him with his contemporaries, with the courtiers, Sir Walter Raleigh and Sir William Berkeley, with Cotton Mather, inciting the magistrates to hang old women for imaginary crimes, and see him wrestling with Cromwell, not for his own gain, but for the help of the downtrodden and the poor, teaching the separation of church and state, protesting against injuring the minds of children by dogma, and with so clear a sense of justice that even the vicious, when driven from the community, were to receive their share of the possessions, we cannot help but recognize his merit and intelligence, and feel for him that sympathy that makes us all akin. When we find him, first of all the colonizers of America, so long ago as 1662, announcing the broad principle that "no lordship or servile slavery shall burden our company," he seems to grow into heroic proportions. Whatever else may happen, certain it is that the events of the life of one, whose book marks the very beginning of the literature and history of the ten millions of people who now live in the States along the Zuid Rivier, must always be of keen interest to them and their descendants. The copy of this book, from which an English translation has here been made, belonged in 1865 to Samuel L. M. Barlow, of New York, and because of its great interest and excessive rarity the Knickerbocker Club undertook its reproduction. The translator, however, met with such difficulty in the rendition of the black letter Dutch that it led to delay and the abandonment of the enterprise.[124]

[124] Growoll's American Book Clubs, p 126

CHAPTER X.

THE PIETISTS—HENRY BERNHARD KOSTER, JOHANNES KELPIUS, DANIEL FALKNER AND THE WOMAN IN THE WILDERNESS.

Arms used by the brother of Kelpius.

GERHARD CROESE, the historian of the Quakers, writing in 1696 of the followers of Spener and the believers in the mystical theology of Jacob Boehm, the inspired shoemaker of Gorlitz, says: "And there is no occasion here to relate how much vexation and trouble their Ministers, and other good men, had in Holland, both from the old Weigelian family, and from this new brood of Teutonicks; seeing this is so well known there and in every body's mouth; But this is not to be past over so far as it has relation to the affairs of the Quakers. Among these few mystical men there was one John Jacob Zimmerman, Pastor of the Lutheran Church in the Duchy of Wirtemburg, a Man skilled in Mathematicks, and, saving what he had contracted of these erroneous opinions, had all other excellent endowments of mind, to which may be added the temperance of his Life, wherein he was inferior to none, and who was of considerable fame in the world; Who when he saw there was nothing but great danger like to hang over himself and his Friends, he invites and stirs up through his own hope about sixteen or seventeen Families of these sort of Men, to prefer also an hope of better things, tho it were dubious before the present danger, and forsaking their Country which they through the most precipitous and utmost danger, tho they suffered Death for the same, could not help and relieve as they supposed, and leaving their Inheritance which they could not carry along with them, to depart and betake themselves into other parts of the world, even to Pensilvania, the Quakers' Country, and there divide all the good and evil that befell them between themselves, and learn the Languages of that People, and Endeavour to inspire Faith and Piety into the same Inhabitants by their words and examples which they could not do to these Christians here. These agree to it, at least so far as to try and sound the way, and if things did not go ill, to fortify and fit themselves for the same. Zimmerman having yet[125] N. Koster for his Colleague, who was also a famous Man, and of such severe manners that few could equal him, writes to a certain Quaker in Holland who was a Man of no mean Learning, and very wealthy, very bountiful and liberal towards all the poor pious and good: *That as he and his followers and his friends designed* [they are the very words of the letter which is now in my custody] *to depart from these Babilonish Coasts, to those American Plantations, being led thereunto by the guidance of the Divine Spirit, and*

[125] Henry Bernhard Koster

that seeing that all of them wanted worldly substance that they would not let them want Friends, but assist them herein that they might have a good ship well provided for them to carry them into those places, wherein they might mind this one thing, towit to show with unanimous consent, their *Faith and Love in the Spirit, in converting of People, but at the same time to sustain their bodies by their daily Labour.* So great was the desire, inclination and affection of this Man towards them, that he forthwith promised them all manner of assistance, and performed it and fitted them with a ship for their purpose, and did out of that large Portion of Land he had in Pensilvania, assign unto them a matter of two thousand and four hundred acres forever of such Land as it was, but such as might be manured, imposing yearly to be paid a very Small matter of rent upon every Acre, and gave freely of his own and what he got from his friends, as much as paid their charge and Passage, amounting to an hundred and thirty pounds sterling; a very great gift, and so much the more strange, that that same Quaker should be so liberal, and yet would not have his name mentioned, or known in the matter.[126] But when these Men came into Holland they sailed from thence directly for Pensilvania. Zimmerman seasonably dies, but surely it was unseasonable for them, but yet not so, but that they all did cheerfully pursue their Voyage, and while I am writing hereof, I receive an account, that they arrived at the place they aimed at, and they all lived in the same house, and had a publick Meeting, and that they took much pains, to teach the blind people to become like unto themselves, and to conform to their examples."[127]

---

[126] After a lapse of two hundred years his name may be now mentioned It was Benjamin Furly.

[127] Croese, Vol. II., p. 262.

BOOK-PLATE OF BENJAMIN FURLY.

ORIGINAL IN THE BRITISH MUSEUM.

Johannes Kelpius opened his Latin journal with a quotation from Seneca "Unto whatever land I come, I come to my own There is no banishment, every country is my country and every where there is good. If a man be wise he is a traveller, if a fool an exile." From it we learn that among these mystical Pietists were Kelpius from Denndorf in Transylvania, Henry Bernhard Koster of Blumenberg, Daniel Falkner of Saxony, Daniel Lutke, Johannes Seelig of Lemgo, Ludwig Bidermann of Anhalt, Henry Lorenz, whose little six-months-old son died and was buried at sea, George G. Lorenz and Peter Schaeffer, a Finlander.

Among the company, which consisted of about forty persons, were also the widow of Zimmermann and their children, Maria Margaretha, baptized Oct. 10, 1675, Philip Christian, baptized Feb 18, 1678, Matthaius, baptized June 25, 1680, and Jacob Christoph, baptized May 14, 1683.[128] They left Rotterdam in August of 1693 and remained in London for six months. In February they went down the Thames in a sloop to Gravesend and there embarked on a ship the "Sarah Maria" armed with fourteen cannon. On the 16th the ship ran aground, and when signals of distress brought no assistance, their prayers prevailed and a great wave lifted it off the bank in safety. On the 21st they arrived at Deal and there waited two weeks for a convoy. Four days they were in the channel in the midst of severe storms which made their ship dance about "like a little ball which most of us were not accustomed to." For five weeks they lay at Plymouth awaiting the convoy. For amusement they had discussions upon the Scriptures and prayer meetings, at which they sang hymns of praise and joy and played upon the

[128] Sachse's Pietists

musical instruments they had brought with them. On the 18th of April they set sail. Though once the gale snapped two of the masts, there was no danger on the ocean because the water was as deep below as the highest clouds were above the earth, and there was nothing for the ship to strike against. Fish of monstrous size spouted water "as fire engines do." One day they caught a big fish which the English called a shark. It had a way "of prowling after ships so as to snap up people." On the 10th of May they encountered a hostile French frigate of twenty-four guns and a merchant ship with six guns The cannon opened fire and the Pietists "abstained of carnal weapons, and taking the shield of faith, sat down between desks behind boxes and cases, and prayed and invoked the Lord everyone for himself." The result was that the Merciful Father caused the balls to "drop into the water in front of the ship," and after one of them had knocked a bottle out of the hand of the Captain's boy, and a Frenchman while aiming with a rifle at the Captain was killed, the Lord struck the enemy with fear and they fled. The battle lasted four hours and one hostile ship with twenty-four Frenchmen was captured. It contained sugar and cider, and an equal share of the "unjust mammon" was allowed to all. On the 14th of June they entered the Chesapeake Bay, and two days before had had their first glimpse of the American coast. There must have been some dissensions among them, probably over some problem presented by the mysteries of Boehm which were not all "Morning Redness," because before they landed, Koster had excommunicated Falkner, together with a woman, Anna Maria Schuchart, who saw visions and had been left behind in Germany. They were pleased with America, because here one could be "peasant, scholar, priest and nobleman all at the same time without interference." They landed at Bohemia Manor, arrived in Philadelphia June 23, 1694, and thence proceeded to Germantown, where in the house of Jacob Isaacs Van Bebber, they held three meetings a week at which Koster spake publicly. He also spoke once a week in English in Philadelphia. In August, of 1694, a gentleman of Philadelphia gave them one hundred and seventy-five acres of ground, three miles from Germantown, upon the ridge and on it they at once began to build a log house.[129] It was a little block house of trees laid one upon another cleared out of the forest, and to save themselves from hunger they planted Turkish corn. They called themselves "The contented of the God-loving Soul"; but since they maintained that the sixth verse of the Twelfth Chapter of Revelations indicated, when properly interpreted, the near approach of the coming of Christ, the name given them by those who surrounded them was "The Society of the Woman in the Wilderness," and like such names as Quaker and Methodist, at first used in derision, it has clung to them. It was their purpose to refrain from marriage, "according to the better advice of Saint Paul," but ere long this rule was broken by Bidermann, who before August had been united with Maria Margaretha Zimmermann, and having separated from the community, had gone to live apart in Germantown. Muhlenberg, who came to Pennsylvania a half century later, reports from tradition that they cared nothing for the sacraments of baptism and the Eucharist, regarding the Holy writ as a dead letter in this respect, but that they busied themselves with the Theosophical Sophia and speculations and practical alchemy. They

---

[129] See Journal Penna Magazine, Vol II, p 427, and Adelung's Life of Koster

were always awaiting and looking for the coming of the Millennium. There is a record at Ephrata that upon the seventh anniversary of their arrival, which they had prepared to celebrate with special effort, and while in the midst of their ceremonies, "a white obscure moving body in the air, attracted their attention, which as it approached, assumed the form and mien of an angel. It receded into the shadows of the forest and appeared again immediately before them as the fairest of the lovely."[130] They watched through the night, and the second night, without further disclosures. The third night the apparition was again present. They fell upon their knees, but alas, the prayers they uttered seemed to repel rather than to attract the ethereal divinity, and so "Kelpius and his brethren remained at the Laurea, wearing out the thread of life in retirement and patient waiting for the final drama they were to enact in the wilderness." The *Chronicon Ephratense* says that after the death of Kelpius, the tempter found occasion to scatter them and that "those who had been most zealous against marrying, now betook themselves to women again."

Johann Jacob Zimmermann, the original founder of this community of Mystics, was born at the village of Vaihingen, on the Entz, in the Duchy of Wurtemburg, in 1644, and displaying great zeal in learning, was taken into the service of the Duke at the age of seventeen. He was then sent to the University of Tübingen, where he was graduated in 1664, as Master of Philosophy, and at once there became an instructor in arithmetic. He entered the Lutheran ministry, and, from 1671 to 1684, was in charge of the church at Bietigheim. He became, however, profoundly impressed with the views of Jacob Boehm, whose influence upon theological thought has been most

[130] Sachse's Pietists.

remarkable and extensive, and regarding the great comet of 1680 as a warning, he prophecied the near approach of the destruction of the world. Getting into controversy with the orthodox, and being accused of trying to elevate Boehm above the apostles, of teaching astrology, magic and cabbalism, he was tried and deposed from the ministry. From 1684 to 1689, he was professor of mathematics in Heidelberg University. He had the support of a prominent minister of state, but persisting in views regarded as peculiar, and maintaining that an invasion by the French was a visitation by the Lord, because of his persecution, he lost position and influence. He was the author of at least eighteen published works upon theology and astronomy. He died on his way to Pennsylvania in 1693. Gottfried Arnold, in his *Kirchen und Ketzer Historie*, Vol. III., p. 913, describes Zimmermann as a very learned astrologus, magus, cabalista, and preacher, and says he was deposed because of his attachment to the doctrines of Boehm, and because in 1689, he published a tract on the extension of common love to the remaining Jews, Turks and heathen. On the 25th of the 10th month, 1694, his widow "was received gratis" into the corporation of Germantown.[131]

Henry Bernhard Koster, who from the exercise of the power of excommunication, would seem to have succeeded Zimmermann, was the son of Ludolph Koster, burgomaster and merchant at Blumenberg, where he was born in November, 1662. He entered the town school of his native city, and when the rector there, Vogelsang, became director of the grammar school at Detmold, Koster followed him and remained four years under his instruction. He was at the gymnasium at Bremen five years, studied law

[131] Among his many descendants in Pennsylvania is Thomas Allen Glenn, the genealogist.

three years at Frankfurt-on-the-Oder, and left the University in 1684 in the twenty-second year of his age. He possessed much talent, which he used for his own advancement and for the instruction of youth. He was first tutor in the family of Aulic Counsellor Polemius, in Kustrin, and by instructing his pupils, not in the ordinary methods, but by attractive discourses, he became known to Privy Counseller Otto von Schwerin, at Berlin, who, in 1685, made him tutor to his three sons. Here he had the advantage of a great library. From Walton's Polyglot he derived a fondness for the eastern languages and for theology. Conceiving a mistrust for the accepted text of the Hebrew Bible, he made a translation from the Septuagint version into the German. His patron had influence with the Prince of Brandenburg, and offered him an important position. But Koster declined to go to the court, where there were so many temptations to sin, and emigrated instead to Pennsylvania. He had been in the service of the Baron von Schwerin for seven years. Just before the arrival of the mystics in Pennsylvania there had occurred the division among the Quakers, caused by George Keith. When Koster began to preach in the English language he was attended by the Keithian separatists in large numbers. His success led him to entertain the hope of establishing a sect based upon his own peculiar views, and no doubt led ultimately to his separation from the community upon the Ridge. He bore an active part in the Keith controversy and caused great commotion among the Quakers. In 1696, taking with him six others, he went to the yearly meeting at Burlington, where there were in attendance about four thousand people and thirty preachers. He asked to be heard, but no attention was paid to him. Finally he insisted while one of their preachers was speaking, and since the preacher had a weak voice, and Koster one which was loud and powerful, he succeeded in making himself heard, although all the preachers got upon the bench and tried to prevent him He cried, "I raise my voice against you with the full witness of the word of God in order to oppose, out of the Holy Scripture, your blasphemous teaching, which is worse than that of the heathens of America, namely, the teaching of your spiritual Jesus, and that the body which Jesus had on earth disappeared in the clouds on his journey to Heaven" And he closed with, "Now to-day has the light of the Scriptures appeared in the second American darkness, and its strength you shall learn, not only here in Burlington, but in all the colonies." He wrote an account of the affair called "History of the Protestation Done in the Publick Yearly Meeting of the Quakers at Burlington in the year 1696," published by William Bradford in New York, 1697. It is pointed out by Sachse that this work, of which, unfortunately, we have no copy, issued in both German and English, has the distinction of being the first book printed in the German language in America. Nor have we the exact title. Pastorius, in his reply, refers to it as "Advice for all professors and writers," and says Koster arrived here "his heart and head filled with whimsical and boisterous imaginations, but his hands and purse emptied of the money which our friends beyond the sea imparted unto him and some of his company." About this time, differing with Kelpius, he endeavored to establish a community, based upon a common ownership of goods, on some lands given to him in Plymouth, to be called "The True Church of Philadelphia or Brotherly Love." A house was built styled "Irenia," or the house of peace. The attempt, however, failed, the people, who never numbered more than four or five, scattered, and the land reverted to the donor. He persuaded some of the Keithians to permit him to baptize them. He chose for the purpose the river near Philadelphia and made an address before a great concourse of people, wherein he sought to show that he had a right to baptize as the apostles did. Then he baptized one after the other and dismissed each with the words, "Go forth and do this all the days of thy life." But he had awakened the animosity of the Quakers; he had become separated from the community on the Ridge, and the Keithians gradually drifted back into connection with the church of England. In December, 1699, he went from Pennsylvania to Virginia, and thence in January, 1700, in a tobacco ship, to London, and soon afterward to Amsterdam. At this time the Duchess Charlotta Sophia had a claim against the Duke Ferdinand of Curland, which Koster undertook to secure for her. He went to Stockholm in 1702, followed the King, who was with his army in Poland, and there in camp before Thoren, succeeded in compelling the Duke to pay a part of the money. For several years thereafter he taught languages at Hamburg. The Baron von Schaak, the Danish Ambassador to England, at this time wanted a tutor for his sons and Koster was selected for the place, and he remained upon the estate of the Count as tutor for seven years. In 1724 he went to Berleburg, where he was under the protection of Count Casimir von Sayn and Witgenstein. In 1735 he was teaching eastern and western languages in Hanover. He claimed to know and to understand most of the languages of the world. But among them all his Holy languages were the Greek, the German, the Bohemian and the Hebrew, in which he at all times repeated his prayers. He maintained stoutly that he would

CAVE OF JOHANNES KELPIUS.

never die, and he came pretty near keeping his word, since he reached the age of ninety-eight years, and retained his health and vivacity until the last. He died in 1749. His publications, in addition to those already mentioned were five in number.[132]

Johannes Kelpius was born in 1673, at or near Denndorf, in Transylvania, and was the son of George Kelpius, a clergyman. When he was only twelve years of age, his father died. Three friends of the family sent

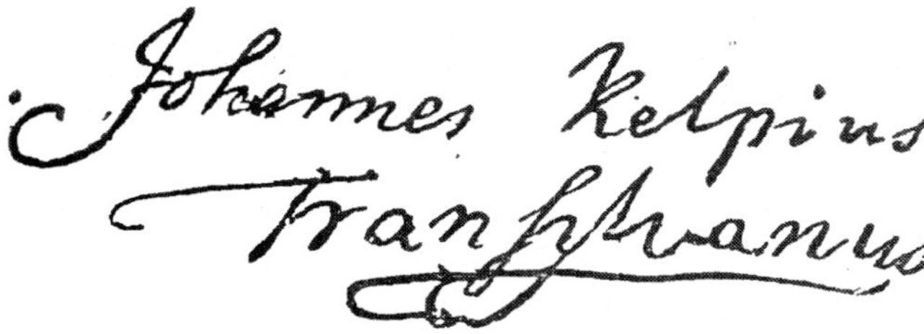

him to the high school at Tübingen, and later to the University, where he was graduated at the age of sixteen as Doctor of Philosophy and the liberal arts. He wrote a Latin thesis, "Theologia Naturalis, seu Metaphysicae Metamorphosis sub moderamine Viri M. Dan. Guilh. Molleri, pro summis honoribus, et privilegiis philosophicis legitime obtinendis, die 15 Jun, 1689. Altforfii." In 1690, together with his teacher, Dr. Johannes Fabricius, a celebrated theologian, he wrote a work in eighteen chapters entitled "Scylla Theologiae, aliquot exemplis Patrum et Doctorium Ecclesiae qui cum alios refutare laborarent fervore disputationis obrepti in contrarios errores misere inciderent, ostensa, atque in materiam disputationis proposita a Joh Fabricio. S. Theol. P. F. et M. Joh Kelpio.

---

[132] Life of Hendrick Pannebecker, p. 107. Adelung's Geschichte der menschlichen Narrheit, Vol. VII., p. 86.

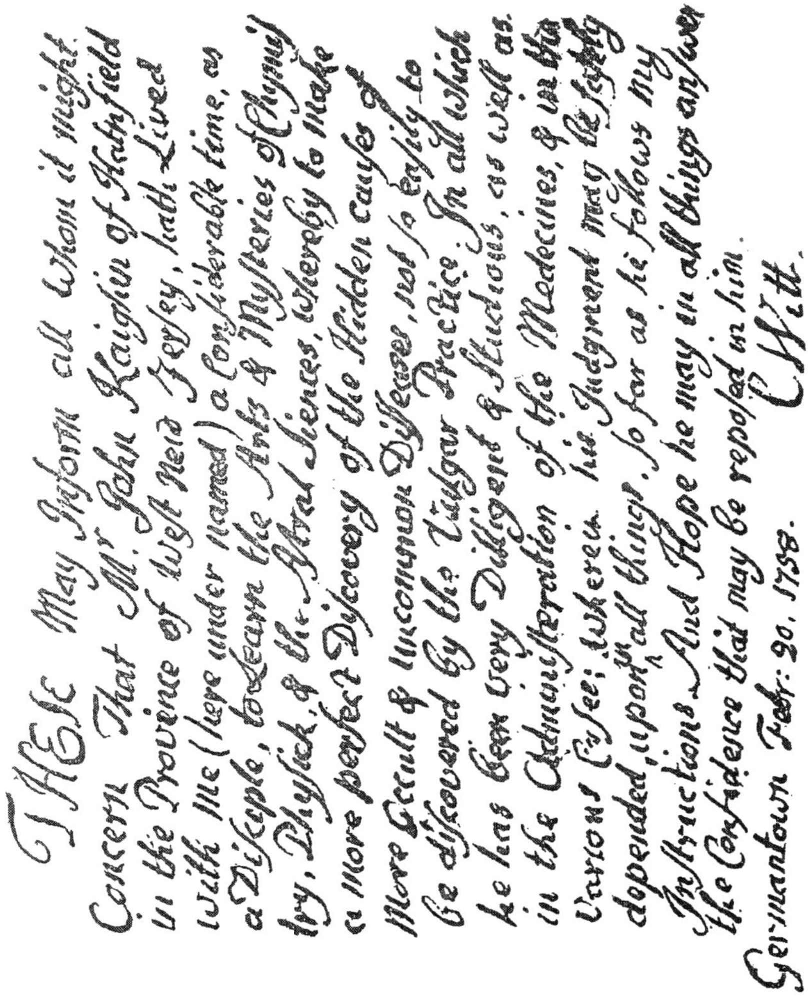

THESE May Inform all Whom it might Concern That Mr. John Kaighin of Hatnfield in the Province of West New Jersey, hath Lived with me (here under named) a Considerable time, as a Dissciple, to Learn the Arts & Mysteries of Chymistry, Physick, & the Astral Sciences, whereby to make a more perfect Discovery of the Hidden causes of more Occult & uncommon Disseases, not so easily to be discovered by the Vulgar Practice. In all which he has been very Dilligent & Studious, as well as in the Administeration of the Medecines, & in the Various Cases; wherein his Judgment may be safely depended upon in all things, so far as he follows my Instructions. And Hope he may in all things answer the Confidence that may be reposed in him.

Germantown Febr: 20. 1758. C Witt.

The original of this early medical diploma is in my library.

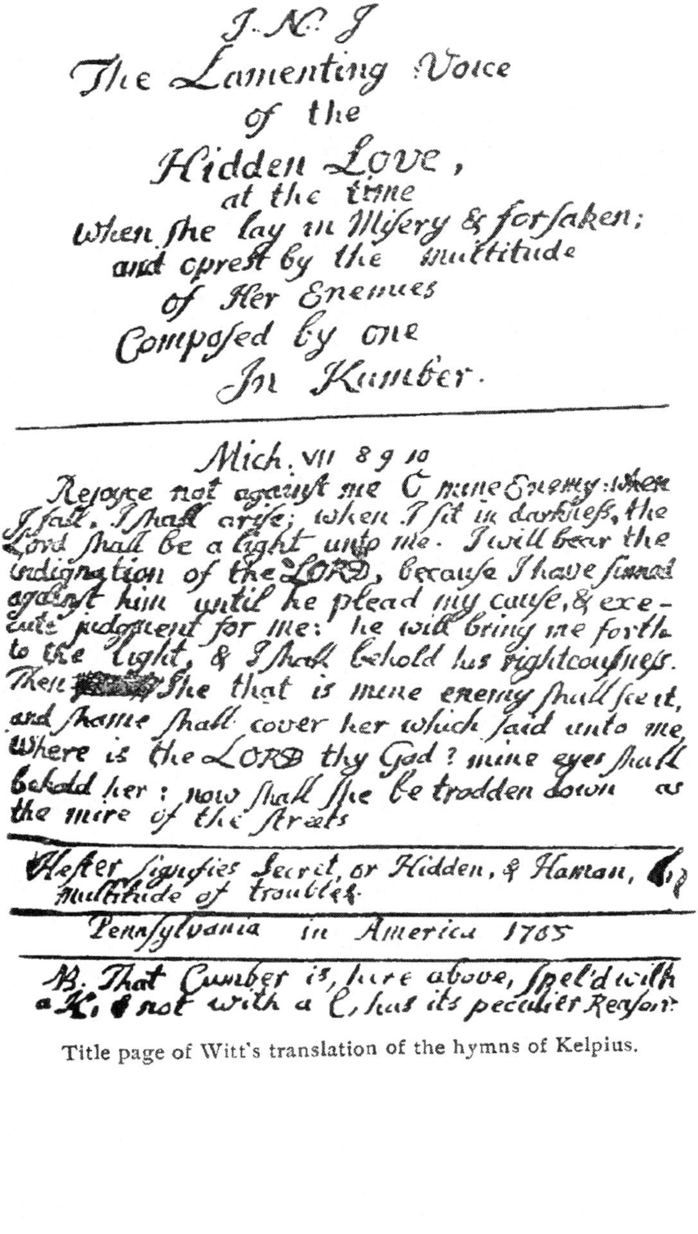

J. N. J
The Lamenting Voice
of the
Hidden Love,
at the time
When she lay in Misery & forsaken;
and oprest by the multitude
of Her Enemies
Composed by one
In Kumber.

Mich. VII 8 9 10
Rejoyce not against me O mine Enemy: when I fall, I shall arise; when I sit in darkness, the Lord shall be a light unto me. I will bear the indignation of the LORD, because I have sinned against him until he plead my cause, & execute judgment for me: he will bring me forth to the light, & I shall behold his righteousness. Then [redacted] She that is mine enemy shall see it, and shame shall cover her which said unto me, Where is the LORD thy God? mine eyes shall behold her: now shall she be trodden down as the mire of the streets

Hester signifies Secret, or Hidden, & Haman, [illegible] multitude of troubles.

Pennsylvania in America 1765

NB. That Cumber is, here above, spel'd with a K, & not with a C, has its peculier Reason.

Title page of Witt's translation of the hymns of Kelpius.

Altdorfii, 1690." The same year he wrote an essay upon the question whether it was fitting that a Christian youth should listen to the heathen philosophy of Aristotle. It was entitled: "Inquisitio an Ethicus Ethnicus, aptus sit Christianae Inventutis hodiernas, sive; An Juvenis Christianus sit idoneus auditor ethices Aristotelieae. Resp Balthos Blosio Norimb. 1690."

Meeting with Zimmermann in Nuremburg, he became a convert and when only twenty years of age, started for Pennsylvania. After the withdrawal of Koster he became the head of the community on the Ridge. Of his work while here we have his Latin Journal of the voyage, a copy of a letter in German to Heinrich Johannes Deichman, of London, September 24, 1697, a copy of a letter in German to Deichman, May 12, 1699, sent through Jan van Loevenigh, of Crefeld, a letter in English, in 1699, to Stephen Mumford, of Long Island, a letter in Latin to the Swede Rev. Eric Biork, a letter, October 10, 1704, in German to Maria Elizabetha Gerber, in Virginia, a letter in July, 1705, to Dr. Fabricius, in German, a letter in German to Deichman, July 23, 1705, and a letter of May 25, 1706, to Esther Palmer, of Long Island, in English. There is also a manuscript volume of hymns, now in the possession of the Historical Society of Pennsylvania, written in German, and translated into English, not very effectively, by Dr. Christopher Witt. Prefixed to this volume is a portrait of Kelpius upon canvas, by Witt and on the title page the hymns are said to have been written by one "In Kummer" thus concealing the initials of the author in an anagram. The volume is dated in 1705, and the portrait, probably taken from life, is evidently contemporary with the book, and is believed to be the earliest extant portrait painted in America. One of the hymns upon the subject of Peacefulness, written, Kelpius says, as he lay in

"Christian Warmer's house very weak, in a small bed, not unlike a coffin, in May, 1706," begins:

> "Hier lieg ich geschmieget
> Erkrancket im Schrein
> Fast ganzlich besieget
> Von sussesster Pein."

and was to be sung to the popular tune of "So wunsch ich nun eine gute nacht." A musical score accompanies each of the hymns. He is also said to have written "Eine kuerze und begreifliche Anleitung zum stillen Gebet," which was translated into English and printed by Sower in 1763.

On the 24th of January, 1700, he was appointed, together with Daniel Falckner and Johannes Jawert, agent for the Frankfort Land Company, but he declined to serve. He was impressed with the belief that he would not die, but be taken to Heaven bodily like Elijah. Being slight and delicate, he caught a severe cold, which ended in consumption and he died in 1708. Muhlenberg gives a strange account of his closing hours from the report of his friend, Daniel Geissler. For three long days and nights he prayed that body and soul might remain united and be transfigured. At last he gave up and said: "My beloved Daniel, I am not to have that for which I hoped. I have received my answer. Dust I am and to dust I must return. It is ordained that I shall die like all the children of Adam." He then gave Geissler a sealed casket and told him to take it to the river Schuylkill and throw it into deep water. Geissler took it to the bank, but concluded to hide it until after the death of his master, and then examine the contents. Upon his return, Kelpius arose, looked him in the eyes sharply, and said, "Daniel, thou hast not done as I bid thee. Thou hast not cast the casket into the river, but hast hid it by the shore." Then Geissler, convinced of his master's occult force, hurried to the bank and threw it into the river. It fell with flashes like lightning and peals like thunder. This story sounds very much like another version of the death of King Arthur, and the experience of Sir Bedivere with the sword Excalibur.

In one of his hymns Kelpius writes:

> "Doch weil ich am Reigen
> Des Todes noch geh'
> Und kan nicht versteigen
> Die Englische Hoh,"

which I translate:

> "And since I am mortal
> Whom death will not slight,
> And cannot mount upward
> The angelic height."

This expresses a thought entirely contrary to the belief attributed to him by Muhlenberg, whose orthodox training sometimes prevented him from getting the measure accurately of the faiths of those not in the church.

Peter Miller, the Prior of Ephrata, who was more sympathetic, gave this account of him: Kelpius, educated in one of the most distinguished universities of Europe, and having had advantage of the best resources for the acquirement of knowledge, was calculated to edify and enlighten those who resorted to him for information. He had particularly made great progress in the study of ancient law, and was quite proficient in theology. He was intimately acquainted with the works of the rabbins, the heathen and stoic philosophers, the fathers of the Christian church, and the reformers. He was conversant with the writings of Tertullian, St. Jerome, St. Augustine, St. Cyprian, Chrysostom, Ambrose, Tauler, Eck, Myconius, Carlstadt, Hedio, Faber, Osiander, Luther, Zwinglius,

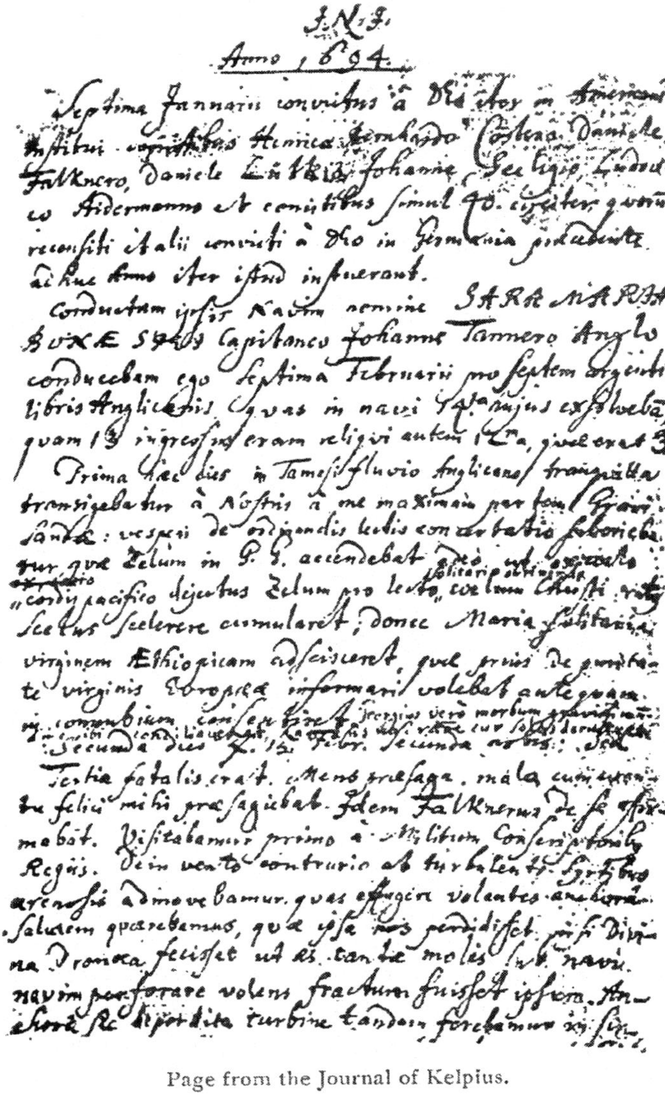

I. N. J.

Anno 1694.

Septima Januarii convictus à Deo iter in Americam institui cum fratribus Henrico Bernhardo Köstero, Daniele Falknero, Daniele Lutkio, Johanne Seeligio, Ludovico Bidermanno et comitibus simul 40. circiter, quorum recensiti et alii convicti à Deo in Germania præcedente adhuc anno iter istud inierant.

Conductam ipsis navim nomine SARAH MARIA BONÆ SPEI Capitaneo Johanne Tannero Anglo conducebam ego septima Februarii pro septem argenti libris Anglicanis quas in navi Sarah Mariæ ejus exsolvebam, quam 13 ingressi eramus, relegimus autem 12ma, quæ erat 3

Prima hæc dies in Tamesi fluvio Anglicano tranquilla transigebatur à Nostris à me maximam per tam gravi. sancta: vesperi de ordinandis lectis concertatio suboriebatur quæ Zelum in P. S. accendebat adeo ut [illegible] solitario [illegible] cordi pacifico dejectus Zelum pro lecto, coelum Christi [illegible] scelus scelere cumularet; donec Maria solitaria virginem Æthiopicam adsciscerent, quæ prius de puritate virginis Europeæ informari volebat antequam connubium consentiret. [illegible] verò morbum [illegible] [illegible] [illegible] Secunda dies X. 12. Febr. secunda [illegible]

Tertia fatalis erat. Mens præsaga mala cum eventu felici mihi præsagiebat. Idem Falknerus de se affirmabat. Visitabamur primo à Militum Conscriptoribus Regiis. Dein vento contrario ob turbulentis syrtibus arenosis admovebamur, quas effugere volentes anchoram salutem quærebamus, quæ ipsa nos perdidisset, nisi Divina Providentia fecisset ut ea tantæ moles sub navi navim perforare volens fractum fuisset ipsum. Anchora ac deperdita turbine tandem ferebamur in [illegible]

Page from the Journal of Kelpius.

and others, whose opinions he would frequently analyze and expound with much animation. He was also a strict disciplinarian, and kept attention directed inwards upon self. To know self he contended is the first and most essential of all knowledge. Thales, the Milesian, he maintained, was the author of the precept, "Know Thyself," which was adopted by Chilo, the Lacedamonian, and is one of the three inscriptions which, according to Pliny, was consecrated at Delphos by golden letters, and acquired the authority of divine oracle.

It was supposed to have been given by Apollo, of which opinion Cicero has left a record. He directed a sedulous watchfulness over the temper, inclinations and passions and applauded very much the counsel of Marcus Aurelius: "Look within; for within is the formation of good."

Kelpius has become widely and popularly known as "The Hermit of the Wissahickon."

Daniel Falckner, another of the emigrants of 1694, was born in Langen Reinsdorf, in Saxony, Nov. 24, 1666, and was the son of Daniel and grandson of Christian Falckner, both of whom were clergymen. He also was educated for the ministry. A description of the voyage to America, from which we get much information, is believed by Seidensticker to have been written by him. In 1698 he went back to Europe in an effort to bring another colony to Pennsylvania. While there he wrote a little volume published at Franckfurt, in 1702, a copy of which I have, entitled "Curieuse Nachricht von Pennsylvania in Norden America," in which he describes himself as a professor, burgher and pilgrim He came back holding authority to represent the Frankfort Land Company, but

his efforts were not very successful, and it appears both from the statements of Pastorius and the court records that he was for a time given to indulgence. He married and separated from the community on the Ridge. His manner of life no doubt improved, since Sachse has shown that he later became pastor of the Lutheran congregations on the Raritan, and elsewhere in New Jersey, where he spent much time in botanical studies, and was living respected until as late as 1741. "Falckner's Swamp" in Montgomery Co., Pa., still bears his name.

Johann Seelig, a teacher and a bookbinder, was born at Lengo, Lippe Detmold, in 1668. Saur, in 1739, published in Germantown a little volume entitled "Ein Abgenothigter Bericht," the only known copy of which I have, wherein he tells of a certain Dr. Schotte, whose letters he prints, and who, he says, preached in 1687 with so much fervor that his hearers were astounded and "fell upon the earth and lay together in heaps as if dead." Schotte stretched out his arm as stiff as an iron bar, so that many men could not move it. He rode through the cities and to the universities of Europe and brought one hundred and forty-five people together, giving them each a distinctive name. Among them were many of the Pietists, Dr. Johann Wilhelm Petersen, as Elias; Spener, as Nicodemus; Johann Heinrich Sprogell, as Philemon; Daniel Falckner, as Gaius; Johannes Kelpius, as Philologus; Johanna Eleanora Von Merlau as Sara; the widow Schutz, as Susanna; and Johann Seelig, as Pudens. Of Seelig's life in Pennsylvania all that seems to be known is that Kelpius was much attached to him; that, May 12, 1699, he wrote a long letter to Deichman, in London, couched in the mystic language of his sect; that he lived the life of a hermit eight miles from Philadelphia, where he bound books and taught the

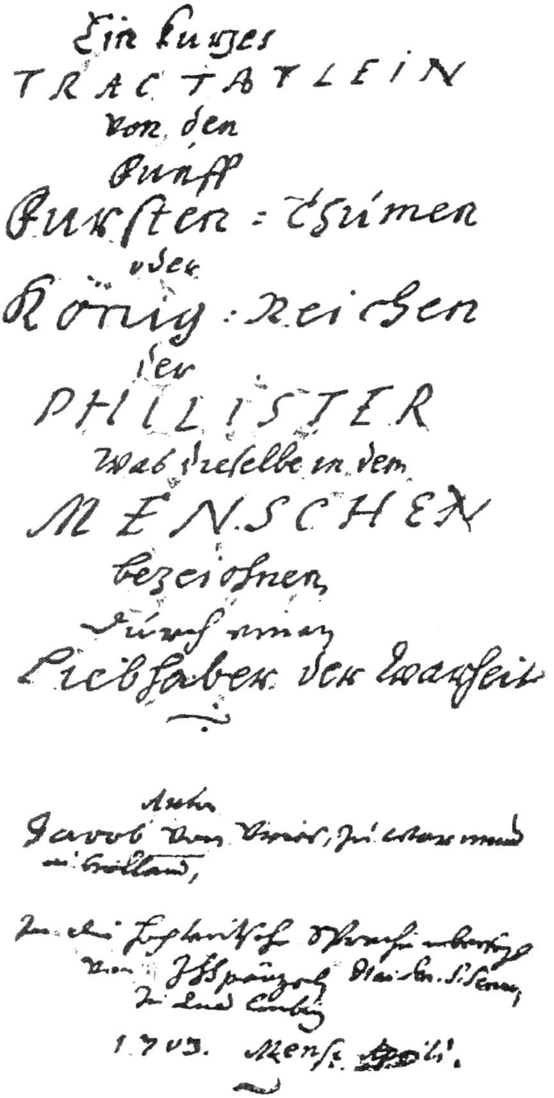

Ein kurzes
TRACTATLEIN
von den
Fünff
Fürsten = Thümen
oder
König = Reichen
der
PHILISTER
was dieselbe in dem
MENSCHEN
bezeichnen,
durch einen
Liebhaber der Wahrheit

Autor
Jacob [illegible]
[illegible]

[illegible]
[illegible] Sprögel [illegible]
[illegible]

1703. Mens. [illegible]

MS. volume by Sprogell in 1703 in my library.

children, and that he died April 26, 1745, aged seventy-seven years.

Justus Falckner, brother of Daniel, was born Nov. 22, 1672, and in 1693 was a student in the University at Halle. We are told by Biorck that he left his home "to escape the burden of the pastorate." He wrote a number of hymns which are still preserved. In 1700 he came with his brother to Pennsylvania. He was ordained by Rudman in the old Swedes Church at Wiccacoe on Nov. 24, 1703, and from that time was pastor of the Holy Trinity Lu-

theran Church in New York, until 1723. In 1708 he published in Dutch a "Grondlycke Onderricht," a catechism, printed by Bradford, in New York, the only known copy of which is in the library of the Historical Society of Pennsylvania and which was long supposed to be the first Dutch book printed in America. He married May 26, 1717, Gerritje Hardick, and had three children.

Despite the earnest efforts of Mr. Sachse, who has given special attention to the subject, and of earlier writers, there is little definite information concerning the community upon the Ridge. Who composed the forty immigrants, beside those named, we do not know. What they did and what was the manner of their lives is for the most part involved in hopeless obscurity. Though men of learning they seem to have given little attention to the affairs of this world, and to have fixed their patient expectations upon the rewards that were to come in the next, because of the self-denial exercised while here.

CHAPTER XI.

THE INDIANS.

THE settlers of Germantown, in making their homes out in the woods, in a new land, were brought into continual contact with the savages. Among themselves there was much of wonderment, and among their relatives in Holland and Germany, much of curiosity with respect to the appearance, origin, habits and manner of life of these denizens of the forest. To this fact we owe the preservation of a series of pictures of Indian life at that early time, the most thorough and complete in existence with respect to the Indians in the neighborhood of Philadelphia, enlivened with anecdote and filled with interesting details, which, because they were hidden in a foreign language and in inaccessible books, have remained almost entirely unknown. The Dutch and Germans at Germantown did not approach the Indians with a purpose of first getting their corn, and then killing them and taking possession of their lands, a course of conduct prevalent in so many of the American colonies,[133] but they seemed to regard the situation as offering an unlimited opportunity for the cultivation of the Mennonite principles of peace and the extension of Pietistic mysticism.

Pastorius says the wild people came to barter fish, birds, deer, and skins of beaver, otter, and foxes, sometimes for drink, and sometimes for their own money, which consisted only of coral strung upon a string, and split mussel shells, some white and some a light brown. This kind of coral money they knew how to twist ingeniously together, and they used it instead of gold chains. The King had a crown of it. Twelve pieces of the brown and twenty-four of the white were worth a Frankfort albus.

They were a strong, active and agile people, dark in color, who at first went naked, except a cloth around the loins, but had begun to wear shirts. They had coal black hair. They cropped the hair on the head, and smeared on fat and let a long cue grow on the right side. The children at first were white enough, but their parents rubbed them with fat and exposed them to the hot sun, so as to make them brown. They are entirely candid, keep to their promises, and deceive and mislead nobody. They are hospitable and are true, and often live together quietly.

---

[133] "And tooke with them parte of ye corne and buried up ye rest. . . . Hear they gott seed to plant them corne ye next year, or else they might have starved for they had none nor any likelihood to get any." "Others fell to plaine stealing both night and day from ye Indians" "Thus it pleased God to vanquish their enemies." Bradford's History of Plymouth.

Their huts are made of bent saplings, which they cover with bark. They use neither table nor bench, and have no furniture, except a pot, in which they cook their meat. He says: I once saw four of them eating together in the greatest pleasure, and all they had was a pumpkin cooked in water, without butter or spice. The table and bench were the dear earth. Their spoons were mussel shells, with which they supped up the warm water. Their plates were the leaves from a nearby tree, which they carefully washed after the meal, and preserved for the future. I thought to myself these wild people have never heard the teachings of Jesus concerning temperance and moderation in their whole lives, and yet observe them much better than Christians. They are earnest and use few words, and express wonder when they hear the continuous and light talk of the Christians. Each has but one wife, and they sorely hate whoring, kissing and lying. They have no images, but worship one almighty and good God, who restrains the power of the devil. They believe in an undying soul, which after the course of their life is run, may expect, through the almighty power of God, a suitable reward. They carry on their religious services with singing, and make wonderful gestures and movements with their hands and feet, and when they remember the death of their relatives and friends, they begin to howl and weep very pitifully. In our meetings they are very still and attentive, so that I firmly believe at the day of judgment, they will sit above those of Tyre and Sydon and put to shame mere name and mouth Christians. As to their manner of living, the men do the hunting and fishing. The women bring up their children with the greatest care, and dissuade them from vice. They plant about their huts Indian corn and beans, but pay no attention to further cultivation of the ground, and to cattle, and wonder much that the Christians are so much troubled over eating and drinking, clothing and houses, as though they doubted that God would care for them. Their speech is very grave, and in pronunciation, like the Italian, but the words are entirely strange They dye their faces, both men and women use tobacco, and spend their time with a pipe in their mouths in continual idleness.

I was the other day at the table of our Governor William Penn, and met there a King of the savages. William Penn told him that I was a German, and came from lands the farthest away. A few days afterwards he came with his Queen to Germantown to see me. I treated them as well as I could with food and drink, whereupon he showed a great attachment to me and called me Carissimo, which is brother. Another time King Colkamicha came to our Governor and showed a great inclination to the Christian religion and to the light of the truth in his heart. He had an unexpected attack of disease, determined to stay with us, and as his illness increased, had his nephew, Jahkiolol, brought to him, and in the presence of many of our people and his, in these words, made him King:

"My brother's son, on this day I give thee my heart in thy bosom, and I will that thou lovest that which is good, and shunnest that which is evil and evil company; also when there is any discourse, do not speak first, but let all speak before thee, and take well in thought what each says, and when thou hast heard all, take that which is good, as I have done. Although I had intended to make Schoppii king in my stead, I have learned from my physician that Schoppii told him secretly since I was sick not to cure me or make me better, and when he was with me in Hulling Schead's house,[134] I saw he was more inclined to be drunk than to listen to my words. Therefore, I said to him he should not be king, and I have chosen thee, my brother's son, in my place. Dear brother's son, I will that thou doest right by the Indians, as well as the Christians, as I have done. I am very weak or I would say more," and soon after he died.

A very cunning savage came to me one day and offered to bring me a turkey hen for a certain price. But he brought me instead an eagle, and insisted upon it that it was a turkey. But I showed him that I knew very well the difference between the birds. Then he said to a Swede standing by that he had not supposed that a German so lately arrived would know these birds apart.

They are much better contented with and more careless about the future than are we Christians. They circumvent nobody in trade or conduct. They know nothing of the proud manner and modes of dress, to which we so adhere. They do not swear and curse. They are temperate in eating and drinking, and if one once in a while imbibes too much, the result is usually with the mouth-Christians, who, for their own profit, sell the cursed strong drink. During my ten years abode here I have never heard of their using force toward anybody, much less committing murder, which they could readily do in concealment in the great and thick woods.

In reply to a question of his brother Augustine Adam, as to how the Indian kings held their courts, Pastorius says: Their royal palaces are so poorly constructed that I can scarcely describe them. There is only a single room or chamber in a tree hut covered with bark, without

---

[134] Hollingshead

chimney, steps or privy. These kings go upon the hunt, shoot wild animals, and earn their living with their hands. They have neither knights nor lackeys, nor maids nor maidens of state, and what would they do with a master of the stables who have no horse and go on foot. No tutor is necessary, where only the bodily wants of wife and children are to be supplied. They live in a state of nature, *quae paucis contenta est.* Their bartering with us Christians consists in this, that they bring to market bear, elk and deer hides, beaver, marten, otter and other skins, also turkeys, game and fish, for which they get powder, lead, woolen covers and brandy, which last with all strong drinks, it is contrary to law to sell, since it is misused by them and leads to their injury. They use no bakeoven, but bake their bread in the ashes So many of these wild people have died since I came here that no more than a fourth remain of those who were here ten years ago.

They are forest people who instruct one another, and the old teach the young by traditions. They are usually long of stature, strong of body, broad of shoulders and head, proud and stern in appearance, with black hair. They smear their faces with bear's fat, and all kinds of dyes, have no beard, are free and open in spirit, use few words, but do it with emphasis They can neither read nor write, but are nevertheless intelligent, keen, earnest and unabashed. They purchase enough and pay readily, can endure hunger long, love drink, work but little, spend their lives in hunting and fishing, and no one of them can ride upon a horse In summer they are covered with nature's covering, but in winter wrap themselves in a great square cloth, and cover themselves in their huts with bear and deer skins. Instead of shoes they use doeskins and have no hats. The women are light-hearted, chatty and proud, and bind their hair in a knot. They have high breasts and black necks, as are also their ears and arms, about which they hang coral. As the men hunt in the woods, so the women plant beans and Turkish corn. They love their children very much. As soon as they are born, they are bound upon shingles, and when they cry, are stilled by moving them rapidly to and fro. While still quite young they are put into the warm streams to harden them. When they are young they must catch fish with hooks, and as they grow stronger, they are exercised in hunting. The maidens when they are grown cover their faces, and thus show that they are ready to marry. All their crimes they punish with fines, even the death blow. If a man strike a woman, he must pay double, because women bring forth children, which men cannot do. They say God dwells in the great sun land, to which, after death, they must hasten. Their religion consists of two kinds of service, singing and sacrifice. The first of the hunt they kill with such rapidity for sacrifices, that their bodies are thrown into perspiration. When they sing, they dance around in a circle, and in the midst two dance and start a sad song. All join in a wierd cry. Then they weep, snap with their teeth, soon crack their fingers, stamp with their feet, and continue this laughable play earnestly and zealously. When they are sick they eat no flesh, except that of a female. When they bury their dead, they throw whatever is valuable into the grave in order to give it to be understood that good will towards the departed has not perished. Their mourning, which continues for a whole year, is shown in their blackened faces. Their huts they build of trees and bushes, and no one of them is so unskilled in the art of building that he cannot construct one for himself and his family in three or four hours.

Their speech is shown in the following dialogue.

Eitanithap,	Welcome, good friend.
A eitha,	You, too, are welcome.
Tan Komi,	Whence come you?
Past ni anda qui,	Not from far.
Gecho lucendi,	What is your name?
	Franciscus.
o letto,	It is good.
Noha mattappi,	Be seated.
Gecho Ki Wengkinum,	What do you want?
Husko Lallaculla,	I am very hungry.
Langund ag boon,	Give me bread.
Lamess,	Fish.
Acothita,	Fruit.
Hittuck nipa,	There is a tree full.
Chingo Metschi,	When do you depart.
Alappo,	To-morrow.
Nacha Kuin,	Day after to-morrow.
Alla,	Mother.
Squaa,	Wife.
Hexis,	An old woman.
Menitto,	The Devil.
Murs,	A cow.
Kusch Kusch,	A pig.
Wicco,	A house.
Hockihockon,	Estate.
Pocksuckan,	Knife.

Pastorius closes this letter and his description of the Indians, by saying: "Whatever professor can hunt out the origin and roots of these Indian words will win my praise. Interim, my paper is small, the pen is a stump, the ink will not run, there is no more oil in the lamp, it is late at

Curieuse Nachricht
Von
PENSYLVANIA
in
Norden=America
Welche/
Auf Begehren guter Freunde/
Uber vorgelegte 103. Fra=
gen/ bey seiner Abreiß aus Teutsch=
land nach obigem Lande Anno 1700.
ertheilet/ und nun Anno 1702 in den Druck
gegeben worden.
Von
Daniel Falknern/ Professore,
Burgern und Pilgrim allda.

Franckfurt und Leipzig/
Zu finden bey Andreas Otto/ Buchhändlern.
Im Jahr Christi 1702.

CONTINUATIO
Der
Beschreibung der Landschafft
PENSYLVANIÆ
An denen End-Gräntzen
AMERICÆ.
Uber vorige des Herrn Pastorii
Relationes.
In sich haltend:
Die Situation, und Fruchtbarkeit des
Erdbodens. Die Schiffreiche und andere
Flüsse. Die Anzahl derer bißhero gebauten Städte.
Die seltsame Creaturen an Thieren / Vögeln und Fischen.
Die Mineralien und Edelgesteine Deren eingebohrnen wilden
Völcker Sprachen / Religion und Gebräuche. Und
die ersten Christlichen Pflantzer und Anbauer
dieses Landes.
Beschrieben von
GABRIEL THOMAS
15. Jährigen Inwohner dieses
Landes.
Welchem Tractätlein noch beygefüget sind:
Des Hn. DANIEL FALCKNERS
Burgers und Pilgrims in Pensylvania 193.
Beantwortungen uff vorgelegte Fragen von
guten Freunden.

Franckfurt und Leipzig /
Zu finden bey Andreas Otto / Buchhändlern.

night, my eyes are full of sleep. Take care of yourself. I close."

Daniel Falckner, whose book, in 1702, is in great part made up of a description of the Indians and their habits, writes: Their number, since they have been attacked by the diseases brought by the Europeans into the country, have been very much decreased, so that where one hundred were seen thirty years ago there is now scarcely one. Others must bend to their humor and follow their inclinations, since they stand fast in their own way, and they do, speak and appear as they choose. The simple plan of going along with them is the best rule. When they are drunk it is better to let them alone.

Their virtue of all virtues is to strive persistently for those things upon which they have determined. They are naturally simple in their wants, and therefore when they take trouble, they do not think of making a profit or benefit for themselves, but it gives them a satisfaction, since it can be seen that they can do it, although the great love for strong drink and the desire for better clothing give them the selfish wish for gain. They are generally sociable, generous, earnest and show wrath, especially towards their own people. The chief of their occupations is hunting and fishing, and their women plant a little Indian corn, beans, pumpkins, melons, etc. They prepare skins and make stockings and liga, that is shoes, and also wooden platters and spoons out of the knots that grow on trees. The women cut wood, cook, wait upon the children, make purses of wild hemp, cards, tapestry of dyed straw, baskets of dyed bark, and covers twisted with feathers. Among the children there is seldom one crippled or lamed. It is remarkable that there is so little unchastity among them, since they go nearly naked and have every opportunity. Among us Europeans we have the punishment of the law and the earnest command of God, and yet the men cannot be made and kept as pure as these are without any law. The marriage ceremony is in this wise · The man gives the woman a deer foot, which imports that he will secure her meat. The woman gives the man a handful of corn, which imports that she will look after the bread and cooking. A man is permitted to have two wives if he undertakes to support them, but it is a reproach to them

It is easy to learn their language, since they have no more words than things. Their verbs and nouns have neither time nor number. The others are mere proper names and appellations. In the want of conjunctions they have taken some from the Swedes and others, to wit, Ok and Ni.

They cannot say R. They talk more with their gestures and accent than with words; therefore those who speak with them, and that of which he speaks, must be present. Thus they say Lanconti, when they want to give something to somebody, and also when they have already given something They cannot keep many things in their minds, and cultivate more the sense of oblivion than of science and memory, and therefore have no monuments of antiquity. But when they want something preserved they call their young people together and impress it upon them, and when they think it worth the trouble they command these that they in turn in their old age tell it and impress it upon the young. In intercourse with them it is important to follow their humor and mingle in their earnestness and laughter, since they are inclined to anger and easily think they are insulted. To secure and keep their confidence we let them come to our houses, and do not let them go without eating and drinking, and when they come in the evening we give them permission to lie by the fire, and so when we go to them they are more kindly and hospitable.

Good and evil are with them nature and custom, and have no certain boundaries. In murder, robbery and adultery, which are capital, the king speaks the sentence. The reward of the good consists in honor and in a present measured by their ability. Punishment is indicated by the words of the king, "Beat him dead," which the accused accepts, since they do not much regard life.

Each king rules over a certain territory, and a king must be the best hunter and the bravest man, so as to be able to give the best counsel. The king's word is absolute, but he is himself the first to obey the command. His service does not differ from the rest, and he has no servants. If he has enemies his retainers are at his command, and remain in their huts by him. He confers with the boldest of his people when anything of importance is to be considered. When there is room they sit around the king's fire. The property of the retainers is at his disposal, but it does him no good, and the king's property is at the disposal of the retainers. Sometimes the retainers bring some of their money, which they call *wampon*, and is black and white, like a kind of enamel or glass pattern, or cut straw, which money is of value to the Europeans also, and Lagio is given for it. But they do not tell how they make it. When they go far upon a hunt, or to war, it is permitted to the women to go along, but the king orders some of the men to protect those who remain at home. Small crimes they punish with a fine. When a man dies in debt the relatives pay it, so that they be not disgraced. Still they ask indulgence.

The king must be the wisest and most skillful, strong and the best hunter, therefore rule is not inheritable. He and his wife have somewhat more of ornament than the others, but it only appears in this, that they string their kind of money together like pearls, according to the shading, and fasten them upon the head like a crown, or upon the breast, or in the top knot.

Concerning their diseases and cures Falckner says: When they have feverish attacks, or do not feel well, they cook the black hulls of nuts in water and drink the extract in great quantities, and they bind themselves about the body and head with bands of coiled hemp. They sweat in the following manner: They make a low hut, just high enough to sit in and cover it to the ground with the bark of trees and skins. Then they heat some stones outside, and carrying them into the kennel, sit upon them and sweat so violently as to wet the earth. A European could not possibly stand it. When they have sweated sufficiently they run out and jump into the cold water. Then they are cured.

They have a root which keeps away the snakes. They bind it upon the bone, and run into the woods and are uninjured by the snakes. If they have not this root, and are bitten, they cut the bite out of the flesh.

To cure swellings, fluxes or sprains of the limbs they let them bleed, and cut with a sharp flint through the skin without touching a vein, which they know well how to avoid, and hold the member by the fire, and scrape off with a piece of wood the blood that prevents the flow till it stops bleeding. Then they wash the wound with water and lay on it a certain root, which they rub between two stones, and some little green leaves. In a single night the wound heals. When they get splinters in their feet they cut them clean out with a knife and smear the wound with snake fat; then it heals.

For inner disorders they eat the small entrails of young beasts with fat.

They are seldom at peace. The fighting happens first in single parties, where man fights with man, or two or three together with bows, axes, reeds and flints, and it generally occurs upon their hunts. They take prisoners and sell them. When their enemies collect and form a battle array they arrange themselves in a circle, so that on all sides their faces are turned to the foe, and when one is shot dead or wounded they draw him inside the circle and make it smaller. When they take prisoners they sell two or three of the fattest to be broiled and eaten. All the southern Indians believe that a man cannot more avenge himself upon an enemy than by eating his flesh. They regard the flesh of the natives as better than game, for the reason that this flesh is not salted, but entirely sweet, but on the other hand that of the English and French is salty and disagreeable. They use all kinds of stratagems to overcome their enemies, whether single or in parties; they examine the bushes and grass, from which they can tell with certainty whether a man, women or child, European or savage, has passed. They go in the night upon the high mountains and look around where fires are made in the woods. Then they go to the other side of the fire, creep up and shoot or kill their foes, while they are asleep. Against parties they make a plan to drive them into a corner, so that they may be taken prisoners.

Their dwelling is in no settled place, and their housekeeping is variable. The house is sometimes made in an old fallen tree, but when complete it stands clear and is only the height of a man. In the middle it is open, so that the smoke of the fire, which is in the center, may escape. The hut is covered with the bark of trees, and in the same way is protected around Inside they put straw or long grass. Some make tapestry of dyed straw and ornament the house, which, in their speech, is called a Wickwam. If they are caught away from home in the rain they take a cover they have with them and spread it out like a roof and get under it, or they make a great fire and throw foul wood upon it to make much smoke, and lie on that side of it toward which the wind drives the smoke, so that the smoke scatters the rain, and that which falls is by the smoke and heat made warm. In the huts they throw quantities of grass or deer skins, and at night cover themselves with them, or with bear skins, or with a woolen cover, or with a cover of turkey feathers, very skillfully worked together, and then they put the smallest child in front of them and one at the back.

Their furniture consists of a piece of a hewed tree, or one which stands with its root in the ground, in the midst of which they burn a hole like a deep dish or mortar, in which they pound their Indian corn. They make bread of this corn, which they call Ponn, and they make soup of it, which they call Sapan. They sprinkle the corn with hot water, and beat it to get the peel off, and pound it small, sift the smallest through a straw basket, and make loaves like great goat's cheeses. They stick these in the hot ashes, and scrape the coals over them, and so bake them. When it is ready they wash the bread off with water. Sometimes they mix red or other colored beans under the bread, which then looks as though raisins were baked in it.[135] They have also a pot in which they cook the deer's

---

[135] I know of no other such graphic description of the Indian women making their pone.

meat, but this they do not wash, and think the strength would thus be taken out. Nor do they skim it, but what runs over they let go. They like the meat bloody and regard it as healthy. Then they cook beans or pounded corn in the meat broth. They cook also tortoises (terrapin?) without a pot under the coals in their own shells. They do not take much time with birds when they are small, but burn the feathers off in the fire. But the feathers of turkeys they use to work into covers. They eat also foxes, fat dogs, civet cats, beavers, squirrels and hawks. For roasting they have nothing except a stake, which they make sharp at both ends. They stick one end in the ground; upon the other end they stick the meat cut thin and at times turn it.

The rest of their furniture is a calibash, or pumpkin, cleaned out to hold drink, wooden spoons which they make in their manner, and in case of need they use mussel or oyster shells. Their wooden dishes are made of the knots of trees and of hard pumpkin rind. Many of them have two or three sacks made of the wild hemp, shaded by dyes, brown, red and white, skillfully put together. They make smaller sacks of the straw of the Indian corn, in which they carry their furniture and a little hatchet, which they call Domehicken. They now get these from the Europeans. Formerly they used hard stones instead. Of this stone they also made their axes. There is a brown stone like a blood stone (jasper?) which they by many blows make sharp and pointed. Their barns they make in the earth, dig a hole the depth of a man, like a spring, line it with long grass, and there put their Indian corn, pumpkins and other things. Their dogs and pigs they accustom to come, not upon seeing them, but by following their voices. At nights they water their swine, and when they are fat, sell them to the Europeans for rum, since they do not much esteem pork.

The women do not help each other at the births of their children, but they go off entirely alone to some previously selected place. Nevertheless there is never seen among them an ill formed or crippled child. The children are soon bound upon a little board, upon which they fasten a skin and cover it with another, so that they can better be carried upon the back, and be held when they suck.

They fish with hooks. They make stone dams and enclose the fish. They bind a long row of twigs with the leaves together and draw it through the water, by which means the fish are driven into a corner, and they then capture them with the hands. They also have boats of hollowed-out trees, with the crevices stopped with moss, in which they chase the sturgeon. They capture wild beasts by their rapid and continuous running, and by shooting them. Some beasts they hunt by night by the clear moon. The wild cats they shoot with arrows. The amphibia, such as rats, martens, etc., they take by night in traps like our marten traps.

They have, by the presence and mode of life of the Europeans, learned to live in a disorderly manner in eating, drinking, cursing, lying and cheating. One has shown the other the way. The Europeans have brought them brandy, beer, and other materials, and now the savages seek them eagerly, and although it is forbidden by law, they find means to secure them to their injury.

They make a hole or grave, in which they bury the dead, to whom they give something to eat, and besides what he especially cared for in life; also his bow and arrows or a flint, so that he can hunt upon the way, since they believe he now journeys toward the warm or cold country, according as he has lived a good or evil life. The grave is covered with wood and grass, and then earth is heaped upon it. The wife and children often go there and lament. They have a certain length of time, in which to think of the dead. During this time they disturb the earth on the grave, so that no grass can grow on it. When the time is over, no man is permitted to call the name of the dead, since he is now forgotten.

They do not observe the seventh day. I once asked one of them why he worked upon Sunday. He gave me for answer that he must eat upon Sunday as upon other days, and therefore he must hunt, but that if he had had something on hand, then he would keep Sunday.

Kelpius tells of a visit that Penn made to the Indians in 1701, at Kintika, and that he endeavored to inculcate in them a belief in the God who rules the Heavens and the earth. Kelpius, who, notwithstanding the assistance of Furly, was none too fond of the Quakers, reported that the Indians listened gravely, and replied: "You ask us to believe in the great creator and ruler of Heaven and earth, and yet you yourself do not believe nor trust Him, for you have taken the land unto yourself, which we and our friends occupied in common. You scheme night and day how you may preserve it, so that none can take it from you. Yea, you even scheme beyond your life, and parcel it out between your children, this manor for one child, that manor for another. We believe in God, the creator, and ruler of Heaven and earth. He maintains the sun. He maintained our fathers for so many many moons. He maintains us and we believe and are sure that He will also protect our children, as well as ourselves. And so long as we have this faith, we trust in Him, and never bequeath a foot of ground."

This friendly intercourse with the natives, based upon the principles of mutual advantage and assistance, and accompanied by an appreciation and recognition of their meritorious characteristics, contrasts forcibly with the burning of the women and children of the Pequods and other similar events, which have stained our American annals.[128]

[128] When Uncas, the Mohican, captured Miantonomo, the Narragansett, the Commissioners of Plymouth advised the savage to kill his enemy and he "accordingly executed him in a very faire manner." Bradford's History of Plymouth, p. 507.

A Germantown Colonial Doorway.

CHAPTER XII.

GERMANTOWN AS A BOROUGH, AND ITS BOOK OF LAWS.

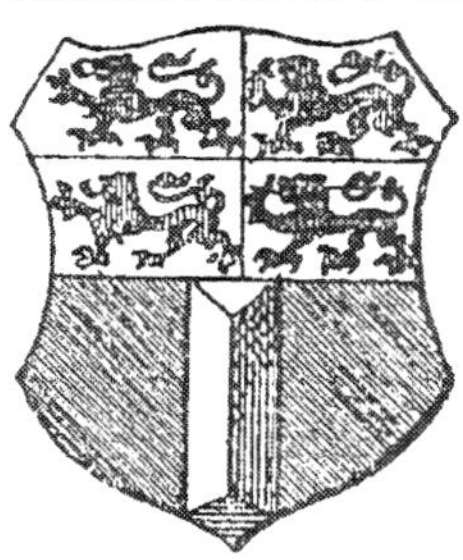

Arms of Rotterdam.

AFTER the town had become populous enough to warrant its having control of its own affairs, a charter of incorporation, dated May 31, 1691, was issued to Francis Daniel Pastorius, bailiff; Jacob Telner, Dirck op den Graeff, Hermann op den Graeff, and Thones Kunders, burgesses; Abraham op den Graeff, Jacob Isaacs Van Bebber, Johannes Kassel, Heifert Papen, Hermann Bon and Dirck Van Kolk, committeemen, with power to hold a court and a market, to admit citizens, to impose fines, and to make ordinances. The bailiff and first two burgesses were constituted justices of the peace.[136] The primitive Solons and Lycurguses of Germantown did not want their laws to go unheeded. They were not keen enough to invent that convenient maxim *Ignorantia legis neminem excusat*. It was, therefore, ordered that "On the 19th

[136] Penna. Archives, Vol. I., p. 111.

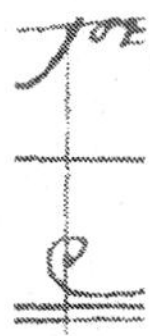

of 1st mo. in each year the people shall be called together, and the laws and ordinances read aloud to them."[137] Oh ye modern legislators! think how few must have been the statutes, and how plain the language in which they were written, in that happy community.

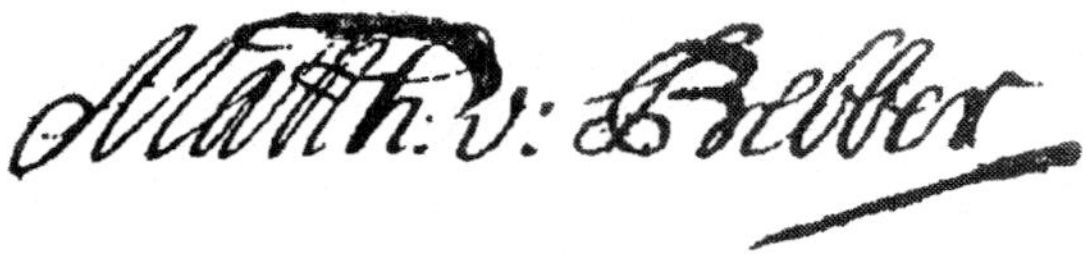

As we have seen, the greater number of the first Crefeld emigrants were weavers. This industry increased so that Frame described Germantown as a place—

"Where lives High *German* people and *Low Dutch*
Whose trade in weaving linnen cloth is much;
There grows the Flax as also you may know
That from the same they do divide the tow;"

and Thomas says they made "very fine German Linen such as no person of Quality need be ashamed to wear." When, therefore, Pastorius was called upon to devise a town seal, he selected a clover on one of whose leaves was a vine, on another a stalk of flax, and on the third a weaver's spool, with the motto, "Vinum, Linum, et Textrinum." This seal happily suggests the relations of the town with the far past, and it is a curious instance of the permanence of causes that these simple people, after the lapse of six centuries, and after being transplanted to a distance of thousands of miles, should still be pursuing the occupation of the Waldenses of Flanders. The corporation was maintained until January 11, 1707, but always with considerable difficulty in getting the offices filled. Says Löher, "They would do nothing but work

---

[137] Raths Buch.

and pray, and their mild consciences made them opposed to the swearing of oaths and courts, and would not suffer them to use harsh weapons against thieves and trespassers." Through conscientious scruples Arent Klincken declined to be burgess in 1695, Heivert Papen in 1701, Cornelis Siverts in 1702, and Paul Engle in 1703; Jan Lensen to be a committeeman in 1701, Arnold Kuster and Daniel Geissler in 1702; Matteus Millan to be constable in 1703; and in 1695 Albertus Brandt was fined for a failure to act as juryman, "having no other escape but that in court in Phila. he was wronged upon the account of a jury." New-comers were required to pay for the right of citizenship, and the date of the conferment of this right doubtless approximates that of the arrival.[138]

The records of the Court occasionally gave particulars which aid us in getting a view of the manner of life and habit of thought of the residents Upon one occasion the Court was adjourned "by reason of the absence of some for religious meeting over Schuylkill." Intended marriages, and notices of things lost and found, were posted up in conspicuous places in the town. Both Maria Margaret Zimmermann, the widow of the astronomer, and Peter Cornelius Plockhoy were given the burgher right "gratis." Johannes Pettinger, on the 19th day of the 11th month, 1694, "did push, and evilly handle" Johannes Kuster, for which he was properly fined two shillings.

On the 7th day of the 3d month, 1695, Peter Keurlis was attested: "why he did not come when the Justice sent for him. He answered: He had much work to do.

"Whereupon he further was attested. Why he refused to lodge travellers? Answer: He only intended to sell drink, but not to keep an ordinary.

"Then he was attested: Why he did sell barley malt beer

[138] Raths Buch and Court Record

4d a quart against the law of this province? Answer: He did not know such a law. Lastly, he was asked why he would not obey the law of Germantown corporation, which forbids to sell more than a gill of rum or a quart of beer every half a day to each individual. Answer: They being able to bear more he could or would not obey that law." This recalcitrance led to a fine of five pounds. Keeping the fences in order and the hogs from running at large caused much trouble. John Silans confessed that on Sep. 6, 1695, "he did beat, wound and evilly entreat" John Pettinger, who apparently had a faculty for getting into scrapes, and was fined ten shillings. A jury found on 24th of 4th month, 1701, "we the jury find that through carelessness the cart and the lime killed the man. The wheel wounded the back of his head and it killed him."

A defendant was brought into the court concerning certain fees and charges and the accounts were produced before him. He said: "The paper was cut off and blotted and that this was done since he delivered it to the Court and that who could trust such a Court?" This was too much, and the Court adjourned for four weeks.

Reynier Peters was fined twenty shillings for calling the Sheriff "a rascal and a lyar" on the open street. George Muller was fined for laying a wager "to smoke above one hundred pipes in one day." Owners of lands were required to put stakes with their names on them along the boundaries. Nov. 28, 1704, Daniel Falckner came into Court and behaved very ill "like one that was last night drunk and not yet having recovered his witts."

No serious crime and no attempt at oppression occurred during the fifteen years covered by the record.[139]

---

[139] Collections of the Historical Soc. of Pa., Vol I, p 245 During the first eighteen years at Plymouth four men were hanged for murder and one escaped. Bradford's History of Plymouth, p 432

The corporation laws, prepared by Pastorius and carefully written by him and others in a volume in German and Dutch script, were supposed to have been utterly lost. The volume met with strange vicissitudes and was a few years ago discovered by accident in the possession of a citizen of one of the states on the Pacific slope. Up to the present time these laws have remained unknown and, constituting as they do the earliest body of municipal legislation extant in Pennsylvania and perhaps in the country, their historical importance cannot be overestimated. These laws and ordinances are as follows:

Leges Pennsilvaniae

h. e.

The Great Law of the Province of Pennsilvania.

Gal. 5 : 14 All the Law is fulfilled in one word in this: "Thou shallt love thy neighbour as thyself. Add Rom. 13 : 3. Matth. 7 : 12

All things whatsoever ye would that men should do to you, do ye even so to them, for this is the law and the Prophets. Add, Caps 22 x 35 etc.

Salus Populi Suprema Lex est.

Francis Daniel Pastorius his book.

1690.

1. Copy of the Germantown Charter.
2. Laws, Ordinances and Statutes of the Community of Germantown, made and published from time to time in meetings of the General Court of that place.
3. The laws of the Province of Pennsilvania antecedent to the said Charter and By Laws.

The law is good if a man use it Lawfully. 1 Tim. 1 : 8.

Summum Jus, Summa Injuria. Extreme right is extreme wrong. Between just laws and righteous men no antipathy. Good laws bind evil people.

The greatest bait to offend is the hope of impunity.

Copy of the Charter.

I William Penn, Proprietor of the Province of Pennsilvania in America under the Imperial Crowne of great Britaine by vertue of Letters Patent, under the great Seale of England doe grant unto Francis Daniel Pastorius Civilian, Jacob Tellner, merchant, Dirk Isaacs Opte Graef Linnenmaker, Herman Isaacs opte Graef, Tennis Coenderts, Abraham Isaacs opte Graef, Jacob Isaacs, Johannes Cassels, Heyvart Papen, Herman Bon, Dirck van Kolck, all of Germantown, yeomen, that they shall bee one Body Politique and Corporate in deed and in name, by the name of the Bailiffe, Burgesses and Comonalty of Germantown in the County of Philadelphia, in the Province of Pennsilvania, and them by that Name one Body Politique and Corporate in deed and in name for ever I doe for mee, my heirs and Successors create, make and declaire by these presents. And that they and their Successors by the name of the Bailiffe, Burgesses and Comonalty of Germantown bee and at all times hereafter shall bee persons able and capable in Law with a joynd Stocke to trade, and with the same or any part thereoff to have, take, purchase, possesse and enjoy mannors, messuages, lands, tenements, and Rents of the yearly value of fifteen hundred pounds p. Ann. liberties, Priviledges, jurisdictions, franchises and hereditaments of what kinde, Nature or Qualitie to them and their Successors, and assigns; and also to give, grant, demise, aliene, assigne and dispose of the same. And that they and their Successors, by the name of the Bailiffe, Burgesses and Comonalty of Germantown shall and may bee persons able and capable in Law to plead and bee impleaded, answer and bee answered, defend and bee defended in whatsoever Courts and places, and before whatsoever Judges and Justices, Officers and Ministers of mee, my heirs and Successors in all and Singular Pleas, actions, Suits, Causes, Quarrels and demands whatsoever, and of what kinde, Nature or Sort soever. And that it shall and may bee lawfull to and for the said Corporation and their Successors to have and use a Common Seale for any Business of or concerning the said Corporation and the same from time to time at their will to change or alter. And for the better government of the said Corporation I doe further grant to the said Corporation that there shall bee from henceforth one of the said Corporation to bee elected and to bee Bailiffe of the said Corporation, and four other of the said Corporation to bee elected and to bee chosen Burgesses of the said Corporation, and that there shall bee from henceforth six persons members of the said Corpor^{n} elected and bee Committeemen of the said Corporation, which said Bailiffe, Burgesses and Committeemen shall bee called the Generall Court of the Corporation of Germantown. And that they or any three or more of them, whereof the Bailiffe with two, or in his absence any three of the Burgesses, to bee always Some, shall bee and are hereby authorized, according to such rules, orders and directions as shall from time to time bee made and given unto them by the Generall Court of the said Corporation (and for want of such rules orders and directions (when desired) as they themselves shall thinke meete) shall manege, govern and direct all the affaires and business of the said Corporation and all their Servants and Ministers whatsoever and generally to act and doe in all other matters and things whatsoever so as they shall judge necessary and expedient for the well governing and Government of the said Corporation, and the Improvement of their Lands, tenements and other estate, joynt Stock and trade; and to doe enjoy, performe and execute all the powers, authorities, priviledges, acts and things in like manner to all Intents and purposes as if the same ware done at and by a Generall Court of the said Corporation.

And I doe by these presents assigne, nominate, declare and make the said Francis Daniell Pastorius of Germantown Civilian to bee the first and present Bailiffe, and the aforesaid Jacob Tellner, Dirck Isaacs opte Graef Herman Isaacs opte Graef and Tennis Coenderts to bee the first present Burgesses, and the aforesaid Abraham Isaacs opte Graef, Jacob Isaacs, Johannes Cassels, Heyvart Papen, Herman Bon and Dirck van Kolck the first and present Committeemen of the said Corporation; the said Bailiffe & Burgesses & Committeemen to continue in their respective offices and places untill the first day of December next, ensuing the date hereof, and from thence untill there bee a new choyse of other Persons duely to succeed them, according as it is hereinafter directed; unless they or any of them shall happen to dye or bee removed by order to bee made by a Generall Court of the said Corporation before the expiration of that time; and in case any of them shall happen to dye or bee removed before the said first day of December, it shall and may bee lawfull to and for the persons assembled at any Generall Court of the said Corporation whereoff the Bailiffe if present with two, or in his absence three of the Burgesses to bee Some to make choyse of any other fit person beeing a member of the said Corporation in the place of such person so deceased or removed, which person so to bee chosen shall continue in the said Place and office during the Residue of the said time. And I doe further for mee, my heirs and Successors give and grant to the said Bailiffe, Burgesses and Committeemen of Germantown and their Successors, that it shall and may bee lawfull to and for the said Bailiffe, Burgesses and Committeemen at and upon the said first day of December in every year successively for ever hereafter (unless the said first day of December happen to fall on the first day of the weeke, and then at and upon the next day following)—to assemble and meet together in some convenient place to bee appointed by the Bailiffe, or in his absence by any three of the Burgesses of the said Corporation for the time being, which assembly and meeting of the said Corporation at such time and place as aforesaid shall bee and shall bee called a Generall Court of the Corporation of Germantown, and that they being so assembled, it shall and may bee lawfull to and for the major part of them which shall bee then present, not being less than seaven in number, whereof the Bailiffe and two of the Burgesses, or in absence of the Bailiffe three of the Burgesses for the being to bee some, to elect and nominate one Bailiffe, four Burgesses and Six Committeemen for the purposes aforesaid, and also such other officers as they shall think necessary for the more due Government of the said Corporation out of the members of the said Corporation, which are to continue in their respective offices and places for the ensuing year, unless within that time they shall happen to dye or bee removed for some reasonable Cause as aforesaid, and upon the death or Removall of the Bailiffe, any Burgesse, or any of the six Committeemen, or any other officer at any time within the year, and before the said first day of December, it shall and may bee lawfull to and for the generality of them the said Bailiffe, Burgesses and Committeemen for the time being, or the major part of them present at any Generall Court of the same Corporation to bee for that purpose assembled, whereof the Bailiffe and two of the Burgesses, or in the absence of the Bailiffe three of the Burgesses for the time being, to bee always some, to elect and nominate a Bailiffe, Burgess or Burgesses, Committeeman or Committeemen as there shall bee occasion in the place and room of such person or persons respectively as shall so happen to dye or bee removed.

And likewise that it shall and may bee lawfull to and for the Bailiffe and two of the Burgesses, or in the absence of the Bailiffe three of the Burgesses of the said Corporation, for the time being from time to time so often as they shall find cause, to sumon a generall Court of the said Corporation of Germantown, and that no assembly or meeting of the said Corporation shall bee deemed and accounted a generall Court of the said Corporation unless the Bailiffe and two of the Burgesses, or in absence of the Bailiffe, three of the Burgesses and four of the Committeemen at least bee present.

And I doe for mee my heirs and Successors give and grant unto the said Corporation of Germantown and their Successors full and free liberty, power and authority from time to time at any of their generall Courts to admitt such and so many persons into their Corporation and Society, and to increase, contract or divide their joynt Stoke, or any part thereof, when so often and in such proportions and manner as they or the greatest part of them then present (whereof the Bailiffe and two of the Burgesses or in his absence three of the Burgesses for the time being to bee always some) shall think fitt. And also that the said Bailiffe, Burgesses and Committeemen for the time being from time to time at their said generall Courts shall have power to make, and they may make, ordaine, constitute and establish such and so many good and reasonable Laws, Ordinances and Constitutions as to the greatest part of them at such generall Court and Courts assembled, whereof the

Bailiffe and two of the Burgesses, or in absence of the Bailiffe three of the Burgesses for the time being, to bee allways some, shall seem necessary and convenient for the good Government of the said Corporation and their affairs; and the same Laws, Orders Ordinances and Constitutions so made to bee put in use and execution accordingly, and at their pleasur to revoke, alter and make anew, as Occasion shall require. And also to impose and set such mulcts and amerciaments upon the breakers of such Laws and Ordinances as to them or the greater part of them so assembled (whereof the Bailiffe and two of the Burgesses, or in absence of the Bailiffe three of the Burgesses to bee always some) in their discretions shall bee thought reasonable; which said Laws and Ordinances shall bee put in execution by such officers of the said Corporation, for the time being, as shall bee by the said Court appointed for that purpose, or in default of such appointment by the Bailiffe and two of the Burgesses, or in absence of the Bailiffe by three of the Burgesses for the time beeing to bee chosen; and the said mulcts and amerciaments so imposed and set upon the breakers of the same Laws and Ordinances as aforesaid shall from time to time bee levied and receaved by such the officers and servants of the said Corporation (in that behalf to bee appointed in manner as aforesaid) to and for the use of the said Corporation and their Successors by distress or otherwise in such manner as the said generall Court shall direct and appoint not contrary to Law, without the Impediment of mee, my heirs and successors, or of any the officers and ministers of mee, my heirs and Successors, and without any account to bee made, rendred or given to mee, my heirs and Successors for the same or any part thereof; or else that the said mulcts and amerciaments or any part thereof may upon the offenders submission or Conformity bee remitted, pardoned or released by the said generall Court of the said Corporation at their will and pleasur. And that the Bailiffe and two eldest Burgesses for the time being shall bee Justices of the Peace, and shall have full power and authority to act as Justices of the Peace within the said Corporation and to doe all act and acts, thing and things whatsoever, which any other Justice or Justices of the Peace can or may doe within my said Province. And further, I doe hereby grant to the said Bailiffe, Burgesses and Comonalty of Germantown, that they and their Successors shall and may have, hold and keep before the Bailiffe and three of the eldest Burgesses of the said Corporation and the Recorder for the time being of the said Corporation one Court of Record to bee held every six weeks in the year yearly, for such time as they shall think fitt for the hearing or determining of all Civil causes, matters and things whatsoever (arising or happening betwixt the Inhabitants of the said Corporation) according to the Laws of the said Province and of the Kingdome of England, reserving the liberty of Appeall according to the same. And also to have, hold and keep one publick market every sixth day in the week in such convenient place and manner as the Provinciall Charter doeth direct. And further to doe and act any other matter or thing whatsoever for the good government of the said Corporation and the members thereof, and for the maneging and ordering of the estate, Stoke and affairs of the said Corporation as they shall at any time or times thinke or judge expedient or necessary, and as any other Corporation within my said Province shall may or can doe by Law not being inconsistent to the Laws of England or of my said Province. Hereby giving and granting that this my present Charter

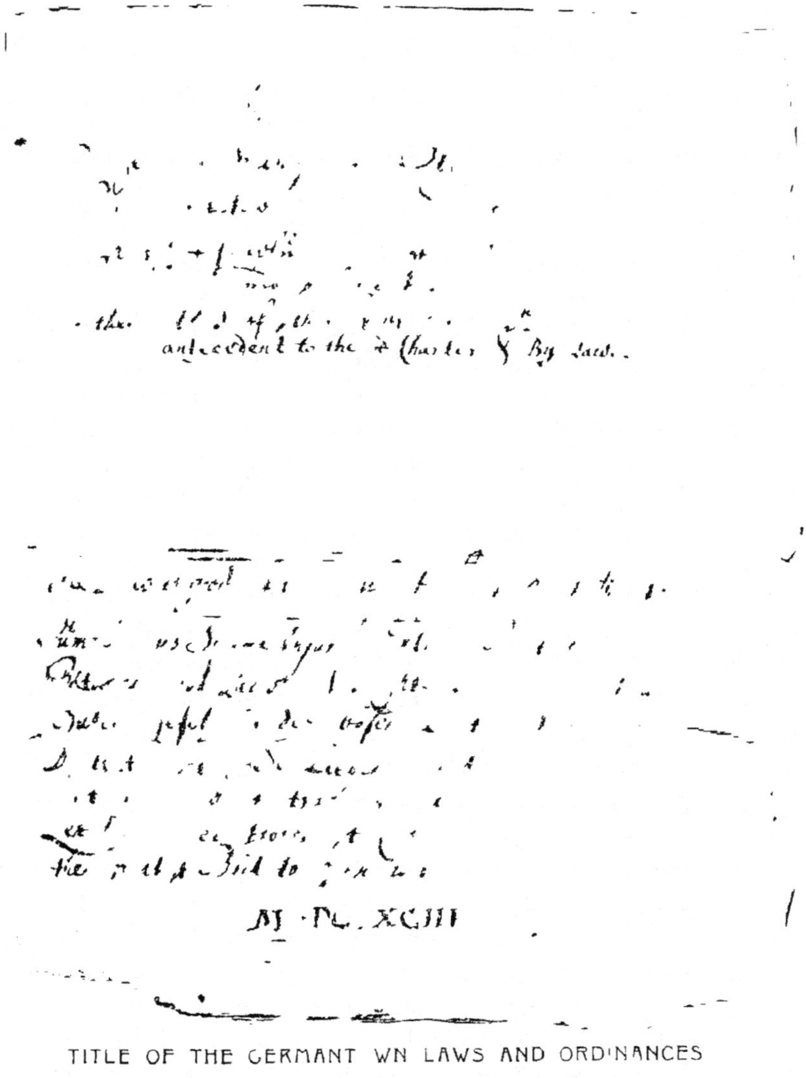
antecedent to the Charter & By Laws.

M · DC · XCIII

TITLE OF THE GERMANTOWN LAWS AND ORDINANCES
IN THE HAND OF FRANCIS DANIEL PASTORIUS

or Grant shall in all Courts of Law and Equity bee construed and taken most favorably and beneficially for the Grantees and the said Corporation. Given under my hand and the lesser Seale of the said Province at London this twelfth day of the month called August in the year of our Lord 1689.

WM. PENN.

Upon the back of the charter Wm. Penn wrote with his own hand 12th of 6 mo. Aug. 89. "Lett this pass the great Seale

"WM. PENN.

"To Tho. Loyd keeper thereof in Pennsilvania."

Past under the great Seale of the Province of Pennsilvania on the thirtieth day of the third month 1691.

Recorded the thirtieth day of the third month 1691.

per Da. Lloyd, Deputy.[140]

LAWS, ORDINANCES AND STATUTES OF THE COMMUNITY AT GERMANTOWN, MADE AND RATIFIED FROM TIME TO TIME IN THE GENERAL COURT AT THAT PLACE.

It is evident, as well from the valuable testimony of Holy Scripture, as from the firm foundation of reason, and daily experience, that the conditions, established by God above, bring to the evil doer punishment and terror, not less praise and reward to the pious.

Moreover it is everywhere recognized that magistrates without eternal laws and reasonable civil ordinances (as long as human weakness and frailty last) often do not clearly see their duty in the punishment of crime, and the

[140] The Charter is here printed as to language, orthography and punctuation as written by Pastorius.

reward of good works, but may easily become tyrannical and arbitrary. Accordingly now William Penn, Proprietor and Governor of Pennsilvania, with power held from the King in England, to the Bailiffe and Burgesses of the community at Germantown, by means of a special charter or grant of franchise of the date 6 mo. 12th 1689 among other things, has graciously permitted and decreed that they may from time to time in their General Court make and establish as many good and reasonable laws, ordinances and statutes as for the salutary government of this community and its affairs may be necessary and advantageous, and may accordingly bring such into effect and perfect them, and also may, when changing circumstances make it necessary, alter their laws, or withdraw them, and establish new ones.

Wherefore, we, the present first Bailiff and Burgesses of the place, do hereby in friendly manner inform each and every citizen, inhabitant and tenant under Germantown jurisdiction that, we, according to the demand of our State, still young, and established only a few years ago, and of its well being, by virtue of the powers given to us in the above mentioned charter, and by the authority of the King, and in the name of William Penn, have in several General Courts (held the 6th, 15th, and 22nd of the 6th month) drawn up the following laws and ordinances, and also unanimously determined that they shall be published and made known to the community by public reading, in order that all may live manfully according to them from this time forth and no one may plead ignorance as an excuse for his disobedience.

And as we now earnestly wish and desire that, towards those who henceforth shall serve in the Magistrate's office here, all citizens and subjects under our jurisdiction may, with just zeal and conscientious obedience, submit to and support such laws and statutes, so long as they are not changed or withdrawn; so we must also warn earnestly, ex officio, the offenders and obstinate delinquents, and also address them separately in the words of the Holy Apostle: "If thou doest that which is evil, be afraid, for he (the ruler) beareth not the sword in vain, for he is the minister of God, a revenger to execute wrath upon him that doeth evil."

Most especially and before all else all the citizens inhabitants and under tenants under Germantown jurisdiction or those who are settled and live here, recognizing with thankful hearts the special providence of the Almighty, as well as the gracious kindness of our King and Governor, (by virtue of which every one may without the least constraint or oppression, serve God unrestrainedly according to the best of his knowledge and conscience, and may worship him more freely than is possible in most other lands at this time) shall keep themselves from all sin and evil, by which the great God of Heaven and earth is displeased and angered, such as these: cursing and swearing by his Holy name, blasphemy against his divine majesty, unchaste babbling talk, which is not befitting for Christians, the dice, cards and other plays, lying, false witness, slander, libelling, insurrection, fighting, duelling, murder, incendiarism, reviling, scolding, especially against parents, magistrates, masters and women, stealing, robbery, fornication, adultery, blood or Sodomitical crime, drunkenness, forgery of a manuscript, or seal, debasement of coin, or false representation of boundary lines, etc., against which and other crimes special provision has already been made in the laws of this land by fines and corporal punishment; whence as well in this case as in regard to the other ordinances contained therein, each and every one is to be informed. And by no means shall any one be pardoned by the excuse that he does not understand the English language and so did not know of such a law, nor by any other kind of pretext or excuse.

Further, the four immediately following fundamental articles, which the founders of this township of Germantown at first unanimously ratified for the greater and more rapid growth of this place shall at all times be inviolably kept, namely:

1. That as well in Germantown as in the villages thereunto belonging, all the properties shall be taken up in regular order and succession, without any exception, both upon the east and west, from beginning to end. But in case both sides are alike, then he who wishes to take up a property must draw lots with the others who have received land in the village, unless they freely grant and offer him the choice.

2. That when a number of them wish to settle at the same time and to take up land together, they shall draw lots, unless it be that they of themselves give the choice to one or more among them.

3. That since Germantown is laid out like a town and every whole property contains four acres, every half property two acres, no inhabitant here shall be entitled to build his dwelling except upon the aforesaid four or two acres respectively, without obtaining first the consent of the community and then that of the General Court. Vid. Num. 52.

4. That, when upon any one's private property, water shall be found suitable for the erection of mills of any kind, the community shall have full right to build such mills, but that for such they must be willing to satisfy the owner of the land according to the decision of impartial

persons. But in case the owner himself should build a mill within a year on such a place, it shall not be taken from him.

Finally the other laws and statutes following shall be valid and remain until the magistrates of this town in the General Court, after finding out further good, shall either change these or abolish and annul them altogether. Namely:

5. No one shall build a dwelling on the side land which he possesses outside of Germantown for the completion of his fifty or twenty-five acres or establish a household there, as long as he has no actual family in Germantown, under fine of twenty-five pounds.

6. Each resident shall keep the long street through the town or village, in front of his property, cleaned and free from all brush (knuysten) as well as from weeds and other trash, at all times. Or if in eight days after the street overseer orders him, he has not obeyed, two shillings shall be imposed.

7. Of the cross streets only two at first, namely the Schuylkill and Mill Street, shall be opened and fenced off, and both shall be cleared by compulsory labor, from this present date on to the end of next October. The other four, any one who is willing to clear and sow them, may hold and use for six years after he has taken possession, provided he leaves ten feet for the public highway.

8. The trees upon the cross and side streets as far as the boundary lines, are for the community, and no one may cut down any of them for private use, under penalty of five pounds fine.

9. The outer cross streets, as long as no division fences are made, shall be fenced and kept in good condition by all those whose land extends through them, each one in

proportion to the amount of his property—also under penalty of five pounds.

10. The posts of the said cross and side fences may stand a foot and a half into the street until such time as each lot in that quarter shall be separately fenced off, but such one and one half foot shall not thereby become the property of the corner lot, but shall also belong to the community for the street.

11. If any one wants to have a division fence made, he shall do it at his own expense, and not demand that his next neighbor pay his share in it, but in case the latter uses such a fence also when completed, he shall make good half of what he enjoys to him who made it.

12. Each and all who wish to keep cattle of any kind, shall fence in before the end of the next month, September, a special enclosure or yard, so that the cattle cannot run into the common fields or through the house door or other doors. Whoever fails to do this must make good all damage thus occasioned, and also pay three shillings fine.

Vide infra, Num. 12.

13. All fences shall be at least five feet high, and strictly, on the lowest foot and a half from the ground there shall be no spaces more than four inches wide; from there to the height of four feet no spaces more than six inches wide, and the top part shall be well guarded with strong rails. Also it shall be permitted to no one outside on the street to lay trees and such things against the rail fence, over which young pigs and other animals could the more easily climb up and get over. Whenever neglect of this on the part of any one shall be made known by the fence inspectors, he shall fix it within twenty four hours, or upon failure shall be fined six shillings.

Vide infra, Num. 13.

14. If the fences are completed after the approved fashion, and yet horses oxen or cows jump over them, those who suffer damage from it are entitled to demand satisfaction from the owner of the animals, and further, if he refuses, to bring it before the sheriff. S.7. But if a young pig or a hog come into fenced off property, and any one on the place makes complaint, and the owner cannot prove that it came in through a gate or a gap which was already in the fence, he shall be fined five shillings for each pig, each time it goes on to the property, of which three shillings belong and must be paid to the community, the other two to him who has suffered thereby.

Vide infra, Num. 14.

15. On the other hand, no one is permitted to kill another's pig, which so runs on to his place, but in case he does, he must pay immediately to the owner the full price which impartial persons consider it to have been worth.

15 et post

Vide infra, Nu. 48 et. post 51.

16. When any one is proven to have accidentally let any kind of cattle into fenced off land, he is bound to make good all damage that they may have done or caused, and besides is to be fined one shilling.

17. But whoever voluntarily and purposely lets any cattle through a gate or otherwise into a field shall be fined ten shillings.

18. Germantown, and the three village communities therein included, (Krisheim, Somerhausen and Crefelt) shall each separately make their paths, roads and bridges, and keep them continually in good repair.

Vide infra, Num. 19.

18. The common service must be done equally by all

who have families. But whoever has one or more properties in addition at any time, must do extra service for each one, when his turn comes.

19. The members of the General Court, together with the town clerk and messengers, in consideration of the length of time which they spend in consultation and the arrangement of the common business and affairs, shall, so long as they are performing such duties, be excused and free from the common compulsory labor.

N. B. This law, after repeated opposition and final solicitation of the community, has been by the General Court repealed and abolished.

20. Every one must plant his trees at least one rod from the furrow of the neighboring property, or else, on complaint being made, be compelled to take them out again.

21. All must, as far as their neighbors clear and plow the land, cut down the trees within four rods on their own ground, (even the community upon the cross and side streets also) or at least make them so that they may not shade the neighbouring cultivated land. Whoever fails to do this in eight days after his neighbor has sent him notice, shall pay six shillings fine.

Vide Num. 56.

22. It is freely permitted to any one living under this jurisdiction, in case of pressing need, to travel over his fellow citizens' cultivated land. Whoever seeks to hinder or hold him back shall be fined six shillings.

23. The dogs are to be kept chained from the middle of the third month (May) until the end of the harvest, or else kept in so that they can do no damage, otherwise the owners of the dog must make entirely good all damage, and besides pay a fine of six shillings.

Vide Num. 55.

24. Chickens shall be free to run about to this extent, that people may frighten them away, but may not shoot them or kill them by a blow, or by throwing anything at them. But whoever, contrary to this, kills anothers' hen, must not only pay the owners for the same, but also for each so killed hen, must pay one shilling fine. S. 2:—Ducks however it is hereby strictly prohibited to keep, together with other injurious things. This on payment of the damage done, and fine of six pence for any one that has done any damage.

25. Oxen and cows which are over three years old, and run with the others in the brush, must have the tips of their horns cut off, so that they may not injure the others by hooking them. Whoever neglects this until the end of next September, must, together with the damage that his cattle in such condition have done, pay eleven shillings for each one whose horns are not cut.

26. Whatever resident of our township of Germantown shall, within the same, shoot or otherwise kill a wolf, and bring its head to one of the justices, shall receive six shillings for every one.

27. At the time when the laws of this land permit the brush to be burned, all inhabitants in Germantown, as well as in the village communities thereunto belonging, shall be required to announce to the neighbors of their quarters twenty four hours beforehand, from house to house, on what day and at what time of day, they wish to burn on their places, but without this neighborly warning they may not make a fire. Otherwise they must make good any damage caused by such burning, out of the proper time. Furthermore, all who own, or inhabit side lands, shall yearly put such under fire.

N. B. This law was thus amended 1st mo. 17, 1696.

28. If any one finds anything, he shall, through the town clerk, have a notice of the same publicly made (and he must have three pence for his trouble) ; but if this is not done the finder shall be severely punished.

29. Poor and old people, under our jurisdiction, who cannot longer support themselves by the labor of their hands, and indigent widows and orphans may make themselves known to the General Court, by which they shall be helped as far as possible.

30. Bills of sale and lease, as well as all contracts relating to land and other immovable property (except for rent for a year or less), which are made within the jurisdiction of Germantown, shall not be valid until they have been acknowledged and delivered in the open Court of record.

Vide infra, Num. 31.

N. B. The foregoing thirty laws and ordinances were read to the community and published, 6th mo. (August) 28, 1691.

32. Each and every one who shall hereafter wish to buy or rent land in the township of Germantown, or to settle within it, shall first procure from the General Court of his fellow citizens the right or privilege of living here, and without such permission no one shall participate in our privileges.

33. In order the better to avoid all possibility of fire, every one is hereby strictly forbidden to carry fire through the streets, or even from his next door neighbor's house to his own, unless it is in a covered pot or kettle. If any one comes to get fire without such pot or kettle he must be refused. If he, however, does this nevertheless, and damage is thereby incurred, the magistrates of this place may hold him responsible for all damage, but if no harm comes from

it, and yet complaint is made, the offender shall be fined six shillings.

34. Similarly, no one may within Germantown or the village communities thereunto belonging, carry upon the open streets, or in stables or barns, a lighted candle, short or long, except in a lantern; and also upon said streets and in stables and barns, no one may smoke tobacco, on pain of repairing all damage, and fine of six shillings, if no harm be done and yet he be accused.

35. Also no one, in said Germantown jurisdiction, shall dry flax, or make it ready for breaking, in the house over a fire, or in a hole in which there is a fire, which is not removed at least five rods from any kind of building. Also no one is permitted to break or swing flax at the lamp or candle. All under the same conditions and fine as are published in both preceding laws.

Vide infra, num. 36.

35. At all times there shall be within Germantown for every sixth lot, a fire hook twenty five feet long, and also a ladder twenty five feet high, namely, in all, four fire hooks and four ladders, and no one shall use these except in case of fire under penalty of six shillings fine.

36. Two of the six members of the council shall alternately every two months inspect the chimneys and hearths, and when they find anything wrong, they must notify the owner of the house of the time within which he must fix it; and if the latter fails to do this, he must be fined six shillings.

Vide num. 36.

37. No one shall take down another's fence or hedge to pass through, until he has obtained permission from the owner of the fence, nor take away any rails from another's

fence; or, in case such a complaint is made, the offence shall be punishable according to the decision of the magistrates then serving.

38. Since when blocks or other wood are laid against a fence, the fence is not only damaged, but also at time of burning brush, is so much harder to save, no one shall lay wood of any kind against another's fence on pain of severe penalty, if accusation is made.

39. When any one cuts down a tree and it falls against the fence, or if a dead tree of itself strike it, he who cut it down, or to whom the tree belongs, shall within twenty four hours take it away from the fence, and set this up as it was before, or pay whatever penalty the authorities shall prescribe, if accusation is brought against him.

N. B. Of the proceeding nine laws, num. 32 anno 1691, Novemb. 20th, numbers 33, 34, 35, 36, 37, 38 and 39 on December 15th were made in full General Court, and the same published by reading them to the community.

40. Those deeds and contracts which, according to the contents of the 30th law, must be acknowledged and delivered in open Court of Record shall be first perfectly valid when they have been sealed by the Bailiff with the common town seal, and recorded by the Court clerk; for no document or contract of any kind shall or may be written of record, which has not thus been sealed. And there shall be paid for the sealing not more than six pence and for the recording one shilling.

Decretum in Senatu 11 mo. 2, 1691. Promulgated to the community 4 mo. 14, 1692.

Vide infra, num. 3.

N. B. Anno 1692/3 20th of 1st mo. (March) were all the preceding laws except Num. 19 again read aloud to the community by order of the General Court.

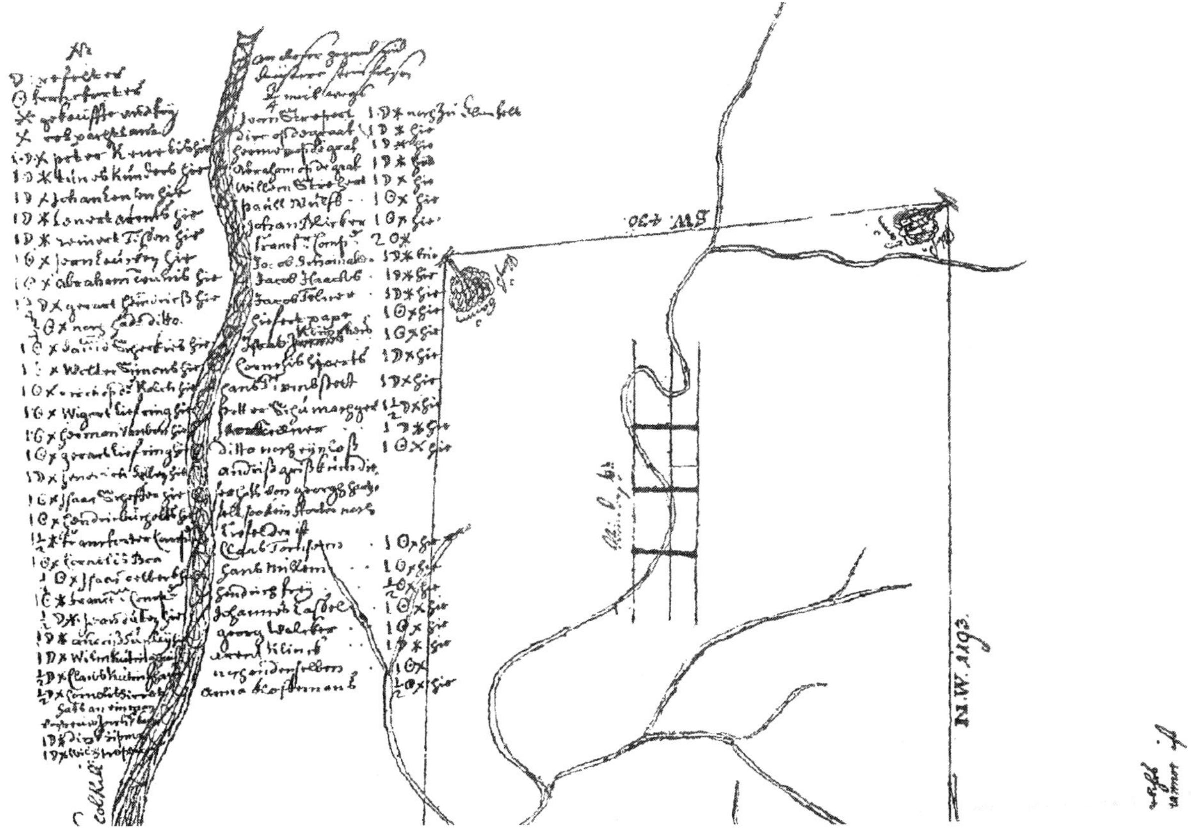

SW. 430
N.W. 1193

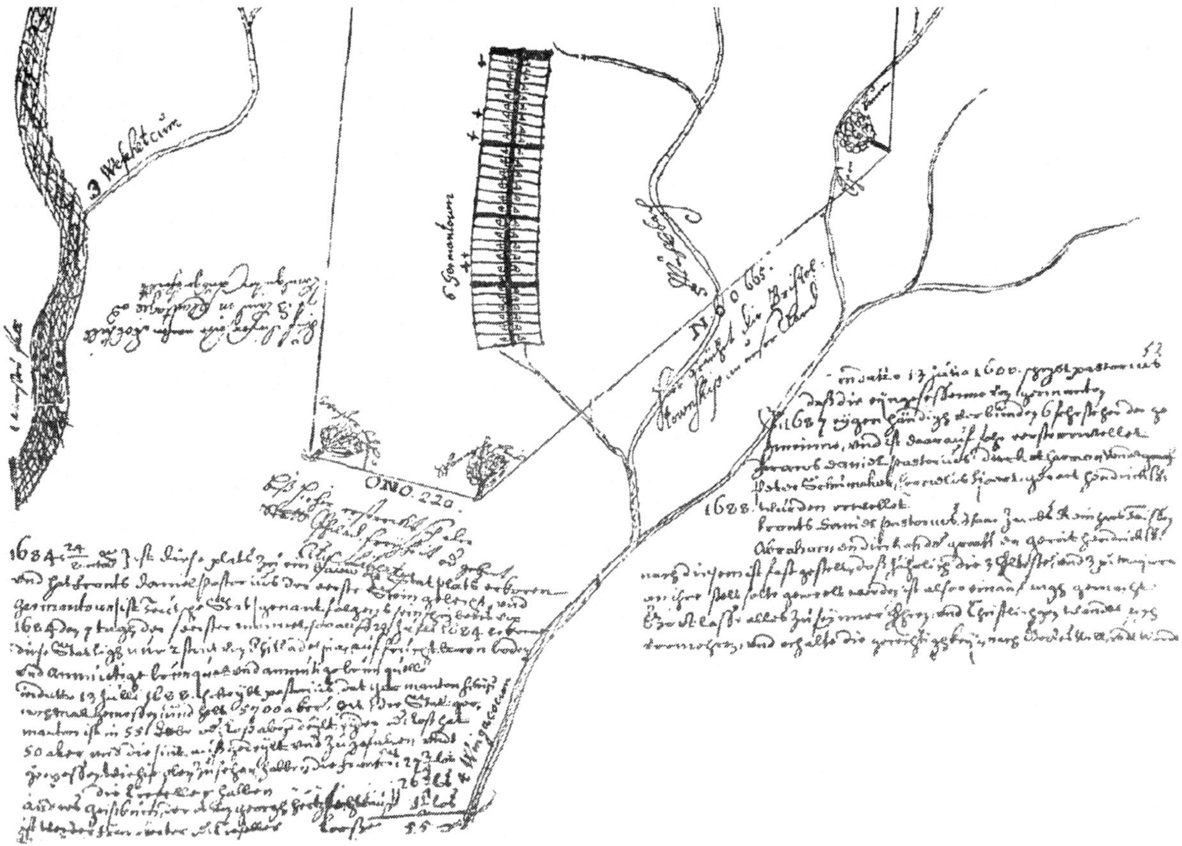
6 Germantown
ONO 220
1684
1688
52

40. The present inhabitants of the village of Krisheim shall according to their undertaking intention and purpose, like those in Germantown, fence their fields in together, but if these or some of them shall prefer to make partition fences, each neighbor shall prepare to furnish half of this fence, or else be required to pay for it.

This law was made 1 mo. 17th, 1696.

41. The 19th day of first month, March, shall be named for yearly reading aloud the laws and ordinances made from time to time by the General Court here, to the community, the members having been previously notified to come together on this same day.

This was also made 1st mo. 17, 1696.

42. On the 20th of said first month every second year, all of the inhabitants of the township of Germantown, especially the young people, shall go around the lines of the common enclosure, and where it is necessary, renew the marks and signs thereof. (Also made 1st mo. 17, 1696.)

The following 43 law is still valid:

43. Each and all who are chosen by the General Court, for any kind of commission or service, shall be compelled to enter on such duties and fulfill them faithfully under penalty of three pounds fine. But the person so chosen may state truthfully with yea or no, if he for conscience sake cannot take upon himself such duties, or if he is under sixteen or over sixty years old, or if the preceding year he held any commission in the general or open court.

N. B. This law was never repealed and should not be crossed out. Also was made 1st mo. 17, 1696.

44. All racing, as well as all other unnecessary fast driving in the streets of Germantown, is hereby strictly prohibited, and whoever disobeys, and thereby causes damage, shall fully repair it, and also pay ten shill. fine.

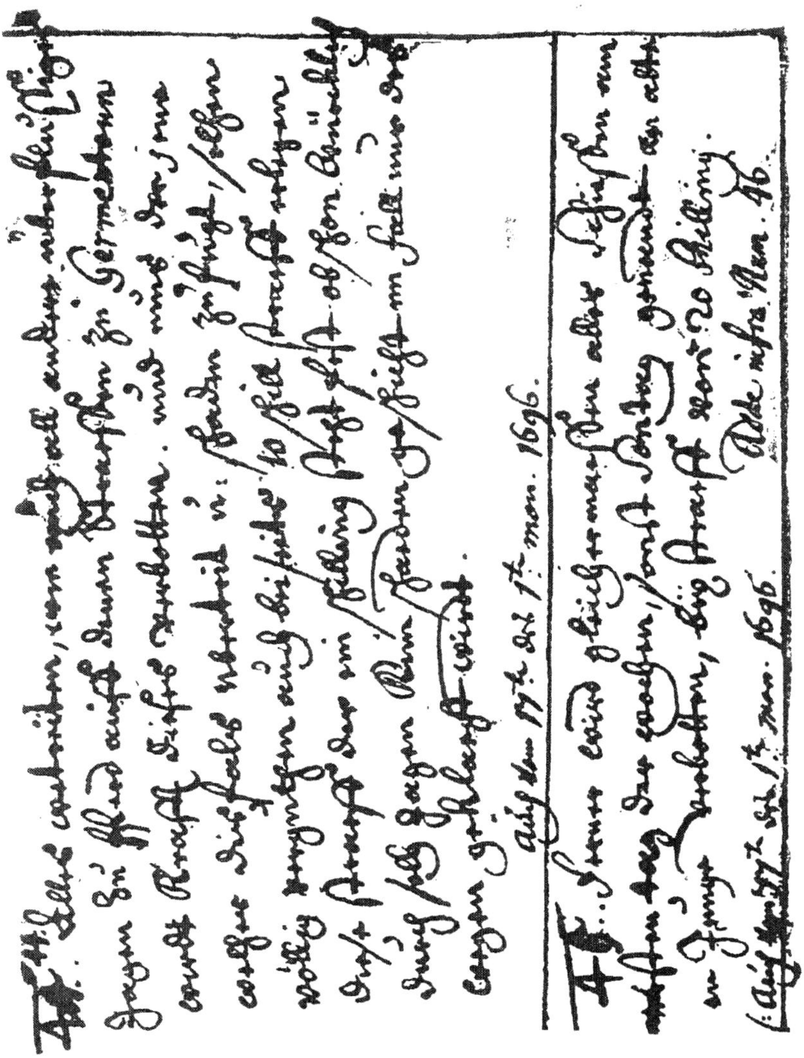

Extract from the book of laws.

Of this fine, one shilling shall be demanded, even though no actual loss is incurred by the racing, in case accusation is made. Also on 1st mo. 17, 1697.

45. Furthermore, all shooting is likewise prohibited to old and young on the first day of the week, otherwise called Sunday, under penalty of twenty shillings fine.

Also 1st mo. 17, 1696. Adde infra, num. 46.

47. In order that the benefit of our best and most complete brand of the clover leaf registered in Philadelphia, may be preserved strictly for the community, all inhabitants of Germantown who sell their own horses, marked with said clover leaf, or exchange them or otherwise part with them to any one who does not belong to our Corporation, shall before parting with the horse, burn upon him in addition to such clover leaf, with the stamp prepared for the purpose, the letter G, under penalty of ten shillings fine. Also all who go away from this jurisdiction on their horses, shall be compelled to do so with their clover leaf so marked, under penalty of the now imposed fine of ten shillings for every animal that is not so branded with the letter G.

This law was made Decem. 18, 1696, by the General Court then assembled, and forthwith published by public reading.

48. No citizen or inhabitant of Germantown after four weeks from the date here set down, shall let any kind of swine or young pigs run in either the fields or streets under penalty of losing all such swine or young pigs that run loose which, after said four weeks, shall by certain persons thereunto appointed, be put up for sale, from which one-fourth part shall go to him who has taken them up, one-fourth to the officer who sells them the next day after the bill of sale has been up, and the other half to the com-

munity. Yet it is expressly directed that in case a hog or young pig shall against the owner's will, break out or run over a field or street, they shall reckon from the first twenty-four hours after the breaking out, before the above order goes into effect. Also if any swine or young pigs, which belong to some one living outside of Germantown, shall be found running loose upon said fields or streets, the owner of the same shall pay for every one, as often as it is caught, ten pence to persons appointed to receive it. In the meantime, before the herein mentioned four weeks are passed, every inhabitant shall have liberty to catch every hog or young pig which comes into his fields, and then the owner of the same is bound to pay to him who has them, two shillings each, or, if he refuse, the finder may bring them to the officer and he may put them up for sale according to a previously posted bill, and may keep the third part of the ransom money for his trouble.

This law was made 5th mo. 20, 1697, in the General Court and publicly put up, and the preceding 15th law repealed and withdrawn.

Vide num. 51.

49. It is ordered by the General Court that no one here in Germantown shall keep an inn without license or permission of the Court, and shall give bond in twenty-five pounds. So as to keep good order in his house no one shall entertain transient guests except only the inn-keeper.

In order to avoid drunkenness, no inhabitant or person within the jurisdiction of Germantown shall be permitted to sell rum or other strong drink to any Indians, or he shall be punished according to the circumstances as the Court shall find good.

Vide seq., num. 50.

50. On the 9th of 6th mo. 1701, the preceding 49th law

was abolished, and the 46th was again established by the General Court with this proviso· That no inn-keepers on the first day called Sunday in God's service, shall hold gatherings of guests, and besides, throughout the whole week, no one except travellers shall be found here in an inn drinking later than nine o'clock at night, on pain of whatever penalty the court of record shall inflict.

51. On Sept. 17, 1701, the 48th law was repealed, and the following two made by the General Court and published with those following: All swine, except suckling pigs, which are found after the 21st day of this month in the fields of Germantown, without a yoke of two feet long, the officer of the corporation, or in his absence, or if he refuse, some citizen with two of his neighbors as witnesses, is hereby entitled to catch or kill, and the half of it shall go to the officer, or in such case as mentioned above, the citizen who in such case has caught or killed the chased pig, for his trouble, and the other half shall fall to the community. For damages, up to the 22nd day of this month, for swine which are now running in said fields, the owner of the land upon which the swine are caught or killed, shall be recompensed' according to the decision of disinterested persons.

Vide num. 55

51. So also was the following ordered: All citizens here in Germantown shall have full right to catch and bring to the officer all horses, cows, calves, and pigs found running loose upon their enclosed fields, and the officer shall pay them one shilling for each head, and shall receive beside from the owner of the cattle so caught two shill. together with all costs for trouble and fodder. But in case he catch them himself, he shall have only the two shill. and said costs. But he who has to pay the officer for his cattle, shall re-

ceive whatever he pays out in this way, provided his own fence is good and regular, from those or him whose fences or fence are not sufficient, besides all lost time and costs of judgment whatever they come to in the dispute.

Horses which can jump the prescribed fence are to be kept with a strong halter around the neck or else kept in a stable.

Num. 12. Each and every property, half property or smaller place upon which any one dwells here in Germantown, shall have a special yard (werf) fenced in so that the cattle may not so easily run into the common field. And such yard fences shall be like the other field fences, strong and sufficient to keep out cattle; also this shall be regularly examined by the fence inspector. Whoever neglects to make this fence or to repair it, must make good all damage caused thereby, and also when accusation is made against him, must pay three shillings fine.

This was made in place of the above 12th law, 1 mo. 17th, 1696.

Num. 13. All fences shall be five feet high, and the highest part protected with strong rails, and otherwise so made and contrived as to keep the cattle out of the fields. Also, no one shall be permitted outside on the street, to leave trees and such things against the fences, by which little pigs and other harmful animals might the more easily climb up and get over. Whereupon any one on being informed of such offence by the fence inspector, shall repair the same within twenty four hours, or on neglect of the same shall be fined six shillings.

This was also made 1 mo. 17th, 1696.

Num. 14. If horses, oxen, cows, etc. come through or over a fence, and do harm, and the fence inspector of that quarter recognize that such fence is firm and in good condition, the proprietor or owner of the cattle shall be indebted and compelled to repair all damage.

This was also made 1 mo. 17, 1696.

Number 15. Any one may set a dog upon swine or young pigs which come upon these streets, but with strict care not to kill them. But if a hog comes into the fenced off land, every inhabitant of this quarter is free to catch it and show it to the owner of the hog, and then the latter shall be bound to pay for every hog or young pig so caught which is one year old six shillings, for one a half year old three shillings, for the good of the community. But if he will not pay in such manner, he who caught it shall bring it to the officer, who at the earliest four hours after he has previously published it shall publicly sell the hog, and give the money received for it to the rent master, but keep back for himself six shillings from every pound.

This also was made 1 mo. 17, 1696.

Vide num. 48.

Num. 19. The road master, as often as common service is needed to be done, shall the day before call upon as many persons as he considers necessary for the present work, and those persons are bound to be upon hand and to work. Whoever does not come himself or send some capable person in his stead, shall have to pay six shillings fine for each day, but if he is so sick that he cannot do his own work, or if he has a wife in child bed in his house, in this case he is not compelled to serve. The aforesaid road master must always keep just and accurate reckoning with all of those who remain in arrears, and give over the same annually in the last court of record in the same year.

This was made instead of the preceding 18th on common service, 1 mo. 17, 1696.

Num. 31. The foregoing deeds and contracts shall be

sealed by the Bailiff with the common town seal and then first copied of record, and for the sealing only six pence shall be paid, but for the recording one shilling.

This was made in place of the 40th, 1 mo. 17, 1696.

Number 36. The general court shall yearly appoint two men of the community who every two months shall inspect the chimneys and fire places, and where they find them imperfect they shall give a certain time to the man living in the house to remedy it, and if the latter neglects doing it, he shall be fined six shillings.

Also made 1 mo. 17, 1696.

Vide Num. 55.

Num. 46. To prevent drunkenness no citizen or under-tenant under Germantown jurisdiction shall sell to any Indians rum or other strong drink, also inn keepers are hereby forbidden to tap more than each half day one quart of beer or a gill of rum for each Indian man or woman, on pain of whatever punishment the court shall find good, according to the magnitude of the offence.

This law also was made in the General Court 1 mo. 17, 1696.

Num. 52. To the foregoing 3rd ordinance was added on the 12 mo. 26, 1701–2 by the General Court:—And any one who already has his dwelling upon said four or two acres may not himself or have any one else build a dwelling or stable upon land lying back of it.

Num. 53. On the aforesaid 26 day of 12 month 1701–2 was substituted by the general court in the 51 ordinance, fifteen inches instead of two feet.

Num. 54. On the same 26 day of 12 mo. 1701–2 the following law was made:—Behind each and every property in Germantown the fences shall stand away forty feet from the line, so that the cattle may pass through. But so long as the neighboring property does not reach the said back fence, every man in Germantown is free to fence in and use the land up to the line.

55. Also on the 26th day of 12 mo. 1701–2 by the General Court, the 23d law about the dogs, the 36th about the chimney inspector, and the last part of the 51st law about the swine, were repealed.

56. On the 11th of 3 mo. 1703 in the General Court, there was substituted in the 21st law two rods for the four rods.

Those who held the town offices during the period of its corporate existence, so far as they have been ascertained, were as follows:

1691. Bailiff: F. D. Pastorius. Burgesses: Jacob Telner, Dirck Op den Graeff, Hermann Op den Graeff. Recorder:, Jacob Isaacs van Bebber. Clerk: Paul Wulf. Sheriff: Andreas Souplis. Constable, Jan Lucken.

1692. Bailiff: F. D. Pastorius. Burgesses: Reynier Tyson, Abraham Op den Graeff, Van Bebber. Recorder: Arnold Cassel. Clerk: Paul Wulf. Sheriff: David Scherkges. Constable: Peter Keurlis.

1693. Bailiff: Dirck Op den Graeff. Burgesses: R. Tyson, J. Lucken, Peter Schumacher jun. Recorder: Arnold Cassel. Clerk: F. D. Pastorius. Sheriff: Jacob Schumacher. Constable: P. Keurlis.

1694. Bailiff: Dirck Op den Graeff. Burgesses: R. Tyson, Peter Schumacher jun., Abraham Tunes. Recorder: Albert Brand, later, A. Cassel. Clerk: F. D. Pastorius. Sheriff: Jan Lucken. Constable: P. Keurlis.

1695. Bailiff: A. Cassel. Burgesses: Arent Klincken, Jan Doeden, Peter Schumacher jun. Recorder: Heivert Papen. Clerk: F. D. Pastorius. Sheriff: Jan Lucken, after May 7 Isaac Schumacher. Constable: Jan Silans and Johann Kuster.

1696. Bailiff: F. D. Pastorius. Burgesses: Peter Schumacher jun., Reynier Tyson, Lenart Arets. Recorder: Thones Kunders. Clerk: Anton Loof. Sheriff: Isaac Schumacher. Constable: Andreas Kramer und Joh. Kuster.

1701. Bailiff: Daniel Falckner. Burgesses: Cornelis Sivert, Justus Falckner, Thones Kunders. Recorder: Johannes Jawert. Clerk: F. D. Pastorius. Sheriff: Jonas Potts.

1702. Bailiff: Arent Klincken. Burgesses: Paul Wulff, Peter Schumacher, Wilh. Strepers. Recorder: Joh. Conrad Cotweis. Clerk: F. D. Pastorius. Sheriff: Jonas Potts.

1703. Bailiff: James Delaplaine. Burgesses: Thones Kunders, Daniel Falckner, J. C. Cotweis. Recorder: Richard van de Werff. Clerk: F. D. Pastorius. Sheriff: Thom. Potts, jun. Constable: Walter Simens.

1704. Bailiff: Arent Klincken. Burgesses: Hans Heinrich Mehls, Peter Schumacher, jun., Anton Gerkes. Recorder: Simon Andrews. Clerk: F. D. Pastorius. Constable, Wilhelm de Wees.

1706. Bailiff: James Delaplaine. Burgesses: Thones Kunders, Lenart Arets, Isaac Schumacher. Recorder: Caspar Hood. Clerk: F. D. Pastorius. Sheriff: Wilhelm de Wees. Constables: Cornelius de Wees, Simon Andrews und Joh. Kuster.

1707. Bailiff: Thomas Rutter. Burgesses: Joh. Kuster, Wilh. Strepers, Peter Schumacher. Recorder: Caspar Hood. Clerk: F. D. Pastorius. Sheriff: Jonas Potts.[141]

---

141 Seidensticker.

CHAPTER XIII.

The Significance of the Settlement.

THERE are many features about the settlement of Germantown, which make it an event not only of local but of national and cosmopolitan importance. Regarded from the point of view of the introduction into America of the results of European learning and cultivation, it is believed that no other settlement on this side of the Atlantic, certainly neither Jamestown, Plymouth nor Philadelphia, had so large a proportion of men who had won distinction abroad in literature and polemics. And it must be remembered that the intellectual thought of that age was mainly absorbed in religious controversy. Those in the advance of theological inquiry upon the continent of Europe, who had begun to forecast the condition of things we now enjoy, and who were thus brought into hopeless conflict with the concentrated forces of church and government, looked to Pennsylvania, not only as a haven, but as the only place in the world, with the possible exception of Holland, where their views might have an opportunity to bear fruitage. Of those interested in the settlement as purchasers Schutz, Ueberfeld, Eleanora von Merlau, Petersen, Kemler, Zimmermann and Furly, and of the actual settlers Plockhoy, Pastorius, Bom, Thomas Rutter, Telner, Koster, Kelpius, Daniel Falckner and Justus Falckner, all wrote books and produced literary labors some of them of magnitude and importance

In Germantown were begun the weaving of linen and cloth, and the manufacture of paper. The great carpet and other woolen industries of the state and the publishing houses and newspapers of the country may alike look back to the clover leaf of this ancient burgh with its motto: "Vinum Linum et Textrinum," with something of the same feeling that inspired the crusader of the middle ages when he gazed upon the cross. At Germantown began the inflow into America of that potent race which under the great Hermann in the battle in the Teutoberger wald overthrew the power of Rome, which in the sixth century conquered and colonized England and now supplies her kings, which in the sixteenth century under the lead of Luther confronted the Pope, and which has done so much to enrich, strengthen and liberalize the state of Pennsylvania and to establish those commonwealths in the west where in the future will rest the control of the nation.

But of more moment than any of these was the lesson taught to mankind by the settlement. The linen weavers of Germantown, no matter how humble may have been their station, or how inconspicuous may have been the events of their lives, were the farthest outcome of the ages, and of the future they were the prophets. Set aloft as an example here were the men who in advance of their fellows, had struck what has become the key-note of American civilization and the hope of futurity for all the races of the world. When Bullinger, the learned and able expounder of the views of the Swiss Calvinists, wrote in 1560 his "Origin of the Anabaptists," he said in describing their heretical beliefs: "But they hold stiffly the opposite and maintain that the government shall not interfere in questions of religion and belief. It appears to these Baptists to be unreasonable that any sword should be used in the church except the word of God, and still more unreasonable that a man should submit questions of religion or belief to the determination of other men, that is, to those who control the government."[142] He unconsciously, and by way of condemnation, marked the lines definitely He believed that heresy was a sin against God and a crime against the state and as such to be punished by the law The Anabaptists, on the contrary, taught that matters of faith were between the man and his God with which the government had nothing to do. The doctrines advocated by Bullinger, extending later into England, led to the organization of the Puritans, and to the founding of the colony of Massachusetts, as a theocracy, where Quakers, Baptists, Antinomians and other heretics were punished and expelled. The doctrines of the Anabaptists carried through Holland to England resulted in the formation of the sect of Quakers and the founding of Pennsylvania, where all were welcome and all were permitted to cherish their own creeds To Germantown as Mennonites came the Anabaptists themselves. Though in England even yet the church and state are united, in America the

[142] Widertoufferen Ursprung, Zurich, 1560, p 165.

contest has been ended, and the constitutions of all the states of the union provide for the exercise of liberty of conscience. When men have once persuaded themselves that the Lord has drawn an impassable distinction, to their advantage, between them and their fellows, the step towards the assumption of intellectual and physical control over the less fortunate is easily taken All peoples have found their bondsmen among the outside barbarians. It is not therefore surprising that when the memorial of the Pennsylvania Society for promoting the Abolition of Slavery, was presented to Congress in 1790, it should meet with the opposition of Fisher Ames and the support of Hiester, Muhlenberg and Wynkoop, the Pennsylvania German contingent then in the House.[143]

When Plockhoy in 1662 declared that no slavery should exist in his colony, it was only three years later than the decree of a Massachusetts court which directed that the Quakers, Daniel and Provided Southwick, should be sold in the Barbados,[144] and when the Op den Graeffs, Pastorius and Hendricks presented their well-reasoned protest in 1688, the other American colonists, as well as the English and the Dutch, were busily engaged in making their annual profits from the trade in slaves.

The settlement of Germantown then has a higher import than that new homes were founded and that a new burgh, destined to fame though it was, was builded on the face of the earth. It has a wider significance even than that here was the beginning of that immense immigration of Germans who have since flocked to these shores. Those burghers from the Rhine, better far than the Pilgrims who landed at Plymouth, better even that the Quakers who established

[143] Journal of the House, p 62

[144] Hazard's Historical Collections, Vol II, p 563

a city of brotherly love, stood for that spirit of universal toleration which found no abiding place save in America. Their feet were planted directly upon that path which leads from the darkness of the middle ages down to the light of the nineteenth century, from the oppressions of the past, to the freedom of the present. Holding as they did opinions banned in Europe, and which only the fullness of time could justify, standing as they did on what was then the outer picket line of civilization, they best represented the meaning of the colonization of Pennsylvania, and the principles lying at the foundation of her institutions and of those of the great nation of which she forms a part.

INDEX.

CPSIA information can be obtained
at www.ICGtesting.com
Printed in the USA
LVOW13*0347010617
536549LV00006B/84/P

9 781296 636081